Praise for *Chasing Excellence*

"Coach Vigil is the ultimate mentor no matter the sport and has the philosophy to ever-learn and ever-share. No matter where you feel you are starting your journey, this book is your gateway to creating purpose and fulfilling your life goals."

—**Deena Kastor,** 2004 Olympic Marathon bronze medalist,
U.S. record holder holder in the marathon,
New York Times best-selling author

"Coach Vigil is an inspiration to me, and now others will get the chance to see the passion and compassion of this remarkable man. I was fortunate to be with him at a time when my life and athletic career were blossoming. He believed in me and he instilled the importance of the nine inches above the shoulders: anyone can get ready physically for a race, but the mental component is also just as important."

—**Meb Keflezighi,** only marathoner to win Boston (2014),
New York City (2009), and an Olympic medal (silver, 2004)

"When I rode with Coach Vigil to my first altitude-training camp, he drove from Tucson, Arizona, to Mammoth Lakes, California, and told me lots of stories all the way. Now, everybody can enjoy Coach's stories and discover what a great mentor, person, and friend he is. He's the coach of every distance runner of my generation. We all have our own coaches, but Coach Vigil is the one we all share."

—**Abdi Abdirahman,** four-time Olympian in 10,000m
and marathon, 2020 Olympic Marathon qualifier

"There are few distance coaches in the world who have as broad of an impact on distance running as Coach Vigil. Like so many, my program was based off the backbone structure of Coach's training philosophy. I am certain that I would have never run at the level I achieved had it not been for Coach Vigil's influence. He is a sage in our sport who has empowered us all to break through, and Pat Melgares has given all of us the opportunity to better know this amazing man and coach."

—**Ryan Hall,** U.S. record holder in the half marathon,
two-time Olympian

"What I admire most about Coach Vigil is the compassion he has to help others with the knowledge he has gathered over 50 years of coaching. Coach's life story being brought to life in this book will inspire others to follow in his footsteps."

—**Brenda Martinez,** Olympian, 2013 World
Championships 800m silver medalist

"I have known Coach Joe Vigil since 1968 and for more than 50 years have observed his many different roles—running coach, life learner, teacher, and compassionate human being. His story and his example are an inspiration to all. This new book will spread his approach and knowledge to many more. There is much to be gained."

—**Amby Burfoot,** 1968 Boston Marathon winner,
longtime editor, *Runner's World* magazine

Chasing Excellence

THE REMARKABLE LIFE AND
INSPIRING VIGILOSOPHY OF
COACH JOE I. VIGIL

———

PAT MELGARES
FOREWORD BY BILLY MILLS

books with *soul* • Flagstaff, AZ

Chasing Excellence:
The Remarkable Life and Inspiring Vigilosophy of Coach Joe I. Vigil

© 2020 by Pat Melgares

ISBN: 978-1-7331887-3-9 (paperback)
ISBN: 978-1-7331887-4-6 (e-book)
Library of Congress Control Number: 2020907891

Cover designed by Lindy Martin
Interior designed by Katherine Lloyd
Proofreading and indexing by Matt Brann
Editorial support by Nancy Schrag, Joe Schrag
Printed in the United States of America

Cover photo is the official USA Track & Field 2008 U.S. Olympic team
  staff photo. Courtesy of Dr. Joe I. Vigil.
"Coach Vigil's Alamosa" map illustration, pgs. 124–5, by Krista Nicole

All photos in this book are used courtesy of Dr. Joe I. Vigil, except: Plachy Hall on page 54, courtesy of the Adams State University Office of Public Relations and Marketing; newspaper headline on page 184, courtesy of the *Valley Courier*; Pat Melgares on page 303, courtesy of the author; the Adams State University logo on page 305, courtesy of Adams State University.

Soulstice Publishing
PO Box 791
Flagstaff, AZ 86002
(928) 814-8943
connect@soulsticepublishing.com
www.soulsticepublishing.com

28 27 26 25 24 23   2 3 4 5

This book honors the love,
dedication, and positive energy
of Caroline Vigil.

"My wife has always encouraged me and supported me in the many projects I have been involved in. She has had a total commitment to me and our lives together. She's been my inspiration for nearly 45 years."

—Joe I. Vigil

CONTENTS

FOREWORD

*C*hasing Excellence will take you on a fascinating and inspiring journey.

You will see how sport and other positive activities—properly taught—can prepare our youth for the challenges they will face later in life better than just about anything else they can do at an early age.

You will be captivated witnessing how Dr. Joe I. Vigil, during 65-plus years of coaching, inspired the dreams of youth, and in so doing, also empowered the visions of the adults.

Reading about Joe's challenges early in life, you will wonder how he avoided the roads that can become misleading, where it's easy to lose sight, direction, and hope.

Your emotions will be touched realizing that to counter the negative challenges young Joe would face, his mother raised him to rely on faith and responsibility. Faith and responsibility became the cornerstones in Joe's life, playing a major role as he matured into a young adult and began choreographing his professional career.

Today, Joe is a legendary physiologist and distance running coach. He is one of the great visionaries of coaching and is also among the most respected individuals in coaching worldwide.

Watching Joe's elite athletes perform was magical to me. It was as if Coach was unconsciously having them draw strength from Mother Earth through the footprints they were so gently laying upon her. I felt as if the strength drawn was challenging their integrity, character, and humility all the while empowering them spiritually.

Joe has made a difference for the betterment of the world. His accomplishments and how he has achieved them are benchmarks for others to aspire to.

How does one describe such a man? I will do so by paraphrasing a quote I once heard used to describe an Olympic athlete from Carlisle Indian Industrial School in the early 1900s, Frank Mount Pleasant. It is just as fitting for Coach:

> To watch Joe Vigil coach is to admire him.
> To coach against him is to learn from him.
> To know him is to love him.

Throughout the history of Native American cultures, including my own, mothers were nurturers, teachers of compassion. These lessons were vital in developing warriors, and that emphasis also goes back to ancient times. To do justice to Coach Vigil's legendary life story, one must reiterate what I call the sacred contribution his mother, Melinda, gifted him. I will do so by asking a question from history: what was the deciding factor King Leonidas of Sparta used in choosing the 300 warriors to stay with him and 700 others to defend Thermopylae Pass against more than 80,000 Persians?

The 300 knew they would be killed, but their sacrifice would allow 7,000 Greek soldiers to leave Thermopylae Pass and defend Sparta from a sea attack, thus allowing Sparta to live. The 300 were chosen because of how their mothers raised them: to be responsible and accountable based on virtues, values, spirituality, and love.

Melinda raised her son the same way. Get ready for an exhilarating story.

Billy Mills was the gold medalist in the
10,000 meters at the 1964 Tokyo Olympics.
February 2020
Fair Oaks, California

PREFACE
AND ACKNOWLEDGMENTS

In the summer of 2018, I was returning home to Kansas from Alamosa, Colorado, where I had attended the celebration of the 50th anniversary of the U.S. Olympic Marathon Trials. In 1968, Alamosa hosted the first-ever Olympic Trials in that event, a remarkable achievement pulled off by Adams State College's young coach, Joe I. Vigil, and former U.S. Olympian Leonard "Buddy" Edelen, among others.

During a late-night social, a few of my former teammates at Adams State and former graduate assistant coach Jim Bevan were urging me to step forward and write a book on Vigil's massive influence on Adams State, American distance running, and countless people's lives. The impact of Coach Vigil's stories, experiences, generosity, and compassion needed to be captured, they said.

I certainly agreed that Coach's life story was extraordinary. But me? Write a book? About Joe I. Vigil? Though I was an experienced journalist, I had never written a book before, and yet my friends wanted my first venture into this area to be about a man so highly revered? It was too scary, I thought. I was intimidated. What if I couldn't capture the spirit of this amazing man? I was insecure.

After reflection and a lot of prayer, I posed the question to my then 19-year-old daughter as we drove home after the celebration in Alamosa. I asked her, "Cara, do you think I should try to do this?"

She said, "Dad, if you don't, you'll regret it for the rest of your life."

At that moment, I wished her mother had not raised her so well. She was absolutely right. I remember thinking about competing for Coach Vigil nearly 30 years earlier. We didn't shy away from competition because it was too tough or too scary. We strapped up the spikes a little tighter and did the absolute best job we could do on that day.

Overcoming my fear was not so difficult thanks to the dozens of fellow "Vigilantes" (you'll hear more about the Vigilantes later in this book; they're everywhere) who gave so generously of their time to talk about the man who often helped to form their moral character at a tender time of their lives. I'm also grateful to many, many coaches and athletes who interrupted their busy lives to talk with me about how Coach Vigil inspired them to greatness. And countless others have shared their stories about how one man's generosity and concern have—in some way—made their lives richer.

I am one of those. I am forever grateful to Coach Vigil and his wife, Caroline, for allowing me to tell his story, but also because more than 30 years ago, he took a young man who was struggling with his own self-identity and guided him past life's rough patches. In the midst of my insecurity, Coach Vigil gave me the courage and support to enjoy a modest college running career (average by Adams State's standards). More than that, he helped me grow into a man of God and a man of service. I am just one of thousands of Vigilantes in the world trying to represent their Coach's legacy.

I am so thankful to my wife, Susan, and my children—Chris, Michael, and Cara—for their support during this project. They believed in me more than I believed in myself. They are my rocks in this life.

I am also thankful to numerous people who reviewed this book while I was writing, including my high school English and journalism teacher, Janice Watkins, and her husband, Kay. My gratitude also goes to Joe Moore, Andy Deckert, Kim McConnell, Peggy Vigil, Patti Vigil, Larry Jeffryes, Larry Fujimoto, Larry Zaragoza, Shirley Melgares, Karen Melgares, Mike Melgares, Bruce Ramundo, Rosemary Ramundo, and others who have read this work in whole or in part, and have shared feedback.

Like Coach Vigil, I was raised by an incredibly loving woman, my mom Shirley. I also know that my dad, Max, who passed away more than 12 years ago, is smiling down on me today, proud of his "Little Rabbit."

Special thanks also to Dan Jaquez, Jim Bevan, and Dan Garcia, who have worked behind the scenes to help this project along. Other supporters who helped make this book a reality are Vicki and Jim Bevan, Pat Devaney, Julie and Milan Donley, Jordan Donnelly and Nancy Yu, Mike Fanelli, Bob Fink, Dan Green, coaches Tena and Peanut Harms, Joe Mangan, Mike McManus, and Dave Shrock.

Thank you to Joe and Nancy Schrag, whose friendship and thoughtfulness led me to their son, Myles Schrag. He happened to co-own a publishing company in Flagstaff, Arizona, with Julie Hammonds—and they both had a special interest in books on running.

One of the fortuitous turns that came by taking my daughter's advice was the establishment of the Joe I. Vigil Scholarship. The Adams State Foundation saw the value in this project and agreed to administer this new initiative that will benefit student-athletes in the ASU cross country and track and field programs. I am grateful for the partnership—a direct outgrowth of this book becoming a reality, and a further reminder of my good fortune to find many others committed to seeing this book in print.

This book is for every single person who has ever been impacted directly or indirectly by Coach Vigil. I am moved by the motto of ASICS, for which Vigil has worked 20 years: *Anima Sana In Corpore Sano*, which means "healthy mind in a healthy body."

That's Joe I. Vigil. Our minds, our bodies, and our world are better for having him in our lives.

Prologue

"LET ME TELL YOU A STORY..."

*J*oe I. Vigil's eyebrows furl above deep, dark eyes as he locks in on you, a stare that grips you like an eagle's claws, commanding your attention. Coming from almost anyone else, it's the type of look that could be construed as confrontation, or at the least, make you very, very nervous. But this glare from Vigil…well, it's quite different. This look excites you. He's found a sweet spot in your curiosity, and you're mesmerized by the intensity of his eyes and his face.

Vigil's mind is revved up. He is about to rehash intricate details of a particular memory from nine decades of living and more than 65 years of coaching. As he talks, you liken his mind to a card catalog, much like the ones in libraries before the Internet age when drawers and drawers of index cards detailed every book in the collection. And Vigil seems to know exactly where he's stored each precious story.

His collection of memories is vast, from humble beginnings as the third child of a single mother, to world-renowned coach of world champion and Olympic medal-winning distance runners.

Nobody doubts that he is among the brightest and most

accomplished coaches in U.S. distance running history. He is the patriarch of one of the most decorated athletic programs in the history of American collegiate sports—Adams State cross country and track and field—where from 1965 to 1993 he amassed a record of 3,014-176 (a winning percentage of .942) and coached 19 national champion teams, 425 All-Americans, and 87 individual national champions. In 2019, the program's bounty reached 56 national team titles in NAIA and NCAA Division II competition.

In winning the 1992 NCAA Division II championship in Slippery Rock, Pennsylvania, his Adams State men's cross country team accomplished the impossible: they posted the only perfect score at a national meet in any collegiate division ever.

"I tease him sometimes and tell him he's the Forrest Gump of running; you know, like in the movie, they tell history through Forrest Gump," said Damon Martin, who has guided the Adams State men's juggernaut since 1995, and the women's programs since 1989.

Vigil's bond with track and field and distance running history is real. He was on the field at the 1968 Olympic Games in Mexico City when Bob Beamon flew 29 feet, 2 inches in the long jump, setting a world record that stood for 23 years. He shook Beamon's hand afterward.

In the 1980s, Vigil formed a friendship with a young Cuban high jumper named Javier Sotomayor, nearly six years before the rest of the world knew him as the first—and only—man to propel his body more than eight feet above the ground. Vigil was one of the first on the field to congratulate Sotomayor in 1993 after his remarkable high jump of 8 feet, ½ inch in Salamanca, Spain.

"I asked him, 'Javier, what motivated you to do this?'" Vigil said. "He said, 'Coach, when I was 10 years old, one of my fellow countrymen, Alberto Juantorena, won the [Olympic] gold medal in the 400 and 800 in Montreal. At that point, 10 years of age, I decided to dedicate my life to bringing glory to my country.' He committed and dedicated and worked until he broke the world record."

Vigil also was trackside when American distance legend Jim Ryun clocked 3:51.1 at Bakersfield, California, in 1967 to set a world record that stood for nearly eight years. Ryun had been training in Vigil's hometown, Alamosa, Colorado, with another legendary physiologist, Jack Daniels, and several of the best middle-distance runners of the time.

"I have been so lucky to have seen so many great things in this sport," Vigil says. "Anytime I saw something great, I developed a bigger love for track and field, and I continued to study it as much as I could."

Vigil has coached American teams at the highest levels, including the Olympic Games, Pan American Games, World University Games, and World Cross Country Championships. From 2001 through 2006, he worked with Team USA California, where his runners won 47 U.S. national championships, set 17 national records, and made the podium at the world track and field and cross country championships. At the 2004 Olympic Games in Athens, Greece, runners with ties to Vigil won gold (Stefano Baldini of Italy), silver (Meb Keflezighi of the United States), and bronze (Deena Kastor of the United States) in the marathon.

Vigil is one of four "founding fathers" of USA Track & Field's coaching education program, serving as national chair for nine years. He is a tireless clinician, having presented workshops in 29 countries on six continents during his lifetime. He has been inducted into 11 Halls of Fame throughout the world.

In 2015, USA Track & Field honored Vigil during the U.S.

national championships at historic Hayward Field in Eugene, Oregon, with the Legend Coach Award, making him just the second person ever to receive that distinction. In a surprise to Vigil, the International Association of Athletics Federations (IAAF) piggybacked on that ceremony and presented him with the Continental Area Legendary Coach Award.

Yet, visit with any of Vigil's athletes, even dating back to the 1950s and 1960s at Alamosa High School, and they will talk of something much different. Instead of the awards, the victories, and the medals, Vigil's athletes talk of a man of compassion and great humility who inspired them beyond their own perceived limits. They talk about having the same feeling of excitement when Vigil calls them 30, 40, even 50 years after they last competed for him just to check in and see how they're doing. If coaching is about relationships—and most think it is whether they have been in the trenches or studied those who have—then Vigil is certainly a master coach, having given his soul to every athlete's physical, mental, and social well-being.

And so you sit with Vigil, sipping coffee and nibbling a scone, blessed with the opportunity to pepper him with question after question. What was your childhood like? How did you get started in coaching? Who were your mentors? And why, at 90 years old, are you still coaching Olympic athletes?

Vigil is neither irritated nor impatient with the volley of questions. Rather, he's locked in. He is eager to share, eager to teach. He genuinely enjoys these moments. And he's giving you that look.

He begins: "Let me tell you a story…"

1

SOUTH
OF THE TRACKS

On a scorching summer day in Tucson, Arizona, Joe I. Vigil is shopping in a local Walmart when a conversation in an adjacent aisle catches his attention. There, a small girl is with her father and mother, scanning the row of bikes, big wide eyes looking for just the right one.

"That's the one, daddy. That's the one!" she says.

The man, of Hispanic descent, is torn between his daughter's excitement and the harsh reality that the family just cannot afford the $80 bike. "Not now, *mi hija,* not now. Daddy lost his job and we'll have to wait until I get another one," he tells her.

Vigil (pronounced "Vee-Hill") has raised two daughters himself, and so the exchange is a little personal to him. He doesn't want to embarrass the man, so he waits a few moments for them to leave the area. Then, he contacts an attendant, who takes the bike down and gets it to the checkout stand.

Outside the store, Vigil catches up with the couple and their daughter. Vigil tells the man in Spanish that he heard his daughter's excitement and he would like to give her the bike. The man is apprehensive; he's never met Vigil and can't seem to figure out why a stranger would do such a thing. Vigil insists they take the bike. He is sincere and friendly and his offer appears heartfelt, so the man finally accepts the gift, and shakes Vigil's hand.

As they walk away, the little girl asks: "Who is that man, daddy?"

It's a great question: just who is Dr. Joe I. Vigil? Google indicates he's a world-famous coach, international lecturer, and brilliant scientist who perfected high-altitude training for distance runners. He's the architect of the world's most successful college cross country and track and field program—in 2019, his alma mater, Adams State University, won its 56th national title in 52 years. He's achieved Legend Coach status from USA Track & Field and the International Association of Athletics Federations, is a member of 11 Halls of Fame worldwide, and has coached 22 Olympians. The accolades go on and on.

But maybe Google gets it only partly right. Maybe he's just an ordinary guy with extraordinary compassion, an ordinary guy with an extraordinary desire to learn and share. Maybe he's a man who followed his love for a sport and for nearly 70 years held true to his values as he climbed from the depths of poverty to the pinnacle of Olympic glory.

Those who know Vigil say they aren't surprised by hearing of his random act of kindness in a Walmart toy section, for they typically describe "Coach" as a simple man with a soft heart and great humility. In his hometown of Alamosa, Colorado, he is hailed by the natives not just as the local boy who made good, but also the kid next door who still drinks coffee at his favorite Campus Cafe restaurant and swaps stories with folks he's known for decades—and some that he met just a few minutes ago.

They say he's still the curious little boy raised by a loving mother who displayed a firm hand in making sure his life was rooted in religious faith. They say he's still the eager Eagle Scout called to service, the teenager who once stood hours on end at the busiest intersection in town to help elderly ladies cross the street, packages in tow.

For many, it may seem a bit too good to be true, this young man of modest means rising to stardom beyond belief. Yet, it's all real. Vigil's upbringing, grounded in family values, service, and religious faith, is likely the root of his remarkable success.

Named after his paternal grandfather, Joseph Isabel Vigil was born November 25, 1929, in Antonito, Colorado, the third son of Augustine and Melinda Vigil. Really, he was the son of Melinda only; by the time of Joseph's birth, she had been seeking a divorce from her husband.

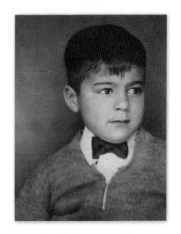

Joe Vigil as a young boy, approximately six years old.

"My mom never mentioned my early years," Vigil says. "And she never mentioned my real dad. She was in the process of divorcing him. From what I was told, he was a *marijuano* [Spanish slang for a pothead]. They used to have to hide my mom in the cellar in Antonito because he was after her to beat her up. Those are the types of things I heard."

"They" included his paternal grandmother—Augustine's mother, a loving woman caught between her son's abusive ways and Melinda's young family—and grandfather, Jose Isabel Vigil.

Vigil had two older brothers, Augustine, Jr., known as Tino;

and John, who the family called Buddy. Just three months after Vigil was born, his father died in Los Angeles, where he had been living, and shortly after that, Melinda moved her three boys 28 miles north to Alamosa, where she had landed a job.

Joe Vigil with his two brothers and mother (circa 1937). Joe is sitting in front. Also pictured are brother Augustine (known as Tino), left; mother Melinda, center; and brother John (known as Buddy).

Vigil has no recollection of ever living in Antonito, a rugged, southern Colorado town of a few hundred residents that formed in 1889 primarily as a water-filling station for steam engines on the Denver and Rio Grande Western Railroad. Most of the town's residents lived in small, flat-roof adobe homes less than 50 yards from the railroad tracks, a matter of convenience for the men who worked the hard-labor jobs. Just seven miles north is the rugged town of Manassa, birthplace of former heavyweight boxing champion Jack Dempsey. His blue-collar persona forever linked him to the region with the colorful nickname of the Manassa Mauler.

What Vigil remembers is that during his first decade of life, the family was barely scraping by, which is not really a surprise given that he was born nearly one month after shares on the New York Stock Exchange collapsed—known to history as Black Tuesday—sending the United States into the throes of the Great Depression.

"My mom, she worked all her life," Vigil recalls. "She walked to work every day. We lived on Ninth Street in Alamosa, and so she was walking five or six blocks to get to work on Main Street. She was working simply to keep us fed. We didn't have much else."

Let Me Tell You a Story

For his entire life, Joe I. Vigil has never forgotten where he came from. Born into poverty, he had particular compassion for those runners with similar backgrounds.

For that reason, he was the perfect mentor for Charley "Pablo" Vigil (no relation), who, like his coach, grew up most of his childhood without a father and watched his mother struggle just to put food on the family table.

"We don't cherry-pick our life happenings," said Pablo, a four-time NAIA All-American at Adams State between 1971 and 1975. "You take the good with the bad, although at the time they sucked so bad. It really sucked to be dirt poor and having a lot of trauma and violence and dysfunctional family and all that. But now I look back and I say, 'You know, I am who I am as a result of all that.'

"I don't want to say they were blessings in disguise; indirectly maybe they were. But there were a lot of great lessons and great happenings that make me who I am as a result of the bad stuff I had early in my life. Ultimately, we are the sum of our experiences and the people we meet."

In the early 1930s, Alamosa offered hope that few towns in southern Colorado could at the time. It was founded in 1878 on the promise of the Denver and Rio Grande Western Railroad (D&RGW), a narrow-gauge line that was best known for connecting Denver, Colorado, to Salt Lake City, Utah, and eventually San Francisco, California. While not part of that main line, Alamosa was an important tentacle in the shorter southern veins of the D&RGW, moving goods west to Durango and the Four Corners area, and south to Santa Fe.

Alamosa's rise was somewhat due to its fortunate geographical location. Because it was a direct shot through the split in the San Juan Mountains to the south, it was the natural route for building the D&RGW into New Mexico. Railroad officials envisioned Alamosa would become its new terminal in southern Colorado and quickly developed plans to build warehouses, maintenance shops, and more. By 1878, 30 miles of rails leading from Garland City—near present-day Fort Garland, a former army outpost—had been laid to Alamosa, forging the way for the railroad and its dozens of workers and their families to continue their westward trek.

Once the rails were down, officials wasted no time. Historical reports indicate that nearly 100 buildings—stores, houses, hotels, and churches—were loaded onto flatbed cars in Garland City and hauled to Alamosa, landing on what is now Sixth Street. One report from the San Luis Valley Historical Society indicates that hotel owner Joe Perry served his guests breakfast in the morning in Garland City, and dinner in the evening in Alamosa...*in the very same building.* Sixth Street was the northern border of the bustling town, and residents were quickly building their homes to the south of the tracks, most of the new residents of Hispanic and Native American backgrounds.

In 1921, Colorado governor Billy Adams—a former mayor of Alamosa—convinced the state's legislature to build a college in Alamosa to become a regional school for training teachers. That year, Adams State Normal School became the first building on Alamosa's northwest side. As the new college's students and staff added to a strong railroad and agricultural economy, Alamosa grew from just over 5,000 residents in 1920 to more than 8,500 in 1930. Despite the Great Depression, the town experienced modest job growth and a steady economy in the 1930s.

But Adams State's location north of the railroad tracks was significant for more than its boost to the local economy. It signaled growth in a new direction for the town. As a more affluent population moved to Alamosa, the railroad tracks began to symbolize the divide between the Haves and the Have-Nots in the community, the north-siders and the south-siders.

For the first time in his life—and it wouldn't be the last— young Joe Vigil would learn to navigate his future with the Have-Nots.

2

MAMA'S
BOY

The town Vigil grew up in was not really a hotbed of racial prejudice, even though growing up as a poor Hispanic kid on the south side of Alamosa was a difficult road to success.

From the time Vigil was a kid and still today, Hispanics and Anglos routinely celebrate Alamosa's Southwest roots, including such Mexican-American traditions as Cinco de Mayo. Alamosa and the surrounding San Luis Valley are rich in the Spanish and Native American arts—including music, dance, jewelry, and textiles—and it's not hard to find some of the best Mexican food you'll ever eat.

In fact, you'd be hard-pressed to find anyone around Alamosa, regardless of ethnicity, who will live without *chile verde* (green chile), a delicacy made with pork, tomatoes, and green chile peppers. Local restaurateurs who offer the best *chile verde* often rise to the status of local celebrity, and routinely are known by a single name: Efrem's, Oscar's, and Mrs. Rios, to name a few.

The dichotomy you'll find in Alamosa has more to do with the swath of railroad yards that spans 10 blocks east–west through the heart of town, and another two blocks deep between Sixth and Eighth streets. From Vigil's days growing up in the 1930s and 1940s through today, kids on the north side of town mostly stayed in their neighborhoods, and kids on the south side in theirs. There was no real animosity between the groups as much as there were divergent lifestyles largely dictated by the mighty dollar.

"Times were tougher then for those living on the south side," Vigil remembers. "Everybody on the north side of the tracks, they had everything. Their kids were going skiing in the wintertime; I never skied in my life. They were playing golf; I never played golf. I knew why I couldn't go, but I never felt sorry for myself."

Vigil's childhood instead was forged on gravel streets playing football and basketball with the neighborhood kids, among them his cousins Amos and Maxi, who lived two blocks away. A small army of boys would get together most days and ride their bikes around the southside streets, often getting home just in time for dinner. The southside kids were proud of their upbringing. When they were asked where they lived, it was a common joke to respond: "U.C.L.A.—Upper Crust, Lower Alamosa."

Life was simple and pure, and Vigil says he loved every minute of it.

"I never owned a new bike," he said. "We just never had the money. I used to buy parts and I would put a bike together."

When Vigil was seven, his mom remarried and moved Joe and Tino to live with their new family. (Buddy, the middle child, by this time was living with his grandmother.) Melinda's new husband, Steve Medina, had three daughters, Juanita, Ethel, and Eva.

"I was just a little tyke," Vigil said. "Juanita [who is seven years older] used to give me my bath each day. We all lived in a house on Ninth Street. I was very close to her. Ethel and Eva [who were younger than Juanita, but older than Joe], we grew up together, but we weren't close."

The blended family was a blessing to Melinda and her boys. Vigil says Steve Medina was "a good, hardworking, honest man." He was a butcher by trade, and Vigil would sometimes travel with him to the slaughterhouse in nearby Monte Vista or La Jara, watching his step-dad labor tirelessly until the work was done. The new family was not flush with money, but they had plenty to eat, enough income to do the things they wanted to do, and a stable, loving home.

"My mom, because of her dad being a Baptist minister, made damn sure that I went to Sunday school every week, all the way through my senior year in high school," Vigil said. "I was in church every Sunday. I loved those biblical stories…all of them. I loved to go to Sunday school. I had good Sunday school teachers who were good men and women in the community."

Vigil's grandfather was John Gabriel Jeantet (pronounced "John-Tay"), whom Vigil admired despite never having met him in person.

"I admired the fact that he was a minister," Vigil said. "My Sunday school lessons and my mother's reminders kept his memory fresh in my mind. My mom had a picture that I wish I still had where he was baptizing people in the river; during his career, he baptized 864 people that way."

Vigil was so enamored by his grandpa's work that, as a youngster, he would often stand in front of a mirror and pretend he was preaching to a crowd of people. "I would preach about the second coming of Jesus Christ," he said.

◇ ◇ ◇

By the time Vigil hit his teenage years, his life was consumed with school, athletics, and Boy Scouts. He especially loved his scouting experience, where he rose to the level of Eagle Scout, earning dozens of badges for service to the community.

"I think you had to be 12 years old to be a Scout," Vigil said. "We didn't have projects back then, but you had to have 21 merit badges to become an Eagle Scout. I still have my merit badge sash and my Eagle Badge stored in my garage."

"What really helped him grow as a leader was scouting," said Vigil's wife, Caroline, whom he calls Kelly. "One of his projects was to help other people, so he'd wait on the corner at State Street and Main Street in Alamosa [the busiest intersection in the town's shopping district] and he'd help ladies across the street with their packages."

Joe Vigil after completing the requirements for Eagle Scout (circa 1945) with stepfather Steve Medina, left, and mother Melinda Medina. They are standing near the steps to the Baptist Church in Alamosa.

Vigil credits scouting with instilling such values as leadership and service into his life: "I became the leader of my company, and eventually became the leader of my Scout troop. I used to have to direct four little companies that we had. We'd go to Scout camp every summer for a week. It used to cost $13 to go for the week, which was a lot of money at the time."

Each summer, Vigil also worked as a laborer in the area's farm fields alongside many of the migrant workers who made their way to the San Luis Valley from Mexico or parts of South America.

"Rich Valdez [a friend who would later be Vigil's neighbor when they were adults] and I would go pick peas, 25 cents a hamper," Vigil said. "If we were lucky, we'd pick 12 hampers a day. So we'd make three bucks a day, and 25 cents of it would go to Scotty Garcia, the manager of our crew who drove us out to the fields.

"As I got older, I went from picking peas to thinning beets, packing lettuce, cutting cauliflower, bucking bales of hay, and picking potatoes. I never had a good job growing up."

In junior high and high school, Vigil immersed himself in his studies. He especially cherished his science classes, and his heroes at the time included his science teachers. "I really liked my chemistry teacher in high school, Rollo Corbutt," Vigil said. "I memorized the periodic table of the 92 elements, including the atomic weight of each, because I wanted to impress him. I was just in high school, you know, and I was a good student in science. I learned to like him because he was giving me attention and I just wanted to do a good job for him."

Vigil was a very good athlete, an All-State caliber football player, in fact. At 160 pounds, he played right guard, giving up 30, 40, 50 pounds or more to most opponents. He was the smallest of the linemen on an Alamosa High School team that went undefeated in 1947, his senior year for the Mean Moose, before losing the state championship game to La Junta. Vigil was a team captain as a senior.

The 1947 Alamosa High School football team.
Joe I. Vigil is No. 66, the fourth player from the left in the front row.

"My dad would talk about him and he would say, 'Shit, he was tougher than hell,'" said Norm Roberts, an Alamosa businessman who ran cross country and track and field for Vigil at Adams State in the early 1970s. Many others described Vigil the same way. Even as the smallest lineman on the team, Vigil was the one guy you did not want to go up against for a 32-minute game. He would figure out the angles, and he'd out-quick you on each and every play. In a game, Vigil was tireless, and after so many snaps, the bigger, slower players on the other side of the line would grow frustrated, never quite figuring out what direction No. 66 would be coming from on the next play.

Football also provided a connection to his past that Vigil says he'll never forget.

"[Coach] Isaac Ortega took a bunch of us guys to Cumbres

Pass south of Antonito before football season to get in shape," Vigil said. "We bought a sheep for three bucks and that's what we ate. We had a big ol' campfire, we were roasting ribs and drinking coffee. All of a sudden, this sheepherder rode down from the mountains on his horse because he saw the fire. Isaac was pretty good with old people. I don't know if he knew him, or what. The sheepherder asked if he could have a cup of coffee and we said, 'Of course.'

"So we invited him to sit down and eat with us. After a while, he looks at me and he says, 'I know who you are.' I was 16, 17 years old at the time, I had never met the guy. He says, 'I used to know your dad.'"

Vigil had never known it, but he was nearly the spitting image of his father.

"That was the only person in my life that ever came up to me that knew my dad," Vigil said. "He just knew who my dad was because he was also from Antonito. And he figured out who I was just by looking at me. That was so strange. It just stuck with me all my life."

Joe Vigil (age 17) in 1946 with Scoutmaster Isaac "Ike" Ortega, a popular principal and community leader in Alamosa through the 1960s. The current middle school in Alamosa carries Ortega's name.

Vigil also tried his hand at basketball and track, though he never could make the high school's basketball team. He was a 56-second quarter-miler, good enough to run on the team's mile-relay squad.

"I always admired people who could run, even though at that time I loved football more than I loved track," he said. "No one is second-guessing what I love more now."

Vigil was the salutatorian of the 1948 graduating class at Alamosa High School, then served two years in the Navy, where he was a Golden Gloves boxer. In 1950, he enrolled at Adams State College, where he studied biology and education. He also played football, earning all-conference honors as a lineman. In one memorable game, Vigil went head-to-head with a 300-pound lineman from Sul Ross State Teachers College by the name of Dan Blocker, who went on to fame as Hoss Cartwright of TV's *Bonanza*.

After graduating from Adams State in 1954, he accepted a job to teach biology and coach football at his alma mater, Alamosa High School.

A young Joe Vigil during the formative decade
before he became "Coach"...

... as a teenager (circa 1945)
in Alamosa.

... as a student at Alamosa High School
(circa 1947) leaning against the car he
drove to school at the time.

... striking a pose as a boxer while
in the Navy (circa 1948). Vigil was a
Golden Gloves boxer during a short
stint in the Navy.

... in Los Angeles (circa 1949) in his Navy
uniform, with brothers Augustine (known
as Tino), left; and John (known as Buddy).

... in his Adams State College
letter jacket (1954), just prior
to beginning his teaching career
at Alamosa High School.

◊◊◊

If you press Vigil on the foundation of his success, it becomes very clear that the groundwork was laid by his relationship with his mother. Ask him if his work ethic came from Melinda, and he's quick to respond: "You hit the nail on the head."

To outsiders, Melinda may have seemed to be a background player as Vigil grew from an energetic little boy to Eagle Scout, hardened farm worker, straight-A student, and accomplished athlete. But she was, indeed, the driving influence behind the young man Joe Vigil was becoming. Her values became his values. Her attitudes became his attitudes. Her drive became his drive.

"Oh, yes, he was definitely a Mama's Boy," said Vigil's oldest daughter, Patti. "She always treated him like a baby, even when he was a grown man. That's her baby. She loved him so much. In Alamosa, she'd always ask people, 'Do you know the Coach?' She was always very proud and wanted people to know him."

Melinda also often referred to Vigil as "My Joe" or "My *Hito*." In turn, Vigil lovingly called his mom "Chata"—a French term that means "pug nose," a loving jab at his mom's short, flat nose. But in Portuguese, the word *chata* also means "my dear one."

"He was a very dedicated son; I think she was very fortunate," said Vigil's younger daughter, Peggy. "My dad would pick her up and take her out to some of the practices with his teams. He always tried to include her, and she loved being around the athletes because they gave her attention. I think she gave him a lot of his qualities of caring; most men would not do what he did for her during her life."

"My mom never expressed her love verbally," Vigil says, "but I knew that I made her happy. And I tried to make her happy; I tried to make her proud of me."

Let Me Tell You a Story

Joe Vigil's mother, Melinda Medina, had a special friendship with Shirley Bervig, a mother of six who was one of the leaders in a running class for local women taught by Vigil at Adams State.

"When we would go places, [Melinda] would say, 'This is my adopted *gringo* daughter,'" Bervig said. "Coach would always tell me that when you take mom somewhere, she's going to embarrass you.

"I remember this one time, I took her to Oscar's Mexican Restaurant for lunch, and there were some men with their suits on, sitting and visiting. Chata goes by them and she grabs one of the French fries from the plate of one of the men as we're walking by. She looks back at him and says, 'I'm Sweet Sixteen and never been missed.'

"Those are the kinds of things I went through with Chata. I miss her something terrible. She was such a sweetie and she would tell me such wonderful stories. She was so full of life; that's how I would describe her."

Chata was something of a local celebrity herself. Many of Alamosa's residents barely knew her name, but they did know about "the nice lady who works at Kavley's," which was a popular downtown clothing store. It was quite common to spend 30 minutes buying a pair of jeans when Chata was your salesperson. She loved to talk and tell you about her son who coached at Adams State. And she also liked to flirt with the male clientele.

However, "She wasn't so nice sometimes to the people she worked with, especially when you took 'her' customer," said Shirley Bervig, a family friend. "When she thought that was 'her person,' that would make her unhappy."

For most of her life, Chata also had zero tolerance for drinking alcohol.

"One time my brothers came to see her, and my middle brother, Buddy, brought a six pack of beer," Vigil said. "She wouldn't let him in the house. That's how strongly she was opposed to drinking.

"Those were the types of values I grew up with. I never drank. Well, maybe I've had a glass of wine at a wedding or toasting someone. But I just never drank alcohol."

There was one occasion, though, when Vigil and Kelly took Melinda to a restaurant named The Outhouse, located five miles east of town and known for its steaks and low-light ambience.

"I ordered her a Mai Tai with little umbrellas and all that; you know, a fancy drink. She was sipping it, enjoying it, and she said, 'Ah, this is good, *Hito*.' And all of a sudden I tell Kelly, 'Hey isn't that the pastor that just came in?' She shoved that drink over to me…" Vigil laughs, remembering the story.

Melinda drove her little brown Chevy to work and to church well into her late 80s, but as the years passed, Vigil, his wife, and Bervig began to take care of her more and more. She remained physically strong and mentally sharp for most of her life, but the family was finally forced to put her in a nursing home in 1998, just past her 94th birthday.

"I called her the day she was going to die," Vigil remembers. "I had her in a nursing home there on Carroll Street—Evergreen Nursing Home [about two blocks from Vigil's house]. I spent the day with her, and I just knew she wasn't going to last the night. So I went home and got a bite to eat and told Kelly, 'I'm going back to the nursing home. My mom's not going to make it through the night.' When I got back there, I'd been gone about an hour and a half, I knew she was going. I grabbed hold of her hand and she asked me to read to her. She had her Bible right there on the table, next to her bed, and I opened it to the 23rd Psalm—that was her favorite—and I read it to her:

> The Lord is my Shepherd, I shall not want.
> He makes me to lie down in green pastures;
> He leads me beside still waters.
> He restores my soul;
> He leads me in paths of righteousness for His name's sake.
> Even though I walk through the valley of the shadow of death, I will fear no evil for You are with me; Your rod and Your staff, they comfort me.
> You prepare a table before me in the presence of my enemies; You anoint my head with oil; my cup overflows.
> Surely goodness and mercy follow me all the days of my life, and I will dwell in the house of the Lord forever."

Vigil closed the Bible, squeezed his mother's hand, and Melinda Medina breathed her last.

3

A NATURAL
LEADER

"*I* am so grateful for those final moments," Vigil said, recalling his mother's passing. "What a great memory to have of your mother." In his grief, Vigil was the man Melinda Medina had raised him to be: tough, yet compassionate. Hardened, yet loving. Realistic, yet optimistic.

"Growing up at the time he grew up, he had many struggles in his life," said Vigil's daughter Peggy. "But I think the thing that has had the most impact in his life is that he tends to focus on the positive instead of the negative. He always tries to find the best out of any situation; you know, to him the glass is always half full. That's one of the things that I've admired about him. I think a lot more people would be a lot more happy if they had that outlook about life."

Those were among the endearing qualities that landed Vigil his first job at his alma mater, Alamosa High School, in 1954. For Vigil, it was a dream job—teaching biology and coaching football. Just six years earlier, he was walking the same hallways and dressing in the same locker rooms. Only now he was the teacher, and like his Baptist grandfather many years before, he, too, had a following of adoring disciples.

"My dad told me the story that when Coach would lecture in his biology classes, kids would leave their other classes, and even teachers would leave if they had a planning period, and they'd sit outside his door to hear him lecture," said Norm Roberts, an Alamosa businessman and former Vigil athlete.

"I never realized what the hell was going on," Vigil said. "I used to have a lot of people standing outside my door just to listen because I talked about everything—not just biology, but also about life in general. I wanted to do a good job of teaching my kids. And you know, I really loved every one of them, even the ones that used to piss me off."

The school's principal trusted Vigil so much that he would often direct troubled youth toward his classes.

"I used to teach a class that the kids called 'dumbbell science' because the troublemakers who had bad grades would get in there," Vigil said. "I used to take them on a field trip to the [Rio Grande] river. We'd collect water and bring it back and talk about amoeba and all that. I actually had them interested in taking field trips."

Vigil was easy for kids to like. For starters, a lot of those he was now teaching still knew him as a local football hero, from his years at Alamosa High and at Adams State. And he was a strong, physically imposing figure. But the teenagers also gravitated to him because they perceived his enthusiasm for people.

"Some people look at you, and they look right through you, like they're looking for the next person to talk to," said Larry Fujimoto, a shy freshman the year Vigil began working at the high school. "But with Vigil, you never felt unimportant in front of him."

At many schools, students walk the hallways or hang out

in the commons area before classes begin each day. Or, maybe they'd flirt with the boys or the girls…typical stuff for teenagers.

But that's not what was happening at Alamosa High School in the mid-1950s. Fujimoto remembers that the cool thing to do before school—or later in the day after you wolfed down your lunch—was to hang out in Mr. Vigil's classroom. Most days, the number of kids—boys and girls—sitting and talking and gawking was 30 or more.

"We would all end up in his room," Fujimoto said. "We would talk about sports, we would talk about life…really about anything at all. It was amazing. It was amazing."

For Vigil, it seems like a simple life, right? Go to school, hang out with kids, teach a subject you absolutely adore, and talk about last night's game. Except with Vigil, there's always more. By the time he began teaching at Alamosa High, Vigil was married, and the couple had just welcomed their first child, Patti. The family moved into a house off the corner of Ninth and State streets in Alamosa. Vigil had bills to pay, and a teacher's salary—in those days, about $8,000 a year—wasn't going to keep the creditors away.

So, he'd get up at 4 a.m. to open the local gas station, and for the next three hours pump gas for anyone who came by. He would head to school at 7 a.m. for a full teaching schedule, coach for a couple hours after, eat dinner at home, then head back to the gas

Joe Vigil in the 1950s, when he was teaching biology and coaching football at Alamosa High School.

station to fill up semi-trucks. He did this, tirelessly, day after day after day. And rarely did anyone fully understand the countless hours Vigil was pouring into the people around him.

"When I was three years old, maybe four, I would go to work with him at the gas station," Patti said. "I remember this one time, it was so cold outside, and my mom had a meeting somewhere, and we were going to walk home. So he stuck me in his jacket and carried me all the way home. I was so tiny."

Vigil's career and his drive to provide for his family had his time, but there's no doubt that his two girls—Peggy was born three years after Patti—had his heart.

"My childhood memories were so awesome," Peggy said. "I loved my childhood. I'm really surprised I didn't go into the field of science or biology because you know my dad was a biology teacher. But because of my dad, that's why I love the outdoors so much. Growing up, I can remember having butterfly collections, ant farms, insect collections—you know, I just loved that stuff. It was because of my dad; he made it fun.

Joe Vigil's daughters, Patti (left) and Peggy, near Garden of the Gods in Colorado Springs (circa 1980).

"We were the house where all of the kids would come and hang out because we were always doing stuff. We even had a little track meet in the backyard. I can remember pole vaulting over the neighbor's three-foot fence, and throwing stuff pretending like we were throwing the shot put; jumping over stuff, pretending they were the hurdles. My sister and I were always outside playing until it was dark. It's not like today. Our parents kicked us outside and said, 'Go play. Come back in when we call you.'"

Patti adds: "We'd go swimming, we'd go running. Both Peggy and I were athletic and loved sports."

In fact, Patti grew to become an All-American gymnast at Adams State. In her adult life, she took up bodybuilding, and at one time held two world records for her weight class—lifting 350 pounds in the dead lift and 300 in the squat. At the time, she weighed all of 97 pounds.

Let Me Tell You a Story

Joe Vigil's older daughter, Patti, fondly remembers taking family trips in the summer as her dad traveled to study.

"The best part of growing up with him was when we would go on vacation in the summers to different schools for education," she said. "We'd go to different places in the summer and it was so fun because we had his total attention then. During the school year, we didn't have his full attention because the track guys were always at the house or he was busy practicing with his team.

"It was hard to share him with his athletes, but we learned to do it, and thank God the track guys were really great people. They had great respect for my dad. They didn't drink, they didn't cuss, and they didn't smoke. They were very close-knit. It was like a big family."

Patti also competed in baton twirling and was the twirler at Adams State football games. As a teen, she dreamed of being a baton twirler.

"When I was training for the baton-twirling championships, I would show my dad my routines and he was very encouraging," Patti said. "He'd want me to march up and down the yard. He'd say, 'All right Patti Jo, go to the end of the fence and I want you to march all the way across. Lift those knees, lift those knees….' It was so funny as I look back on it."

Peggy was a good high school athlete, but as she grew, she took on her dad's thirst for knowledge. She earned master's degrees in exercise physiology and curriculum and instruction, and in the early 1980s was hired as the head coach for distance runners at Stephen F. Austin University in Nacogdoches, Texas, where she coached for seven years. She had a stint as the U.S. women's coach for the multistage Ekiden Relay in Japan and served on the NCAA rules committee.

"When you coach at the Division I level," she said, "you don't have a life. I'd come home to visit and people would ask what I did for fun. I'd say, 'Fun? What's that?'"

Today, like her dad, Peggy is still working when many would be thinking about retirement. Since 1993, she's been writing curriculum to teach ethics in U.S. schools, lessons that are currently being taught in K–12 schools across the country.

"Back in 1993, it was better known as character education or life skills," she said. "I became very interested in that because I think there's a direct connection between sports and life. Athletics can teach you a lot about life, teach you a lot about integrity, respect, being a good teammate and those types of things. I still wanted to be connected to athletics, but in a different way."

She helped to develop the U.S. Olympic Training Center's Champions in Life program, which promotes the Olympic

Games and supports athletes in becoming positive role models in their communities.

"Later on," she says, "I started writing curriculum for the U.S. Anti-Doping Agency, thanks to Lance Armstrong because he had been their big ambassador and so they had to throw all of that away when he was found guilty of doping. I came in and helped to write the new curriculum."

Asked what it was like growing up with a father who was a driven coach, Peggy laughs. "He was pretty much a hard-ass. He expected the same thing out of my sister and me as he expected from his athletes, in that he wouldn't settle for anything less than perfect. So I think it was kind of tough being his daughter. You had some big shoes to fill. As an adult, I understand it better, and as I got into coaching, I understood it even more than my sister, even though she was an athlete. But I understood his expectations, and I now understand the commitment that it takes to succeed at a high level, and that it takes away from family time."

Both girls became a reflection of their father: able leaders who were determined to succeed and fiercely motivated to help others along the way, which were precisely the qualities that set in motion Vigil's path from small school football coach to the pinnacle of track and field and distance running success. In 1954, he was the assistant football coach at Alamosa High School; he had no other duties in the athletic department. But that was about to change. Vigil tells the story:

> Everybody knew I loved football; I had nothing to do with track. The head coach for football, Joe Harrell, was also the head coach for track. That spring, he put out the first call for track. I went to the gym that day just to see

what was going on. I was always interested in what was going on. And I did like track a little bit.

Well, only three boys showed up: Luther Quintana, Cletus Arrellano, and Dave Miller. Harrell looked around and said, 'Well, if this is all there is, then we're not having track this year.' I looked back, because I was sort of sitting toward the front and the tears started rolling down from their eyes.

I went home and I told my wife, 'I'm going to see if I can help those guys somehow.' I didn't know what I was going to do. I went to Harrell the next day and said, 'Would you feel offended if I tried to help those guys?' He said, 'No, but you better go through the administration,' which was good advice.

So I went to the principal, who sent me to the superintendent, John Evans, and I told him what I wanted to do. He said, 'We'll let you know.' In about two weeks, they said I could coach those kids. When I left, [Evans] said there will be no budget and no money for you. I said, 'That's all right, that's not what I'm after.' I just wanted to help those kids. I didn't have anything to do after school in the spring.

I started working with them a little bit; I didn't know much, but I helped them out. I'd take them to meets all over the San Luis Valley, you know, every Saturday I would throw them in the car. It didn't take much gas to go to Monte Vista or Sargent or Del Norte [all were within 30 miles]. And there were no entry fees at that time.

And then something great started happening: those boys were winning medals. Every week. All the way up to the district meet in Salida, where all three qualified for the state meet in Boulder.

"But we had no money to take them to state," Vigil says. "So I went home and I raised money; I think I raised $175, and we went to the state meet."

Bundled up in a single hotel room, getting by on just the bare minimum for meals, the boys and their coach represented Alamosa High School at the 1955 Colorado State Track and Field Championships. Quintana won a medal in the mile run. And when the results were reported in local newspapers on Sunday, it surprised many—including the school's principal.

"I got to school on Monday and he called me into his office," Vigil said. "He tells me, 'I didn't give you permission to go to the state meet.' I reminded him that he said I could coach these kids and that's what I did. It didn't cost the school any money, just my time. He couldn't say much to that."

Vigil continued as an assistant coach for football in 1955 and head coach of track in 1956. Early in 1956, he was offered the job as head coach for football. But the school's administration claimed to have a "rule" that individuals were allowed to be the head coach for only one sport, even though coaches before him—and after—had led more than one sport. Vigil said he suspected he was being denied an opportunity to be the head coach for two sports because he was Hispanic. Nonetheless, Vigil faced a dilemma: follow the sport that had been his love to that point, having earned many honors and accolades, or meander on over to this peculiar sport that he had come to coach by happenstance.

He chose track and field.

4

THE MEAN
MOOSE MACHINE

*I*t took just a little under two years for Vigil to put together a track and field team at Alamosa High School that was capable of winning the Colorado state championship. Vigil was giving every ounce of his energy to the rising program and finding that his little hometown was ripe with kids who had talent for track and field. In 1956, his first year as an official high school head coach, he had his first state champion, a muscular shot putter and discus thrower named Dale Pruett. Vigil says Pruett provided the impetus for wanting to learn all he could about the sport:

> I didn't know much [about track and field], but I cared about those kids. I had developed a fondness for track and I was attached to the kids I was working with. I'm sort of a creampuff that way; I've always liked the kids I worked with.
>
> One day, Dale Pruett comes up to me and he says, 'Coach, I want to be able to throw the shot put 50 feet. How do I do that?' I didn't know what to tell him. And

it embarrassed me. I thought, 'Damn, this kid wants me to teach him how to throw the shot put farther and I don't know what to tell him.' So, I started looking for all the material I could get my hands on. I tried to study an event or two every year, you know, areas where I thought I had a weakness, and read up on it. If I had talented kids in an area, it motivated me to study a little bit more. I became a much better coach over the years because of that.

Eventually, I went through every event and learned as much as I could, and I subscribed to a couple magazines that were out in the field at the time. One of them was the *Yessis Sports Review*, a Russian document that used to come out every month [the forerunner to the *Soviet Sports Review*, published in the 1960s by American biomechanist Michael Yessis]. And that's what started my routine for reading every day. I think the first thing you have to do to be a leader is to set an example for your kids that you know what you're talking about. The reading that I did, I was able to learn a few things and I was able to answer a few questions, as opposed to not being able to answer Dale Pruett's 'how can I be better' question.

The high school's sports teams were called the Maroons but were better known by their scowling moose mascot, a raging heap of smoke billowing through its nostrils. The pep squads warn opponents to watch out for the Mean Moose Machine. And from 1956 through 1965, that's exactly what Vigil's track and field teams became.

Pruett, also a high school football and basketball star, was one of the early anchors of Vigil's track and field program. The locals called him "Fluff," maybe not the toughest nickname you'd give to the local high school stud. But it was reflective of Pruett, a gentle soul who—like Vigil a decade before—was a guy you didn't want to cross on the athletic field.

"His dad was a police officer in Alamosa," Vigil remembers. "This one day, he comes knocking on my door, with Dale right behind him. I answer the door, and I say, 'How can I help you?'

"His dad asks me, 'Coach, is my boy a good kid? Does he have respect for others?' And I tell him, 'Yes, yes, he's a good kid. He's a hard worker.' And then his dad tells me, 'Well, OK, but I want you to know that if he acts up, I give you permission to give him a kick in the ass.'"

Vigil never had to do so. Pruett, who also competed in the high jump and 880-yard run, became a leader for the Mean Moose teams that in the mid-1950s made a quick ascent up the state rankings.

◊ ◊ ◊

By 1958, Alamosa entered the Colorado state championships as the team favored to win the Class AA division—the middle of three classifications in the state.

When it was time for the finals of the 180-yard low hurdles, Larry Fujimoto was an imposing figure. He had transformed from the wide-eyed freshman to a terror on the track as a senior.

"He was the best runner in the state at that event, and he also ran the sprint relays," Vigil says. "He was leading the race the whole way until he tripped over the last hurdle."

Fujimoto never made it to the finish line. He limped off the track, perhaps more devastated emotionally than physically. Pruett jumped out of the stands and hugged his teammate as they walked through the infield. And Alamosa ended up in second place, ½ point from winning the state championship.

"He was heartbroken," Vigil remembers. "And the team was feeling pretty bad because we would have easily won the meet. When he got off the track, I gave him a big ol' hug and told him, 'There's always tomorrow.' And his mom was sitting with me when I told him that. He felt like he let the team down, but, nah, we got the second-place trophy."

Even so, more than 60 years later, Fujimoto still gets choked up reliving that moment.

"I ran those hurdles for four, five, six years going back to junior high, and the only hurdle I ever hit was the last hurdle of my last race and I would have won the state championship," he said. "I hit the hurdle and it flipped me.

"That moment was…" Fujimoto's voice cracks. "You know, well, I did feel like I failed the team because we would have won. And I do remember that Dale Pruett came and talked to me and my uncle came down from the stands and my parents were in the stands. But Coach Vigil, he was so compassionate. Oh yeah. You know, just the thought of him making me feel important. He was my holy spirit; he was my greatest mentor in life."

Six decades later, Vigil recalls that story often, to coaches at running clinics, at Hall of Fame induction dinners, and during a ceremony to unveil a bronze statue in his honor. Still a young man—he had not yet reached his 30th birthday—and a young coach, Vigil's perspective in a moment of an excruciating defeat was honorable and humane.

"Larry was close to me; he's still close to me," says Vigil, who also was Fujimoto's and Pruett's Scoutmaster when the two boys received the Eagle Scout badge in 1955. "We call each other up every now and then. He became a doctor of Oriental medicine, providing acupuncture to his patients. For many years, he would go to Altea, Spain, to work in a clinic and all of the rich oil men from the United Arab Emirates would come in. He'd spend a month there treating those people, and they loved him there."

Let Me Tell You a Story

In 1958, Denny Nash fell just short of qualifying for the Colorado State Track and Field Championships as a senior at Alamosa High School. It was a disappointing finish for the young man, who had a good shot at a state medal.

He remembers the compassion of his coach, who recognized the young man's disappointment. Vigil found a way to take Nash with the team, a reward for his dedication to the team that season.

In 2018, Nash wrote a letter that recognized the impact that particular instance and others have had on him and many of Vigil's athletes.

"Your biography," Nash wrote, "does not include the significant impact you had on hundreds of students and athletes, which has spanned more than 60 years. It only highlights those athletes who reached the pinnacle of their sports.

"You must also be recognized for your support for and rewarding of the athletes who didn't win the ribbon or medal. You encouraged, guided, supported, and recognized that each of us performed to the best of our abilities, and in doing so, you have played a significant role in who we have become."

Despite the narrow loss in 1958, the Alamosa track and field engine was just revving up. Bill Heersink won the state title in the discus in 1959, and John Phillips won the 100, 200, and shot put and ran a leg on a gold-medal-winning 880-yard relay in 1960, leading Alamosa to another runner-up finish.

"Have I told you about John Phillips?" Vigil asks, itching for the opportunity to share the memory of one of his greatest athletes, a 6-foot-2, powerful man-child who "was fast as grease," Vigil said.

"His dad was a farmer in Sargent [a small town 15 miles northwest of Alamosa], but during the drought in the 1950s, his family went broke. So his dad came to Adams State as a freshman, the same year that John was a freshman at Alamosa High School. They graduated the same year. His mom had also graduated [from Adams State] and they got jobs in Durango [Colorado, 150 miles west of Alamosa]. John's dad became a science teacher and his mom became a music director in Durango.

"He was a great athlete, but he also loved music. His mother had taught him to sing and play the flute. His senior year, he landed a part in the school musical, which so happened to be on a Friday night before we were to compete in the Colorado Relays in Boulder on Saturday."

"Coach Vigil always encouraged my participation in other school activities," Phillips said. "It wasn't just studied tolerance on his part; he actually meant it." Phillips decided to stay in Alamosa and sing in Friday night's musical, "but before I knew it, Joe Vigil pulled an airline ticket from his hat, and following Friday night's performance, I was on the next Frontier Airlines flight from Alamosa to Denver to join the track team the next day."

Phillips never knew nor questioned where that plane ticket came from; 48 years later he found out.

"Joe Vigil buttonholed the good merchants of Main Street in Alamosa to come up with the cash for that ticket," Phillips said. "I was floored when I learned this. And for 48 years he never volunteered to tell me…I had to ask."

With Vigil's blessing, Phillips practiced just three days a week his senior year because he needed to work and help his family pay the bills.

"During the spring of my senior year, things became so tight that I had to seek an after-school job," Phillips says. "I mentioned my dilemma to Coach and he instantly said, 'Do what you have to do.' So I took the job, and a few weeks later, four gold medals at the state track meet."

"After John won his four state championships in 1960, he got a full-ride scholarship to play football at Colorado State University under a coach by the name of Don 'Tuffy' Mullison," Vigil says. "The players used to show up two weeks before school started for practices and tryouts. Based on those two weeks, John made the team. When school started, Mullison had a team meeting and told all of the players that they needed to attend study hall every night."

Phillips was a straight-A student who had his heart set on studying music and science. The commitment to a big-school football program in the Skyline Conference was more than he wanted to take on, so he went to Mullison's office and quit before the season began. He stayed a year at Colorado State, then transferred to the College of Emporia in Kansas, where he also received a full-ride scholarship to study and play football.

A dominating force on the Emporia football team, school record holder in the shot put, and conference champion in both the 100-yard dash and the shot, Phillips was later named to that school's athletic Hall of Fame. He earned a post-graduate degree in molecular genetics, eventually teaching for more than 45 years at the University of Guelph in Ontario, Canada. "He was just one heckuva guy," Vigil says.

By the early 1960s, Vigil's track and field teams had become one heckuva program, as well. The school's home meet, the Alamosa Relays, had become a premier track and field meet in southern Colorado and northern New Mexico.

"All the judges wore maroon blazers," Vigil remembers. "I had the superintendent of schools out there timing races, the principal, several of the teachers that wanted to help, and some of the guys from the college. Every year, we'd get 30 teams to come to Alamosa to compete, from Pueblo and Colorado Springs, south from New Mexico, north from Buena Vista and Salida, and all the way from Durango in the west. It was a big meet.

"I was building a culture of track and field and running, and we had established a pretty good tradition. Track was an important sport; it wasn't like a second thought at Alamosa, you know, like it is at some other schools. I remember getting a Christmas tree in my biology room one year, and I had ordered a new shot put and discus, and I put them under the tree for some of the guys on the team with a note that said, 'Merry Christmas, Santa Claus.' Those were little things I did that made the track people feel special."

Alamosa's reputation in track and field had grown so much that in 1963, the Colorado State High School Activities Association selected the town to host the Class AA State Championships.

"The meet was held at Adams State [about three blocks from the high school]," Vigil says. "Dale Pruett's brother, Dave, was my quarter-miler, which he won that day. And Harvey Carter was my half-miler, which he also won. And they both ran the mile relay, which won the state championship."

The week before, Pruett and Carter had finished third at the district meet, barely qualifying for the state meet. When Vigil asked them how they were able to turn their fortunes around in just one week, they said, "You told us we would win at state!" Simple as that.

The meet was broadcast on the local radio station, KGIW. Alamosa had never won a state championship in track and field, but powered by Pruett and Carter, Vigil's 1963 Maroons became hometown heroes.

"I remember going downtown that afternoon and because the meet had been on the radio, everyone knew we had won and they were so happy. It was pretty exciting," Vigil said.

By now, kids were flocking to Vigil's track and field program, a far cry from the three dejected teens who had begged for a chance to compete eight years earlier. Vigil was a trusted adult and a master motivator, and he had a cadre of kids who were clinging to his every word and his every command.

"I was just myself. I was just myself..." Vigil says when asked about his tactic for motivating young athletes.

"I grew up caring about things. I just carried it over into my work. I knew that people had problems. I knew that my mom had problems. I knew the problems that people on the south side had. I tried to get them all to the next level of success, something you could be proud of. And I just practiced the same principles on the team. You're here; your parents are sacrificing to send you to school. Don't let them down. Work a little harder. Be account-able. Be an impact person for your team. Help your teammates out. You know they're not machines; they're going to have a bad day every now and then. Sometimes for the first time in their life, they were being treated like human beings. And everybody had different problems. Sometimes I'd tell them to come to the office and visit with me about it. Sometimes I'd tell them to come to the house. I had an open-door policy."

At Alamosa High School, Vigil had two rituals at the beginning of each season. First, every senior on the team had to adopt a freshman. "If the freshman didn't show up to practice, I would tell the senior, 'Where's your son? Go get him.'"

The second ritual: before the first meet of the year, every track and field athlete had to state their individual goals in front of their teammates. Most of the athletes' dads were also there to witness their commitment. Vigil memorized the standard each kid had set. Then, when an athlete reached a goal, Vigil would buy an apple or an orange, sign it—right there on the outer peelings—and give it to the kid as recognition of a job well done. That would continue on for three more goals until the young athlete eventually reached a fifth goal and the ultimate prize: a chicken dinner with Coach Vigil at the Campus Cafe, the popular local hangout located directly across the street to the west from the high school track.

"He was also doing that with kids in his classroom," says Larry Jeffryes, who ran two years for Vigil in high school and four years at Adams State College. "My wife was in the Medics Club, which was for people who wanted to go into medicine. He was the faculty sponsor and they would have fundraisers, which was mainly selling candy. The person who sold the most candy would get to go to a chicken dinner with Coach at the Campus Cafe. She worked her butt off so she could have a chicken dinner with Coach.

"Well, she and I had just started dating, and about the same time that she got that award, I had achieved a time or something, so I got a chicken dinner too. He took us both out for a chicken dinner at the Campus Cafe."

◇◇◇

Jeffryes was a horse on Vigil's greatest team at Alamosa, the 1965 season when the school oddly was moved to the state's highest division, Class AAA, where the Maroons would compete against teams from Colorado Springs and Denver, many of them twice the size of the small southern Colorado school. It didn't matter. In 1965, Alamosa was every bit the match of the big-city schools.

"That year, we went to the Duke City Relays in Albuquerque," Vigil says. "Highland High School had not been defeated in 11 years in New Mexico. We went down there with 11 boys and won the Duke City Relays. Everyone was just amazed that we beat Highland High School. The coach who had started that program, Hugh Hackett, went on to be the head coach at the University of New Mexico."

Alamosa was loaded, for sure. Jeffryes ran 9.6 for 100 yards and 21.4 for 220 yards. Fellow senior Dave Bartelt, a 6-foot-3, 240-pound goliath, was a 50-foot-plus shot putter who also ran 21-flat for 220 yards. Wayne Stribling was one of the state's best in the 440-yard run, running sub-:50 for the event. Mike Carter was a sub-2:00 half-miler, and Vigil had a couple milers who ran about 4:30—which, at 7,500-foot altitude, was usually a good enough time to score points at the state meet.

"And we had great relays," Jeffryes says. "You'd be exhausted from running your events during the day and they'd need someone to run the mile relay. Coach would say, 'Jeffryes, you're running the mile relay. Get ready!' What was I going to say? 'Yeah, all right, Coach.'"

One time during the 1965 season, the high school boys got to talking to the college boys at Adams State and began a debate about who had the best 440-yard relay squad. Vigil and the

Adams State coach, Duane Mehn, got in on the argument. So they all decided to settle it on the track.

"We went over to the Adams State track and ran against their 440-relay team, and somehow we beat them," Jeffryes says. "We beat their team, and it really ticked everybody off."

A few weeks later, Alamosa rode the Mean Moose Machine into Boulder for the Class AAA State Championships. The mile-relay squad won in state record time (3:19). The 440-yard relay won in near-record time. The 880-yard relay placed second. Jeffryes was runner-up in the 100 and 220, and Bartelt won the shot put. But the Maroons fell just a few points short to the state's track and field beast at the time, Denver East.

"We all wanted to win that title for Coach," Jeffryes remembers. "We came so close."

No matter. Vigil was doing all right. He was enjoying a pretty lofty status among the state's high school coaches, and bigger schools were soon calling. Days after the 1965 Colorado state meet, Vigil was offered and accepted a job at the newly built Billy Mitchell High School in Colorado Springs to teach science and coach track and field. It was an imposing school, with a budget to match. He would likely have an abundance of great athletes to build his team. More, Colorado Springs was a bustling city that could provide a nice standard of living and numerous amenities for Vigil and his family.

Joe I. Vigil was, it would seem, leaving the ranks of the Have-Nots.

5

LOYALTY WINS

There's something everyone should know about Dr. Joe I. Vigil: his dreams are not like others' dreams. Many of us spend an inordinate amount of time thinking about how we can earn more money, live in a bigger house, get a better job, drive a nicer car, become more famous...it's easy to be lured by external trappings.

Oh, Vigil likes those things, too. He's lived a nice life, has a beautiful, 2,600-square-foot desert home in southern Arizona, and has enough money to travel anywhere he'd like and do the things he wants to do. His world today is certainly a long way from the unassuming life he began 90 years ago. But Vigil never forgot what it was like growing up in south Alamosa, where he learned to believe that life's riches were more closely connected to such virtues as loyalty, friendship, honesty, humility, and service.

In fact, even as his stature as a world-famous coach grew, Vigil was known to meet the local boys down at Mack Pierotti's pool hall on Alamosa's State Street, a joint known as Mack's Place and located a block and a half north of the railroad tracks. Vigil would belly-up to the bar not to drink beer, but rather to grab a hot dog and a Dr Pepper and swap stories with some of his buddies. At the time, State Street between Fifth and Sixth streets was a bar district, but Mack's Place was the one business on the strip where under-age kids were allowed to play pool, pinball, Pac-Man, or air hockey, and grab a bite to eat and Coke to drink.

"One time, Coach came in and said, 'I won't drink a beer, but anybody who wants a hot dog, I'll buy them a hot dog,'" says Frank "Boogie" Romero, who grew up on Alamosa's south side with Vigil and worked for a short time at the pool hall. "Mack says, 'No, Coach, you don't have to do that,' but Coach tells him, 'I want to do that. These kids, they're all good kids and someday they're going to do something good.' He was always saying that about people."

Vigil's dedication to his roots is true to the core. He and Boogie have been friends for nearly 80 years, and Vigil speaks just as fondly about his experiences with him and dozens of others from his hometown as he does about traveling the world with Deena Kastor and Pat Porter and many other giants of track and field and distance running.

So it should come as no surprise to anybody that Vigil happily opened the door when Fred Plachy, John Turano, and Jack "Doc" Cotton arrived unexpectedly at his Colorado Springs apartment in July 1965.

Days before, Duane Mehn had resigned as track coach at Adams State College, and Plachy, the school's president, had zeroed in on one guy for the opening. Vigil was clearly a coach on the rise, as evidenced by his success at Alamosa High School the previous decade. And those in the know remembered how he brought his 440-yard relay team and beat the college men just a few months earlier. Thus, Plachy and Turano, the vice president for academic affairs, and Cotton, the school's basketball coach and a former player for the ABA's Denver Nuggets, hopped in a car for the three-hour drive, hoping Vigil was interested in coming back home.

"I had already signed the contract to be the first track coach at Billy Mitchell High School and to teach physiology," Vigil says. Vigil's contract paid him $10,000 at Billy Mitchell, $2,000 more than he was earning at Alamosa.

"We were even looking for houses in Colorado Springs, but I took the job at Adams State," Vigil says. "I considered coaching in college a challenge, and I liked challenges."

Let Me Tell You a Story

Boogie Romero remembers his boyhood friend Joe Vigil asking him to go to a coaching conference at the University of Colorado in Boulder.

"Naturally, I said yes," Romero said. "There were hundreds and hundreds of coaches from all over the country.

"The night before, he tells me, 'Boogie, at about four o'clock in the morning you're going to hear somebody talking in the restroom.' I asked him what he was talking about, and he tells me, 'Yeah, that will be me. I'm going to start memorizing my speech.'"

Boogie was impressed. "When I heard him talking that morning, I said, 'Oh my God!'

"That day, I went with him to the conference and for about six hours, that man talked and talked, and he had those coaches' attention. It was an experience that I will never forget."

Vigil's first contract at Adams State was for $12,000, roughly $99,000 in today's dollars.

Vigil also initially signed on to coach Adams State's linemen in football, but had his sights on starting a cross country program, which Turano allowed him to do in 1965. Thus, Vigil coached the linemen for a year while getting his cross country program started. Plachy retired after the 1965–1966 school year, but not before fulfilling one of his goals of opening a new athletic facility on the college's north side. Known as Plachy Hall, the facility was a jewel in the small town, and perhaps unique for an NAIA school, with an Olympic-size swimming pool, two basketball courts (one for games and one for practice), a wrestling room, a practice area for gymnastics, a weight room, and a 150-meter indoor track.

Thus, Vigil came home to a shiny new facility and a modest budget to build a small-college program.

Vigil soon convinced one of his high school stars, Larry Jeffryes, to shun a scholarship to the University of Colorado and follow him back to Alamosa to compete for the Adams State track and field team.

"In the transition from Alamosa High School, Coach arrived at Adams State and there's great promise and so on, but what I remember is that it was a constant battle with the other coaches and the athletic director," Jeffryes says. "Coach is Coach, after all. He came in and he's pretty self-assured and he says what he believes, and they weren't used to that. You know, here he was a high school coach coming in, and they had to think, 'What do you know?'"

If Vigil's talk was tough, his actions soon backed it up. He and Cotton developed a strong friendship, perhaps because both never believed that living in a small town was a barrier to achieving greatness. They were, perhaps, an odd pair—Cotton, a lean, 6-foot-7 Anglo and former professional basketball player from Montana, and Vigil, a husky, 5-foot-10 Hispanic and local football hero from the town's south side. But they shared an undying love for their small school and their small community; they were two tenacious coaches who believed that Alamosa and Adams State were the Little Engines that Could. And neither felt threatened by the other's tireless energy and relentless drive, nor jealous of the other's success.

Joe Vigil in the 1960s, about the time that he accepted a job to teach physical education science classes and coach cross country and track and field at Adams State College.

"Around 1966, Cotton was talking about getting the USA basketball team to come to Alamosa to train before the [1968] Mexico City Olympics," Vigil says.

Alamosa, at an altitude of 7,544 feet, was about 100 feet higher in elevation than Mexico City. Vigil began thinking that if Cotton was going to bring basketball players, why not invite the country's best distance runners to train in Alamosa's high altitude as well.

At about the same time, a young man by the name of Leonard Edelen, an elite runner who had just retired from international competition, came to Alamosa to pursue a master's degree in psychology at Adams State College. Better known as Buddy, Edelen was the first American ever to break 2:20 in the marathon and 30:00 in the 10,000 meters. He first broke the American record in the marathon in 1962, finishing fourth at the Fukuoka Marathon in Japan in a time of 2:18:57.

In June 1963, Edelen set the world record at the Polytechnic Marathon in England with a time of 2:14:28. He was the first American to hold the world record since 1925, and he has remained the only American-born runner to hold that record since then. [American Alberto Salazar, who was born in Cuba, set what appeared to be the world record at the New York City Marathon in 1981 but the course was later ruled to be 148 meters short. Khalid Kannouchi, a naturalized American originally from Morocco, set the world record at the London Marathon in 2002.] In 1964, Edelen placed sixth in the marathon at the Tokyo Olympics.

Edelen's clout and name recognition, and Vigil's personality and energy, soon combined to form something of a dream team for attracting distance runners to Alamosa. Along with Cotton and Adams State wrestling coach Frank Powell—who was also working to bring USA team members to train in Alamosa—the men formed a local Olympic Training Committee to bring many of the country's greatest Olympic hopefuls to Alamosa's thin air. Adams State's recently opened Plachy Hall was a centerpiece facility that could adequately meet many of the elite athletes' training needs.

The newly built Adams State athletic facility, named Plachy Hall after longtime school president Fred Plachy, played an important role in Alamosa's turn as an Olympic training ground in 1967–1968.

On Edelen's and Vigil's encouragement, a few of America's best runners began trickling into the small town during the spring and summer of 1967. Most notable among them was Jim Ryun, an established star at the University of Kansas but perhaps best known at that time as the first high school runner to break 4:00 in the mile. Noted exercise physiologist and coach Jack Daniels came to Alamosa to train Ryun and a handful of other middle-distance greats of the day.

But that was simply not good enough for Vigil and Edelen, who had bigger ideas. The two men were putting a full-court press on the Amateur Athletic Union (AAU)—the leading governing body for U.S. track and field then—to establish a marathon to determine the three spots on the U.S. Olympic team for Mexico City. Up to that point, U.S. marathoners were chosen by the U.S. Olympic Committee from their performances at select, established races, such as Boston; Culver City, California; or Yonkers, New York. Why not, the two men thought, forget those races and let the country's best marathoners go head-to-head for the Olympic spots in Alamosa, Colorado?

To prove its capability, the Alamosa Olympic Training Committee staged a midsummer marathon in 1967, inviting two-time Olympic gold medalist Abebe Bikila to come run. He couldn't make it, but fellow Ethiopian Mamo Wolde came in his place. Wolde ran off-course in Alamosa and never finished, but the following year in Mexico City he won gold.

Maybe it was fate, maybe it was Edelen and Vigil's persistence, or maybe it was just dumb luck, but at its annual meeting in Chicago in late 1967, the AAU chose Alamosa as the site for the first-ever U.S. Olympic Marathon Trials. It came with a caveat: the AAU could provide only minimal organizational help, and no budget. Vigil had certainly heard that before. No problem.

Except that it could be a big problem, certainly a big headache, putting on an event at the scale of an Olympic-qualifying race. The AAU demanded that physicians be on hand to conduct pre- and post-race medical examinations of all the runners. There were the logistics of lodging, meals, drinks during the race (Gatorade had just been introduced to the sporting world), volunteers, timing, course safety, road closures, and much, much more. And there was no template in place for the local organizing team.

"Buddy and I had to do everything," Vigil told noted American track and field journalist Amby Burfoot, one of the participants in the original Marathon Trials, in a 2018 story for the Road Runners Club of America. "We were running around ragged. I remember one time, we looked up at each other and just about started crying."

Vigil leaned on the people in his hometown to help out. "He got me in on that when I was still in college," remembers Jeffryes. "I was a junior and senior, and I'd go to the meetings and he named me the head timer for the U.S. Olympic Marathon Trials in 1968."

Think about that for a moment: Vigil assigned 21-year-old Larry Jeffryes, who had never timed a race in his life, to be the head timer for the first-ever U.S. Olympic Marathon Trials.

"Well, he had a way of knowing who he could trust," Jeffryes says. "It certainly made me feel special, and I wanted to make him proud. I think he treated a lot of people like that. There are a lot of people that thought they were pretty special in Coach's eyes. And I think they were."

Vigil says: "You trust people if you have faith in them. But they have to have earned it through the life they have lived, to put that trust in there."

In the months and weeks leading up to the August 18 Alamosa trials, runners began filtering into the small community. Australian Kerry Pearce. Irishman Pat McMahon. Americans Frank Shorter, Steve Gauchpin, Ron Daws, Hal Higdon, Bob Deines, Steve Matthews, Ed Winrow, Tom Laris, Nick Kitt, Bill Clark, George Husuark, Tom Heinonen, Dave Costill, Burfoot, and others. Some came the week of or just days before, such as 1964 Olympic 10,000-meter gold medalist Billy Mills and 1968 Olympic hopefuls George Young and Kenny Moore.

"Frank Shorter came to Alamosa, and it was the first marathon he ever ran," Vigil said. "He was going to school at Yale, and his dad was a retired surgeon from the U.S. Army. He was actually born in Munich. When he came home that summer, his dad bought a ranch in Ranchos de Taos, New Mexico [90 miles south of Alamosa]. He heard about the race. He was a distance runner but had never tried the marathon, so he came and tried it. Four years later, he's an Olympic gold medalist."

Shorter dropped out of the 1968 Alamosa trials with blisters, but he went on to win the U.S. Marathon Trials in 1972 and 1976, winning Olympic gold in 1972 and Olympic silver in 1976.

There were 129 men who entered the race in Alamosa, many of them staying in modest college dorm rooms and eating cafeteria food. The only qualifying standard was that you could get yourself to Alamosa by August 18. Those who arrived early explored new running areas, favoring the levee that lined both sides of the Rio Grande River, dusty country roads framed by 14,300-foot-plus Mount Blanca, and a shaded area on the town's north side that locals called Carroll's Woods. For speed workouts, they hit the college's cinder track or a 700-meter grass loop in Cole Park, just a mile from the Adams State campus.

All the while, Vigil was watching the elite runners closely. Where are they running? How fast are they running? How do they warm up? How do they recover? What are they wearing? What are they eating? What are they drinking? How much are they sleeping? Every movement, he thought, is an opportunity to understand more about what it takes to train elite distance runners.

Vigil already was having some success with his own Adams State team. Including the upcoming 1968 fall season, his cross country squad won the first four recorded Rocky Mountain Athletic Conference (RMAC) championships (1965 through 1968), and had the individual champions at each of those meets: Bob Henry, Rick Vafeades, Mike McDonald, and Robert Montoya. McDonald was a four-time All-American in cross country—the only one to accomplish that in the history of the program. But beyond the conference, the budding Adams State program was mostly an also-ran. Vigil, aware that he had a lot to learn if that were to change, recalled his mindset at the time:

> Really, I didn't know anything about training distance runners. I was learning, but I didn't really know. When I started at the college in 1965, nobody ever thought the program would develop as it did. You know, I'm just a Latino. I felt at the time that it was sort of a token job, that maybe the only reason they hired me was because I could teach anatomy and physiology, not to coach so much.
>
> But I had a hero at the time, Alex Francis, the coach at Fort Hays. And I used to call him up because he had the best team in the NAIA at the time, and good runners. He'd give me tips here and there and he became my hero and my leader. I went to an NAIA convention and at that time the U.S. Olympic Committee for track and field was composed of four members from the NAIA,

four from the NCAA, four from the high school federation, four from the junior college federation, and four
from the Catholic Youth Organization. Out of the clear
blue, Alex Francis recommended me as one of the four
from the NAIA, and I got voted in. After three years as a
college coach, here I was on the Olympic Committee for
track and field. What a shock that was to me.

I came home and I said, 'Damn, I'm going to have
to contribute if I'm going to be a member.' So I started
reading and studying as much as I could, and that's been
going on for more than 50 years.

That was 1967, and that summer, Vigil flew with Daniels
and the middle-distance runners who had trained in Alamosa
to the AAU National Track and Field Championships in Bakersfield, California. Vigil watched on June 23 as Ryun set the world
record in the mile, running a 3:51.1 before a raucous crowd, a
mark that would stand for nearly eight years.

A chance meeting at that same meet would later open more
doors for Vigil.

"At the time, foreigners could run in our national championships, and the Mexican coach was a guy from Poland, Thaddeus
Kempka," Vigil said. "He was a brilliant coach, but he was having trouble speaking English when he went to enter his athletes,
and I just happened to be standing there. I asked him in Spanish,
'*Puedo ayudarte?*' [Can I help you?] He told me what he was trying to do, so I helped him enter his people in the various races
he had."

◈◈◈

Vigil returned home to Alamosa to coach his team, teach his
classes, and continue his work on the Olympic Marathon Trials,

which were held the following year on a hot day in the middle of August. The people of Alamosa came out in waves and fired up the small-town charm to cheer on the runners. Vigil even had appointed a marathon queen and her princess court to ride in the lead vehicle, waving at the spectators ahead of the runners.

The marathon consisted of five loops around a 5.2-mile course, a course called "The Loop," with the final .2 miles stretching to the finish line in front of Plachy Hall. There were 113 runners who started the race; just 60 finished the entire distance.

When it was done, George Young—the country's best steeple-chaser at the time—had won the first-ever U.S. Olympic Marathon Trials, followed by Kenny Moore and Ron Daws. The three men earned their right to represent the United States at the Mexico City Olympics, which would be held just over two months later. Young finished 16th in the Olympic marathon but was the bronze medalist in the steeplechase. Moore was the top American marathoner at the Olympics, placing 14th.

Vigil, exhausted from working on the trials for many months before, admitted he needed a break:

> I said to myself, 'Gee, it would be nice to be going to the Olympics.' I had never even dreamed about it before that. So I asked my administration at Adams State if I could go. Keep in mind, I didn't have tickets. I didn't have a hotel. But they said, 'No, you can't go. We can't afford to have two people gone from the (physical education) department,' because Jack Cotton had a sabbatical and he had applied for it to go to the Olympics. I understood that; I was the teacher of the science classes in the PE department.
>
> But two weeks later they call me up and said, 'Coach,

we thought it over and we think it's OK if you go for two weeks.' I didn't have tickets and I didn't know anybody in Mexico City. So I called Thaddeus Kempka, and I told him I needed some help. He remembered me. And he says he'd call me back the next day. He did, and he tells me that he's got a hotel room for me, but I was going to have to pay for it. I said fine. Then he says, 'We're going to let you into the infield to watch the events.'

For the record, Vigil was a meet official at the 1968 Mexico City Olympics, but he had very little in the way of official duties. From the infield, he experienced the roar of more than 80,000 spectators in Mexico's *Estadio Olímpico Universitario* as Olympic drama unfolded right before his eyes. He watched the remarkable 1500-meter final in which Kip Keino of Kenya stunned Ryun, running an Olympic record 3:34.91 to win by 20 meters. He watched Bob Beamon soar 29 feet, 2 inches in the long jump, the first human ever to exceed 29 feet in that event. He saw Jim Hines of the United States become the first human ever to break 10 seconds in the 100-meter dash. And he watched as Dick Fosbury of the United States revolutionized the high jump, for the first time using a back-first technique in Olympic competition, to clear 7 feet, 4¼ inches and win gold with a new Olympic record. Today, the standard form for all high jumpers is the Fosbury Flop.

"The 1968 Olympics was also the first time that they had an all-weather track," Vigil said. "There was an engineer from England who was coaching David Hemery, that country's 400-meter hurdler. He studied the surface and noticed that it was giving energy back to the runners. So he changed Hemery's stride pattern from 15 strides between hurdles to 13. And Hemery not only won gold, but he set the world record at 48.12 seconds."

That year in Mexico City, 14 world records and 12 Olympic records were set in track and field. It's also known as the Olympics when distance runners from the African nations made their first significant breakthrough on the world stage; it was thought at the time that having spent their lives running in their countries' mountainous regions made them better adapted to Mexico City's altitude. Since 1968, African distance runners have remained dominant forces in every Olympic and World Championship event.

Vigil also witnessed Americans Tommie Smith and John Carlos—the gold and bronze medalists, respectively, in the 200-meter run—raise their black-gloved fists in protest during the playing of the American national anthem, a silent gesture aimed to show support for human rights.

The 1968 Olympics were rich with history; seeing it up close energized Vigil. He headed back to his hometown with even more enthusiasm for the job ahead of him.

6

THE GUINEA PIGS

 *B*ack in Alamosa after 14 exhilarating days in Mexico City, Vigil capitalized on the momentum started by the Olympic Marathon Trials to launch his hometown into distance-running relevance, even if it was just a flicker compared to the better-known and established distance meccas in Eugene, Oregon, and Boulder, Colorado.

"After 1968, a lot of people wanted to come to train at high altitude," Vigil said. "I was contacted by national federations, including the Finns, Italians, Japanese, and others, and my workload increased because I had to take care of them. All of these foreign runners were coming in and my athletes were motivated by them, too. I would tell them, 'You're running on the same trail that Frank Shorter ran, or Billy Mills ran.' And that made them feel good, you know."

Though his cross country program had the Rocky Mountain Athletic Conference's first four titles under its belt heading into the 1969 season, Vigil knew he had to work harder than other coaches on the recruiting trail. The top runners in Colorado and New Mexico weren't likely to choose his small NAIA school.

Instead, they were lured to the University of Colorado, Colorado State University, or the University of New Mexico, all of which had strong and established programs with more flashy facilities. Vigil figured he'd chase the kids with potential and convince them he could turn them into national-caliber athletes.

One thing working for him was that he already had a reputation as a solid college coach. One athlete, Rick Vafeades—a superb all-around athlete from Denver South High School who won the conference cross country championship in 1967— embodied Vigil's early success.

"They called him the 'Galloping Greek from Cherry Creek (a suburb in south Denver),'" Vigil says. "He originally came to Adams State to play football and basketball and had asked me if he could run with the cross country team to get in shape. I only had a handful of kids then, so I said, 'Sure.' He started running with us (during his junior year) and never went out for football or basketball again."

After his final season at Adams State, Vafeades ran the 1968 Olympic Marathon Trials, finishing 36th in 3:01:40.

But enticing promising 17- and 18-year-olds to come run for a program that had yet to join the ranks of the big leagues was fraught with hits and misses—more of the latter, though Vigil had the kind of relentless attitude that was needed to overcome those.

In fall 1967, Vigil showed up to the Aurora Invitational near Denver to watch a young man from Cherry Creek High School who was tearing up the state's running scene early that season.

"I happened to win that race by a large margin," says Lance Harter, "and as I walked through the finish chute, there was a man at the end who greeted me."

Running junkies know Harter as the Hall of Fame coach from the University of Arkansas, who in 30 years with the

Razorbacks' women's cross country and track and field programs has coached more than 500 All-Americans, including 25 NCAA individual champions and four NCAA team champions. Prior to that, he was the head coach of the dominant women's cross country program at Cal Poly San Luis Obispo that won a record 10 straight NCAA Division II titles from 1982 to 1991. Harter was the head coach for the first eight of those titles before taking the job at Arkansas.

Before his coaching success, Harter was a pretty good runner, too. And so Vigil hopped in his car and drove nearly four hours to try and convince the young high school star to join the green and gold of Adams State.

"Hi, my name is Joe Vigil. I'm the coach at Adams State in Alamosa," Vigil said as Harter exited the finish chute.

"I said, 'Ah, OK,' and I chatted with him for a while about the idea of college," Harter says. "Up until then, no one in my family had gone to college, so the idea of going to college was a little bit of a backburner thought for me. Was it even possible? Coach Vigil was the one who introduced me to the idea that you could go to college and run.

"Well, I ended up going to school at Texas Tech, but I wish I had followed up with Coach Vigil, because I think my determination to be as good as I could have possibly been would have been a perfect marriage with his style of coaching. I ended up floundering through college, and did some racing as a post-collegian, but knew pretty quickly that coaching was my avenue versus trying to be an elite athlete."

A few months after trying to recruit Harter, Vigil was on the recruiting trail again, this time finding himself in a steamy gymnasium in Lafayette, Colorado, to watch a brash high school senior playing point guard for the local basketball team. Larry Zaragoza had won the state 800-meter championship as a junior, and college coaches were already circling, including Vigil, who sent handwritten letters ahead of his visit.

By his own admission, Zaragoza was self-assured in his athletic abilities. He was definitely a feisty one. He says now that his tough exterior was likely due to the fact that his father was an alcoholic, and he had spent most of his high school years living with his uncle, Ray Vigil (no relation to Joe Vigil). In sports, he found a comfort zone. He especially loved track and field, where he grew up idolizing Jim Ryun and other American greats such as Glenn Cunningham, Tommie Smith, Lee Evans, and John Carlos.

"After the game that night, Coach Vigil comes out of the stands and he says that he wanted to meet me and Uncle Ray in person," Zaragoza said. The three left the gym for a school office where they could talk more privately.

"He says, 'I like you, Uncle Ray, because of your last name… Vigil, you know,'" Zaragoza said. "Then he looks at me and he says, 'Tell me something. I watched you run all over that court tonight, and isn't the objective of that game to put the ball in the basket?'"

The two older men had a laugh. Zaragoza wasn't so sure he thought it was funny.

"Anyway, we just start talking about recruiting," Zaragoza continued. "I said, 'Well, should we tell him, Uncle Ray? I've already signed with Colorado State.' He looks at Uncle Ray, and he looks at me, and he says, 'It doesn't matter. It's nonbinding. They're NCAA and we're NAIA. If you're interested in Adams State, we can work it out.'

"When I talked to him during that meeting, what really convinced me that the man cared about me was when he looked at Uncle Ray and said, 'If Larry comes to Adams State, Uncle Ray, I'll make you a promise. If this man doesn't complete his degree in four years, I'll put my foot in his ass.'

"I thought, 'Wow, nobody talks to me like that.' But on the way home, Uncle Ray and I talked about that. I asked Uncle Ray what he thought about that man. I liked him, because he cared about me as a person. He was the first man that talked about getting an education—not track, running, teammates…ah, he talked a little about that—but education was the bottom line. That was the convincer for me. I'm Adams State–bound. And it was because of him and his personality in that meeting. He was so confident, so caring, and so concerned about me as a person, not so much being a runner."

Adams State was slowly climbing the NAIA ranks in cross country, stringing together six top-10 finishes at the national meet in as many years from the program's genesis in 1965 to 1970. Vigil was learning more about training distance runners, spending his summers traveling to visit the world's top coaches and international sports federations, mostly in Europe and on his own dime.

"We used to joke that our group, and many of those in Coach's early years at Adams State, we were the guinea pigs," said Norm Roberts, who was recruited from nearby Del Norte (Colorado) High School in 1971. "He tried everything on us. One hundred-plus miles a week. Repeat miles. Sprints up the Sand Dunes National Monument. We rarely rested, not like the teams do now. We ran a race every week, and then we went straight from cross country to indoor track and then outdoor track. Case closed."

"A lot of the workouts we were doing were just totally crazy," said Charley Vigil, who was also a freshman in 1971. Vigil—no relation to Coach Vigil and better known as Pablo—looked at those hard workouts as a blessing, even though "we questioned where the heck are all of these workouts coming from."

In the early 1970s, some of the workouts Pablo Vigil recalls included 10x1 mile repeats at 4:50–4:55 pace (at 7,500-foot elevation), 20x400-meter repeats in 65 seconds (one-to-one rest), and 30 one-lappers at Cole Park (a loop of just over 700 meters) at 2:00 with a 50-meter jog in between.

"By the time we finished the workout and got back to the cafeteria, all the good food was gone," Pablo said. "You know, we were all learning, and Coach was a young, up-and-coming coach and he was learning a lot. We just so happened to be his guinea pigs. During that time, a lot of coaches were experimenting with a lot of stuff.

"But I tell people that Coach Vigil lit a fire under me like nobody else did. He made me believe I could walk on water, and I'm not talking frozen water. He was still learning, but he could make you believe stuff that you didn't even think of yourself. And I think in a lot of ways that makes for the better coach, the one that taps into your psyche and makes you believe. He may not have known a whole lot at the time, but he was studying and working and later on became excellent."

Coach Vigil wasn't alone in learning on the fly, according to Pablo. He names legendary coaches of that era from the United States, Australia, and New Zealand to make his point.

"To put it all in context, you're talking about the 1960s, so there was a lot of stuff happening at that time other than all the craziness of Vietnam," Pablo said. "(Bill) Bowerman was experimenting a lot, (Percy) Cerutty and (Arthur) Lydiard and all of these coaches all over the world were trying new things. It was the running boom. And people were trying to figure out how do we make our runners go faster. And of course you need guinea pigs to test all this out."

What Joe Vigil wanted was to lift Adams State to the level of a pair of schools one state to the east, Fort Hays Kansas State

College (now Fort Hays State University) and Kansas State Teachers College (now Emporia State University), which together had won eight of 12 NAIA championships between 1958 and 1969. By the latter part of that decade, Alex Francis was the standard-bearer for NAIA coaches, having led Hays to national titles in 1963, 1965, 1968, and 1969, and to four national runner-up finishes around the same time.

"He was one of my heroes," Vigil said. "He was winning all the time and I wanted to be like him."

That door began to open in 1971. During the indoor track and field season, Zaragoza became the first-ever national champion coached by Vigil when he won the 600-yard dash at the NAIA championships on the banked boards at Kansas City's old Municipal Auditorium.

"The year before, I finished second…nipped by a nose. Can you believe that?" Zaragoza said, subtly noting his protruding honker. "On the podium, the guy from South Dakota that beat me, Paul Blalock, shook everyone's hand but mine. So I said, 'OK, you son of a bitch, I'll be back next year and I'm going to beat you.'"

Vigil and Zaragoza practiced their strategy on the flat indoor track in Plachy Hall. "Here's what you're going to do," Vigil said. "Don't try to take the lead right away. Let them take the lead for the first two laps, then they're going to start coming back to you on the third lap. And then at the finish, get up on the shoulder and I want you to swoop to the right just a little bit and let the momentum of the bank take you to the finish line."

Zaragoza visualized his race time and again, even though they had no banked track to work on. It didn't matter. He knew the feel of the boards. He had heard the clickety-clack of runners speeding around the 150-yard Municipal Auditorium track enough to know the sound. And he had his podium memory from one year earlier.

But Vigil had one more ace up his sleeve. "Zamagoza?" the coach said as the young man answered the phone in his hotel room the afternoon before the semifinals and finals. Vigil rarely called Zaragoza by his real name, instead giving him a nickname by inserting an "m" for the "r" in his last name.

"Yeah, Coach…What's up?"

"I want you to come down here and meet me in the restaurant," Vigil said.

The 600-yard semifinals were just a few hours away, and the finals were about 90 minutes after.

"He's sitting in the restaurant and as I arrive, he tells the waitress to bring him two cups of coffee," Zaragoza recalls. "'Two cups of coffee? You're going to drink two cups of coffee at the same time, Coach?' That's what I'm thinking."

The two cups arrived and Vigil pushed one of them toward Zaragoza. "I want you to drink this."

"Drink it?" Zaragoza responded.

"Yeah, put a little cream and sugar in there. It tastes good. You ever drink coffee?"

"Nah. Well, maybe I've tried it, but I don't know."

"Zamagoza, it's got caffeine in it. It's a stimulant," Vigil said. "You'll be ready for tonight."

Zaragoza tells the rest of the story: "So, I drank that coffee and I was buzzing. I whizzed right through the semifinals. I remember meeting with Coach just briefly as I was warming up for the finals, and he tells me, 'You're not as fast as these guys, but you know, it's a four-lap race. They're not in as good of shape as you are, either.'

"In the finals, I did exactly what he said and what we had practiced in Plachy Hall and when we came off that final turn on the last lap, I whipped up high and rode the bank of the curve to the finish and I nipped that sucker at the line."

Let Me Tell You a Story

In 1971, the Adams State men's track and field team was heading home from the NAIA indoor championships in Kansas City.

"We were in the 'weanie wagon' (a nickname for the school van) and it's late on a Saturday night, snowing, and the road is icy," said Larry Zaragoza, the national champion in the 600-yard run that year. "We're coming to the toll booth on Interstate 70 and Coach is hauling ass. I tell him, 'Coach, you better slow down, you've got to pay the toll.' He says, 'Oh yeah.'

"So, he hits the brake and we go into a spin, doing a complete circle. Our van slides right into the tollbooth. Calmly, Coach pays the toll and then takes off again.

"I'm thinking…How the hell? Only that man could have that kind of luck. Only that man…I'm like, what the hell did I just see?"

Win number one only made Vigil all the more hungry as a coach. He was ready to put more science behind his love for coaching distance runners, so he applied for a sabbatical from Adams State, even though it meant he wouldn't be able to coach the 1971–1972 cross country and track and field seasons in person.

"At that time, you couldn't do the sabbatical in the summer, and I had to have 21 hours of research and a foreign language to get my PhD," Vigil said.

Adams State granted his leave. He submitted his proposal, titled "The Concentration of Catecholamines in Myocardial

Tissue," focusing on the effects of training on the response of catecholamines in the heart. Catecholamines, such as epinephrine or norepinephrine, are hormones made by the adrenal glands that regulate such physiological functions as heart beat and breathing rate. Essentially, Vigil's theory was that conditioning the body makes the heart stronger and better able to resist the presence of stress-causing catecholamines.

"My subjects were 60 albino rats that I flew in from San Francisco," Vigil said. "They were one year old, and one year of rat life is comparable to a 65-year-old American man. The first thing I did was give them a shot of penicillin to boost their immunity, because there was a lot of money invested. I divided the rats into two groups, the experimental group and the control group. The experimental group swam 30 minutes every day in a homemade pool, three feet wide by three feet long by three feet deep. Once they adapted to the workout, I would tie 6 percent of their body weight in lead washers to their tail to simulate a training overload. They were very smart. Sometimes they would fake being tired. They would sink to the bottom as if they were drowning. I'd pull them up and give them artificial respiration."

Vigil controlled all of the variables during the 10-week study—the type of food the rats were given, how much they ate and drank, and the time of day they worked out. He had three assistants to help him administer the rats swimming and keep track of the data.

"At the end of the experiment, I had a rat guillotine. I sacrificed them," Vigil said. "I'd take their hearts out and put them in liquid nitrogen to freeze until I was ready to analyze them. But before I sacrificed them, I put the exercised group of rats and the non-exercising rats on a rat treadmill—a wheel—to see how much they could run."

Vigil and his assistants analyzed the hearts for catecholamines, namely norepinephrine and epinephrine, to test whether exercise had made a difference.

"The hearts of the exercised rats had a lower concentration of epinephrine, which is a stimulant that makes the heart beat faster," Vigil said. "In other words, they were healthier. And I related that to human life."

Meanwhile in Alamosa, Vigil had asked Larry Jeffryes to oversee his cross country team while he was away. Jeffryes had followed up his successful high school career under Vigil's guidance with an All-American sprint career at Adams State. At the time, the NAIA was something of a powerhouse in the sprints, sometimes rivaling the top NCAA Division I sprinters. Jeffryes remembers one time beating Willie Davenport, an Olympic gold medalist in the 110-high hurdles, in a preliminary heat of the 100 meters; and at another meet, running just behind 1968 100-meter Olympic gold medalist Jim Hines.

After leaving Adams State, Jeffryes coached at Rangely High School in northern Colorado up to the summer of 1971, when Vigil called him on the phone.

"Jeffryes!" Vigil said. When Vigil calls you in his stern voice by your last name, you know he's about to spur you into action. "I want you to be the coach at Adams State while I'm gone."

"I was young enough, or maybe stupid enough, so I said, 'OK, Coach,'" said Jeffryes, then just 24 years old. "It helped that Coach had faith in me and supported me, but looking back on it now, I say, 'Wow, that was way over my head.'

"Coach met with me before he left that fall, and he mapped out all the workouts. Early in the season, I would talk with Coach Vigil two or three times a week. Eventually, we deviated from his training plans because somewhere along the line I realized I was not Coach Vigil. I modified things the way that I felt after talking with the guys."

Let Me Tell You a Story

In 1971, Milt Place ran one of the best races of his career as Adams State pulled off a stunning win at the NAIA cross country championships in Liberty, Missouri. Joe Vigil was on sabbatical that season, but Place recalls how his Coach was ever-present.

"When I was running at Adams State, I noticed how well-respected Coach Vigil was," said Place, who has coached for 38 years at Medina (Ohio) High School. "He had a commanding presence wherever he went and we knew that we were in the presence of someone who was not the average coach and professor.

"I remember that he did not play favorites and that you had to earn his respect. He worked hard at whatever he was doing and he expected everyone else around him to do the same. I try to emulate Coach in that regard by being a good role model as a coach and doing a lot more than what I imagine other coaches are doing with the athletes in their charge. I am constantly thinking about the workouts, motivational tricks of the trade, and whatever else my mind can dream up to make my runners run closer to their potential."

The 1971 team had high hopes for a top-five finish at nationals, and they had a solid squad to make that a reasonable goal. Pablo Vigil led the team for much of the season, and they were winning or placing high at each meet. They finished third at the RMAC Championships, grabbing the last qualifying spot into the national meet in Liberty, Missouri, north of Kansas City.

Eastern New Mexico was the odds-on favorite to win the 1971 NAIA championship. The team was led by coach Bill Silverberg, who in some circles has been credited with bringing African runners to U.S. universities, and who was Billy Mills' roommate at the University of Kansas. Silverberg's prized runner at that time was Mike Boit, a 22-year-old freshman from Kenya and bronze medalist in the 800 meters at the 1972 Munich Olympics, the same race where American Dave Wottle rallied from nearly 20 meters back of the pack and then lunged to beat Soviet Yevhen Arzhanov for the gold medal. Eastern New Mexico also had a young star in Rex Maddaford, who represented New Zealand in the 5000-meter run at the 1968 Mexico City Olympics.

Adams State's cross country team had no visions of running in Eastern New Mexico's stratosphere, and two miles into the national championship race, all seemed normal. Boit and Maddaford and some of the other prerace favorites loped along.

But things changed very quickly. One and sometimes two runners from every contending team—Malone (Ohio), Edinboro State (Pennsylvania), and Eastern New Mexico—began dropping back. Pablo Vigil suffered from the early pace, eventually finishing as the last man for Adams State that day, but Roberts ran the race of his life. So did others on the young Adams State team. Maybe, just maybe, it was good enough for that top-five finish.

"And then it became one of those miracle stories," Jeffryes said. "Remember, this is before automatic timing. It took them a while to figure out the results. We really had no idea who had won the national championship, even sitting at the awards banquet afterwards. We were in our jeans, ready to get out of there."

Team member Milt Place was the numbers guy of the group. "Milt was keeping track of things mentally," Jeffryes said, "and they announced the third-place team. Milt says, 'I'm pretty sure we came in ahead of them.'"

"Then, second place was Eastern New Mexico and Milt says, 'Well, maybe…no…I don't know.'

"And then they announced us as the national champions."

The final tally was Adams State 196, Eastern New Mexico 210. It was the highest winning score ever and remains so to this day.

"Bill Silverberg was pissed," Jeffryes remembers.

"It was phenomenal…I was speechless," Pablo Vigil said. "On a personal level, I was sad that I wasn't able to contribute point-wise, but we all contributed and I was ecstatic that we were able to do something that nobody from our school had ever done."

Jeffryes rushed to the nearest phone. "Coach Vigil, this is Larry Jeffryes," he said. "We won!"

"You won what?" responded Vigil, who was in Albuquerque.

"Coach, we won nationals."

"You're kidding."

"That's about all of the conversation that I remember," Jeffryes said. "It was one of those days where the stars aligned for us, I guess. It was one of those magical moments."

The seven men and their interim coach climbed back into the school's small van for the 13-hour drive back to southern Colorado, pulling up to a lonely Plachy Hall in the dark hours of the morning. They unloaded their gear, an NAIA banner, and a championship trophy, then stumbled off to their dorm rooms.

"We'll see you at practice Monday," Jeffryes told them as they wandered off. "We've got indoors to start."

7

THE ADAMS STATE
WAY

A springboard is only good if you use it to get to a new level, so Joe Vigil, spurred by the program's national success in 1971, returned to his newly adorned national championship program on a mission. Fresh from his sabbatical and a PhD in hand, the coach became consumed with the idea of moving Alamosa and Adams State into distance running and track and field prominence:

> For me, everything became running-involved. I was establishing a culture of running where people accepted it as a major thing. And that's what I was proud of. We involved not just our athletes and our school, but also the community. Bankers, farmers…really, the whole San Luis Valley.
>
> We'd put together indoor track and field meets and people from the community would come to see our athletes run. We'd get members of the community involved as timers, judges, and other things. Some of my students were officials. My job was to involve people and help

them learn about track. I used to like to tell them stories about great track performances. Kids used to like to hear stories. I was a storyteller.

Vigil was also his own fundraiser. He routinely drove downtown to talk to local business owners—many of them his friends and people he grew up with, some of whom he had taught at Alamosa High School—and convince them to help the young program. For many years, he persuaded the locals to "sponsor" a runner, committing five cents or ten cents or more for every mile the athlete ran during the summer. He'd build the fund and then when he wanted to send athletes to a meet, or needed equipment or travel or meal expenses, he'd have the money to make it happen. Many viewed Adams State track and field and cross country as Vigil's program, but in his mind, it was the college's program, Alamosa's program…the San Luis Valley's program. He was simply the funnel that brought the groups together.

"People forget about him going out and selling pledges and making kids do the same, and he would try to do more himself than all of the team combined to raise money for the team," said Damon Martin, Adams State's current coach, who was a graduate assistant for Vigil in the late 1980s. "There are so many of those things he did that went unnoticed so that you don't realize how he accomplished what he did."

The Adams State track and field program had little maintenance support for its facilities; in fact, the outdoor track on which they ran did not have permanent lines, and every so often Vigil would have to get out and paint the lines himself…though he didn't do it alone.

"Boogie Romero would get up with me at four in the morning to help drag and lime the track," Vigil said of his childhood friend from the south side of town. "Then, after he went to work all day [by this time, Boogie worked for Adams State in the maintenance department], he would meet me out there again at five o'clock so we could finish the work. He wasn't getting paid to come out and help me. He was doing it out of the goodness of his heart."

"He would tell me, 'Boogie, I'll never forget you, buddy,'" Romero said.

Vigil would often direct some of his runners to work-study jobs with Romero because he knew his friend would make them earn their money but would treat them well.

"To me, Coach Vigil is like a father," said Romero, who is five years younger. "Anytime I could help him, I would help him. To me, he is the man of the century."

Joe Vigil talking with marathon great Juma Ikangaa of Tanzania (left) and Ikangaa's coach. Ikangaa trained in Alamosa in the mid to late 1980s, during which time he won major marathons in Melbourne, Tokyo, Fukuoka, Beijing, and New York. He was also runner-up in the Boston Marathon three times.

Vigil also was known to buddy up to the director of Adams State's business office, who controlled the college's purse strings but also had authority over the use of many of the campus's facilities and vehicles. As one example, even after Vigil resigned his post as coach in 1993, business director Jim Campbell gave him a sweet deal on using carpool vans to transport post-collegiate athletes and the visiting foreign delegation to rigorous runs in nearby Alamosa Canyon, the Great Sand Dunes National Monument, Fort Garland, and other spots. When Tanzania's great marathoner Juma Ikangaa—winner of the 1989 New York City marathon and three-time runner-up in Boston—came to train in Alamosa in the late 1980s, Vigil and a few others would often accompany him in a school van on his 35-mile-long runs down U.S. Highway 285 to the New Mexico border.

In 1974, Adams State's then–business director, Leonard McLean, agreed to let Vigil use the Plachy Hall fieldhouse to begin a running class for women in the community, though a few men also joined the group. Vigil believed that building a successful college program included building a vibrant running culture in the community. Many of his students were stay-at-home moms wanting to get some exercise. Over the next 20 years, Vigil's running class would involve nearly 500 local women who came out to run several times a week.

"I had the fieldhouse at 10 in the morning for the moms that stayed at home with the kids, and at six in the evening for the working housewife. My track runners used to be the babysitters," Vigil said. "I would teach all day, have the women's classes, coach track, and then have the six o'clock class and go home. That's a full day.

"I would test all of the students briefly: first, I'd give them a bench press test, then check their heart rate and their flexibility. They'd show up and I'd have an educational component for five minutes, something they could learn about themselves. From the test results, I'd tell some of my runners, 'You take these women out for a 20-minute mile,' or a 15-minute mile, or 10-minute, whatever they could do, and I'd have one runner out front and one runner in back."

The groups would often head out along Alamosa's First Street, one mile out to Cole Park and back.

"I wasn't what you'd call heavy, but I wanted to lose 20 pounds, and so I signed up for that class," said Alamosan Shirley Bervig, who was raising six kids at the time. "As soon as I walk into Plachy Hall, I see these shirts that read, '10-Mile Club.' I met Coach Vigil, and I asked, 'Do people actually run 10 miles without stopping?'"

Vigil told her: "Sure. You'll be doing that any minute," to which Bervig replied, "I don't think so."

"Have you done any running?" Vigil asked.

"No, I don't run," Bervig said.

"Well, today is the day!"

"So I started running around the Plachy Hall indoor track and the kids would play on the high jump mats," Bervig said. "Well, I loved it so much that I went to the evening class also. I would get supper ready, go down there and run, then come home and we could eat."

After several months, Bervig made the 10-Mile Club, then set her sights on running a marathon.

"I told Coach what I was going to do and he set up a schedule that I kept up on my refrigerator, and I used that faithfully," she said.

The two became good friends and even on days when class was not held they'd meet at Plachy Hall to run several miles together.

"I felt like I was getting a free education," she said, "because he would just share so much information with me, like he would share in his biology class, and I would get so much wisdom from him. I thought this is almost as good as going to college."

"I remember this one winter day, a horrible day, it was not only snowing, but it looked like there was ice under the snow. I knew that we had always run outside, but I thought, 'Ah, we'll just run inside today.' Coach Vigil shows up and he's dressed warm, and I say, 'Coach, are we running outside?'"

Vigil responded: "Bervig, is there tea in China? Yes, we are going outside!"

"We take off running and he is doing worse than I am," Bervig said. "He is slipping all over the place, and I thought, there is a point where this is just ridiculous. Why am I out here like this? My eyelashes are frosted over and it was like, ah, Coach, I don't know about you!"

The two friends would often tease each other, but whenever Bervig questioned running in bad weather or anything else, Vigil would respond with his signature, "Get tough, Bervig!"

"Or," Bervig said, "he loved to tell me, 'Bervig, you're a mass of corruption!'"

Vigil also formed a great friendship with Bervig's husband, Farris, who was a successful businessman and later the town's mayor. On one occasion, Farris questioned the amount of time his wife was spending running, including the cost to pay babysitters while she was away.

"I told Coach my sad story: 'I don't think I can be running this much anymore because Farris doesn't like me paying for babysitting.' And Coach says, 'Bervig, you just tell him it's a lot cheaper than having you go to the doctor to get tranquilizers!' I thought about that, and he was right. There are so many women who are raising their families and they're overwhelmed.

"So I tell Farris, 'This is what Coach says.' And Farris kind of backs off, and says, 'Well, I guess he's probably got a point.'"

While the residents of Alamosa and the surrounding San Luis Valley were becoming more literate in the world of track and field and distance running, Vigil was molding the Adams State program in his values. Work hard. Study hard. Be honest. Serve others. Love your teammates. Be humble.

He was a demanding coach but also a master motivator, something he seemed to come by naturally. He gathered his team most days at 2 p.m. to outline the day's workout. Most of his runners likened those meetings to receiving a bolt of electricity.

"Mike Streeter [a graduate assistant in 1981] warned me about the meetings he'd have with the cross country team," said Milan Donley, a college hurdler at the University of Southern Colorado in Pueblo before he joined Vigil's staff as a graduate assistant in 1981. "Streeter said, 'You're going to get blown away.' I said, 'Whatever…our coaches talked to us too on a daily basis.' Then, after that first meeting, I wanted to go for a run. And I'm not a distance runner. He just motivated you to want to be better all the time, no matter what it was, and just be committed to being better."

Donley continued: "I truly believe that Coach Vigil could stand up in those team meetings and if he told you, 'We are going to run one mile a day every day and we are going to win the national championship,' those guys would have believed it. And they might have run just one mile a day because that's what he said. He would have given you all the right reasons for why it was going to work."

Vigil learned the right buttons to push with each individual athlete. He had a knack for barking out the right expression aimed at the right athlete at just the right time.

"I remember one year running at Cole Park and I was struggling," said Tom White, a three-time cross country All-American between 1978 and 1980. "In retrospect, I was just being a baby, feeling sorry for myself; school was hard and running was hard and I was tired and all this. And I remember Coach's voice coming all the way across Cole Park, yelling, 'White, you creampuff! Pick it up!'"

Vigil's tough love got White going that day. Then, some weeks later, White said he got another dose from Vigil.

"Tom Gilfillan and I lived in an apartment that is right next door to the Campus Cafe, and around the corner there was a bakery," he said. "One Sunday morning, Tom and I got out of bed and we walked over to the bakery and bought three or four of those creampuffs.

"We brought them back to our apartment and we are sitting on our couch in our pajamas biting into these creampuffs. All of a sudden, the front door flies open, and here comes Coach Vigil and the assistant coaches, who had been eating breakfast next door. Coach says, 'I knew it...you are creampuffs!' We were busting up. We had whipped cream on our faces and we were just laughing so hard."

Joe Vigil standing at a podium during a team meeting in Adams State College's Plachy Hall. U.S. Olympian and eight-time U.S. cross country champion Pat Porter is seated in the front row.

Much of Vigil's vernacular centered on a theme many coaches use: get tough. In fact, Vigil was known to tell certain athletes just that: "Get tough, Porter!" or whoever he thought needed a minor attitude adjustment at the time. He'd use variations of that, including calling an athlete a "candy ass" or a "mental midget" or threatening to "put my size 9½ up your bazooka!"

Athletes who would make an excuse for not running that day? Vigil might exclaim, "Poppycock!"

Sleep in too late in the morning? "You're a sack rat."

"One year we were in South Africa for the World Cross Country Championships and one of the girls on the team from Oregon knew Coach," said Jack Hazen, who has coached at Malone College in Ohio for 53 years. "Coach had been flying all night so he went to bed early. We called to ask if he wanted to go to dinner and he told us that he was already in bed. She called him a sack rat."

Vigil had a solution for sack rats on his team: the Flying Dutchman. Legend has it that Vigil threatened to get a running start and just before reaching the bed, he would jump through the air and land on top of the unsuspecting sack rat.

No one recalls him ever actually giving a Flying Dutchman, but he had the tables turned on at least one occasion.

"One time we were in California. Me, Coach, and Jeff Pope [an assistant coach] were in the hotel room," said Damon Martin, Vigil's graduate assistant and the coach who succeeded Vigil at Adams State. "Coach said something like, 'Dammit Martin, you're a candy ass.' And so I ran and gave him a Flying Dutchman in the room. Then we start wrestling and I grab his leg or something and he squeals because he had bad knees.

"So I always tell people about how I threw his ass through the wall and there's a cartoon outline through the wall in that hotel room."

Vigil's light side also served him well even when he may not have been too happy with his team.

"There was one meeting that resonates with me and it was after an indoor conference meet at the Colorado School of Mines," said Martin Johns, a 15-time All-American at Adams State between 1989 and 1993. "We won the meet, but no one really ran very well. It's the only time I can recall that Coach actually went around the room and singled out some people. He had a purpose behind it, because he literally never did it, and maybe didn't do it ever again.

"There was one kid that he singles out: 'John T., you only have one gear, son, and it's slow!' And then he tells Brian Blazek: 'Blazek! Son, tell me, isn't the purpose of an indoor 800 to get out and get the lead? What were you thinking, son?'"

For context, both of those athletes were fast…really fast. Vigil knew he could motivate fast kids by suggesting their effort was slow.

"And he does that to four or five other people," Johns said. "I've got to tell you that the energy in that room was definitely different. And I know from that, we never again went through the motions at a meet. That was the way he chose to get his point across that day. He was disappointed. I tell that story because there was a certain amount of arrogance potentially being shown in those events that day, and he wouldn't stand for that. You have to get out there and earn the win, earn your place. You can't just show up in the green and gold striped shorts and expect people to lay down for you. I think that was probably the motivation behind that particular instance. It was definitely one of those memorable occasions that I have with Coach."

◈◈◈

Whether serious or in jest, Vigil established a culture in which athletes were accountable to the team.

"When I first started coaching at Adams State, I wrote down my philosophy on what I thought the program should represent," Vigil said. "Every runner got a copy of this, and they had no excuse for not upholding the standards we had set as a program."

Let Me Tell You a Story

Lance Harter, who won eight NCAA Division II women's cross country titles as coach at Cal Poly San Luis Obispo and four NCAA Division I women's track and field titles at the University of Arkansas helm, calls Vigil one of his coaching mentors.

"I think the summation of Coach Vigil is that he is a coaches' coach, and there are very few of those in this business," Harter said. "The ultimate compliment that any coach has is that you have a go-to person—and we call those mentors. But then you have a person like Coach Vigil, who is a step ahead of the vast majority of coaches in the United States.

"As developing coaches, if we need someone as a go-to, Coach Vigil is that person."

Vigil's original document was etched on paper with a manual typewriter, every click-click-click-click carefully thought out and representing the values he was first taught by his mother, and later refined while coaching high school athletes and teaching misfits. The 2½-page document outlines what Vigil expected from anyone who came to compete for him in the early 1970s through today. As such, it is the common thread that ties all of Vigil's athletes together, from those who competed at Alamosa High School and the beginnings of the Adams State years, all the way to his championship teams of the 1980s and 1990s and nearly two dozen Olympians.

Vigil's approach never strayed; he decided who he was as a young man and how he wanted to help others, and for more than six decades, he fiercely pursued excellence in what he stood for as a man and a coach, never accepting mediocrity in himself nor in those he led.

"His philosophy and his values are very person-oriented," Larry Jeffryes said. "He really did believe people could be more than they were, and he knew instinctively how to get the best out of people. And that hasn't changed. The Joe Vigil I met in 1964 is the same man he is today. He might have learned a lot of scientific stuff along the way, but his relationship, rapport, ability to support and motivate people and athletes…that's who he was when I first met him."

Including some minor changes over the years, here's the path Vigil set early on:

Philosophical Dimension for Track and Field and Cross Country at Adams State College

If you decide there is to be no turning back, you will have to be ready for many difficult experiences, simply because training and competing is at the least very difficult and time-consuming. Many times injuries delay progress; it does not stop it. Also, illness may prevent training; the training can be resumed under these conditions. Athletes don't give up, they work harder and dig deeper. One thing is certain, that the farther along the road you get, the more confident you become and, therefore, the more able to go on. For most athletes, there is one step back for every two forward. But this need not be so; the firmness of the forward movement will restrict the backward one.

In the beginning, our athletes do one thing; they take a thorough look at what they wish to achieve, how they think it can be achieved and how long it will take them. The time that we spend surveying our ambitions is time well spent. We have to understand and study carefully the factors involved in long term preparation.

Intelligent forethought is the foundation of success, and positive pride its creator. The thinking will map out a route and the pride will ensure progress along that route. Intelligence, seeking and using knowledge, is a necessary quality of an athlete. The more you know about training and competing, the better you will be as a competitor. The more self-respect you have, the more you will stay on the route that you have worked out. It certainly helps in all states of your training to have somebody to persuade and support you, but in the end you will train and race successfully because you want to, not because somebody else wants you to.

The strength of mind and character is perhaps best seen in those men and women who do essentially solitary deeds, or who carry out solitary responsibilities. The genuine athlete must have a strong spirit, vigorous and sane, not easily demoralized or defeated. This resolute balance allied to intelligence is the mixture necessary for success.

The culturation of this will power, or spirit, is possible. It is capable of tremendous development under training and stimulus, or of near extinction under neglect.

This development may not be purely mental. It is possible to train the nervous system, to nurture the reserves, to increase the body's durability. It is also possible to deplete the nervous energy and produce a malnutrition of spirit as well as of the body. All defeats do this and unintelligent overexertion of the will can break down the physique, and in turn, demoralize the athlete, thereby he defeats himself.

It is necessary to accept the very severe limitations under which the animal body must work—need for sleep, rest and proper diet, capacity to function only within a narrow range of temperature, sensitivity to any heavy and repeated loads of chemical fatigue. He must disregard slight signs of discomfort, learn to judge when you have started to break yourself down rather than to build yourself up. The history of the sport is littered with the bodies of men who believed that all they had to do was exert an even will in order to succeed. Their successes finally were not much greater than that of men who lacked the necessary will; their disappointments and frustrations were bigger.

Nature cannot be hurried. There are no crash programs in the preparation of an athlete, though the iron-willed athletes who lack intelligence think there are. Men like Virén, Moses, Ovett, Rono and their kind believed and lived by the notion that years of training was necessary for athletic greatness to emerge. Cultivate your physical resources; don't try to thrash them into life, or you may end up destroying them.

The pride which has been mentioned as an integral part of the athlete's character operates to make him or her want to carry through whatever plans have been conceived. It also operates to make the athlete want to beat other athletes. This, after all, is what sports is all about.

There is satisfaction in beating a watch, there is more satisfaction in beating other runners. While this kind of pride should not become an arrogance that sees defeated opponents as necessarily inferior people, it will be a pride which, though unobtrusive, remains nevertheless, stubborn and evident to its owner. Such lack of modesty will belong to the athlete's nature. It need only function in training and competition, and even there, silently. The noisy athlete does well to remember that most of the world is not listening, and the interested public applauds the arrogant competitor who leaves his arrogance behind when he steps off the track.

Finally, the young athlete would be well advised to keep athletics in its place. Be passionately involved in the activity, exert yourself to succeed. Gain from competing the massive satisfaction that competing offers. Yet be a well-rounded, sensitive, literate human being. It is not the job of athletics to produce people who know or care for nothing except athletics. Keep it in its place, behind your family, your concern for the general life of the world, and your education. There are athletes and coaches who prepare to act as if athletics were life; it is not. It is but a corner—and a rich one—of life which will contribute immensely to the holistic development of the individual.

—Joe I. Vigil

8

RISE OF
THE VIGILANTES

O ne summer day in 1967, the phone rang in Joe Vigil's Plachy Hall office. "Joe," said the voice. "This is Alex Francis."

Ever since Vigil became the head coach at Adams State in 1965, he had been flooding the phone lines talking with Francis, who had built the Fort Hays Kansas State College cross country and track and field programs into an NAIA terror. From 1946 to 1980, Francis—who grew up in a small Kansas town and graduated from Fort Hays—won four NAIA cross country championships and had five runner-up finishes at the national cross country meet. He coached 139 All-Americans, had 28 top-two conference finishes in track and field, and held 27 conference titles in cross country. At one point during his tenure, the Fort Hays track and field team won 33 consecutive dual meets. Francis was known by his athletes for a simple phrase: "Go beat somebody." He was the coach for the U.S. distance runners at the 1968 Mexico City Olympics.

He had taken a liking to the curious, hungry new coach at Adams State College, who would routinely inundate him with questions about training and coaching. But this phone call was different. On this particular day, Francis needed something from Vigil.

He tells Vigil: "Let's do something different."

"Alex, what do you have in mind?" Vigil said.

Francis went on to describe an idea he had. He and his team would jump in a school van and begin driving south on U.S. Highway 183 to U.S. Highway 50 in southwestern Kansas. At the same time, Vigil and his team would take a school van and head east on U.S. Highway 160 to US 50, meaning each team would drive about 200 miles before they would meet up somewhere in western Kansas. There, they'd get out of the vans, do a short warm-up, and hold a dual meet on a course set up by one of Francis's former runners. (In future years, as the challenge continued, they'd sometimes race out-and-back on an isolated country road.)

This was in the days before cell phones. Each team would keep an eagle eye out for the other after about three hours of driving. "We would synchronize our watches before we left, and we would meet somewhere by Lakin, Kansas," Vigil said. "Alex always had former athletes in western Kansas who were available to conduct a meet on the road. We decided that whoever won the dual, the other team would have to buy them lunch afterward."

When the duals began, Adams State's program was just two years old, and while they were having success in the Rocky Mountain Athletic Conference, they were no match for Fort Hays, which had finished in the top two at the NAIA national meet in five of the previous seven years—including national championships in 1963 and 1965. Maybe Francis saw Adams State as easy prey, but maybe he already viewed Vigil as a worthy competitor, someone who would soon lead his team to NAIA greatness as well. Whatever the case, Francis's gesture was a bit like North Carolina basketball inviting pre-Mike Krzyzewski Duke over for a friendly pick-up game. Championship teams don't typically work very hard at building up the next threat to their dynasties.

"We started meeting in 1967, and they would beat us pretty easily," Vigil said. "But after a few years, I started beating him, and he couldn't believe it. I showed him we knew what we were supposed to do, you know, because he had a great program."

Francis certainly showered Vigil with respect. At the U.S. Olympic Committee meeting in Chicago in 1973, Francis again nominated Vigil for a national position—this time as head coach for the World University Games.

"Can you imagine that? As a head coach...I just about choked," Vigil said. "I couldn't even imagine being a national coach. Well, at the time, the AAU and the NCAA were having a power struggle with each other; they each wanted the power to run track and field in the country. It turned out that all of the AAU coaches voted for me to be the head coach of the World University Games because they weren't going to vote for a coach from the NCAA. So, I got the assignment, without ever having any national coaching experience before."

Fort Hays Kansas State College won the last of its NAIA titles in 1968 and 1969 under Francis, but through 2019 the Tigers have never finished in the top two again. Adams State—and others—gradually caught up to them. The Indians pulled out an unlikely win for the 1971 NAIA title when Jeffryes was the interim coach, but as that decade progressed a seismic shift was occurring in the balance of NAIA power—and it leaned sharply toward the school located in southern Colorado, a mile and a half above sea level. Vigil described that evolution as only partly by his design;

mostly, he credits the runners themselves for graduating from the program having left it in better shape than they found it:

> The people we recruited all got along for the most part. I wasn't doing that on purpose. It just happened. They came to a program that had a little culture. I tried to tell them stories about people who had run in Alamosa and some of the hardships we endured to get to where we were going, because you know, we never had much money. I think they bought into the program totally and we never had a lot of blue-chip kids, but they were all kids who were hard workers, you know.
>
> They started relying on each other and believing in each other and helping each other out, whether it was academically or little problems they had on their plate, or whatever. They relied on each other. And they weren't just teammates in running, they were teammates in life. And that has transcended to today; 50 years later some of these guys still rely on each other. They respect each other. And I see it every time we have a gathering, how happy they are to see each other, how faithful they are to the team they ran for and even the school they went to, even if they had a few bad experiences when they were in school.
>
> They always get together to talk about the sweat and tears they had in training, whether we were running up to Rock Creek, or a 15-mile run, or the Trinchera Run [near Fort Garland, to the east of Alamosa], or whatever it was. The highlight of the day was talking about it afterwards. No matter how bad they felt, they would go and try their best, always try to make the team better. It was never about themselves; it was about making the team better.

I didn't really consider my job as a coach to just coach a team, because I was getting paid for it. I wanted those guys to be a success. I never cut anyone from my teams. They'd come in, I'd recruit them, and they were part of a program. I wanted them to be successful. And I tried to learn as much as I could to help them out. I was always studying things, trying to find ways to make them better and work better as a team. I think they understood what I was trying to do. And they would talk about it, and pass the word on. The big thing was that the upper-classmen would always help the underclassmen along. Because, you know, the freshmen would come in and they didn't know shit about the program, and before you know it, they had the same goals in mind.

Vigil filled his early teams with proud men, tough men, appreciative men…men dedicated to his blue-collar persona. Many of them were from a similar have-not background as their coach, but they became the backbone of Adams State College cross country and track and field. They were trailblazers: the men—and later, women—who established a Vigil-like mind-set and culture and opened opportunities for those who would come to their coach's program over the next two decades.

"I first met Coach Vigil at the state cross country meet, right after I won that race my senior year," said Charley "Pablo" Vigil, who ran for Moffat County High School in Craig, Colorado. "I hadn't done anything in running, really, other than I was doing fairly well in the Moffat County area, and in the conference."

College coaches were not lining up to recruit Pablo Vigil. He was probably a better high school wrestler than he was a run-ner; his older brother, Roger, was an All-American wrestler at Adams State at the time (and later the head coach at Alamosa

High School), and Pablo thought he would naturally fall into wrestling, if he even decided to go to college at all.

Then, a letter arrived in the mail:

Dear Mr. Vigil,

I'd like to take this opportunity to congratulate you on a fine performance in the state cross country meet. I saw a real potential in your ability and would like very much the opportunity of trying to develop that potential over the next four years.

I don't know if you have any desire to go to college, but I know that you could be a real success. If you do want to attend college and if you think you'd want to attend Adams State College, we would try to get you the maximum amount of aid possible.

We have an excellent track and cross country program at Adams State and we have ranked in the top ten in the nation (NAIA) the past six years. I am sure you have many questions about our school and our athletic program, therefore, feel free to write and ask. I am sending you a questionnaire, so please fill it out immediately. I will try to make it to Moffat County to see you.

Yours truly,
Coach Vigil

Fifty years later, Pablo Vigil treasures that letter and the faded yellow envelope it's tucked into like it's his lifeline. In 1970, the letter was, indeed, something of a lifesaver for the young man, who grew up in extreme poverty. When Joe Vigil later decided to visit Pablo at his home in Craig, he witnessed subsistence-level living conditions, right down to the dirt floors, leaky windows, and wood stove—which was the family's only source of heat and the only way they could warm water for a bath. The house had no running water and no plumbing, and an outhouse in the back yard was the only toilet for the family of seven.

"We were poor, and both of my parents were illiterate," Pablo said. "They were farmers from the Mora Valley in New Mexico; good, hardworking people, but they never really had any opportunities to go to school. In the early 1960s we left Mora to move to Craig, where my dad got a job herding sheep. Not long after we went up there, he left the family. It was my mom, me, my three brothers, and my little sister...we were stuck in Craig. But the thing about Craig was they had better schools, and they had Little League programs in baseball and sports programs for kids in the summertime.

"I tell you the thing that saved us is that our mother [Aurora Lucero Vigil] was an amazing, religious, very strong-willed lady that kept us in line, because we were four wild-ass boys and a newborn baby girl, so she had to be tough," Pablo continued. "She had an incredibly strong work ethic and she really instilled that work ethic in us. We were all doing gardening jobs, collecting aluminum cans and beer bottles and recycling them. Back in the day, you could recycle a Coors bottle for a penny. In the wintertime we'd go to the other side of town where the rich people lived and after we'd deliver newspapers, we'd go out and shovel walks before we'd go to school.

"I loved it when I got to middle school and started wrestling and playing basketball. They had this amazing thing in middle school called a shower. You could shower for PE class. It was heaven. Warm water, and the school was warm and safe. You didn't have to worry about drunken people coming into your house, and dealing with all of that insanity."

It's no wonder Joe Vigil quickly came to like the younger Vigil. "His mom sort of reminded me of my mom, you know, working hard just to feed her kids," Coach Vigil said. But there was also a certain grit to Pablo that he wanted to add to this team, a working-man's attitude that represented what Coach Vigil wanted Adams State College to be about.

"I remember asking him, 'Pablo, what motivated you to want to be a good runner and to win the state championship?'" Vigil said. "He said, 'Coach, you don't understand, being in sports and doing well was the only way I could take a hot shower.'"

Thus, Vigil showing up to his house one cold winter day in 1970 meant a lot to 18-year-old Pablo. "The part in that letter that says 'I think you really have potential and I'd like to have a part in developing you...' I thought, 'Are you kidding me?'" Pablo said. "Coach Vigil wants to coach...me? I had heard of Coach Vigil. I knew of Mike McDonald and Larry Zaragoza and some of the other guys down there. I was thinking that they have a really cool bunch of people down there. And Coach Vigil being a Latino, I thought, 'This is so amazing.'"

So, Pablo Vigil headed to Alamosa in the fall of 1971, and immediately became the No. 1 man on the cross country team— leading most workouts and all of the races up until bonking at the national meet in his freshman try.

"Vietnam was breathing down my neck; I was No. 2 in the draft lottery," he said. "I was struggling with acclimating to the academic workload, the running workload, and all that. It got to a point where I couldn't go anymore. Physically and emotionally, I had nothing left in the tank. I was running on fumes."

But the early experience served to give Pablo more of a steely resolve. He earned NAIA All-American honors in cross country as a sophomore, on the way to becoming a four-time All-American at Adams State. He moved to Boulder to train with Frank Shorter and others after graduating in 1975, later made the U.S. World Cross Country team in 1978 (which won the silver medal behind France), and from 1979 to 1982, became the only man

to win four consecutive world championships in mountain running—a grueling 31-kilometer (approximately 19 miles) race in
Sierre Zinal, Switzerland. He was mountain running's equivalent
of Shorter, who won Olympic gold and silver in the marathon.
If mountain running were an Olympic event, Pablo Vigil surely
would have been celebrated as an American hero, maybe even
a gold medalist. Instead, even having never won a collegiate
national title, he is arguably the greatest runner that much of the
world has never known.

"I used to give him a pair of shoes to run in and he was in
heaven," Joe Vigil said. "He was just an easygoing guy, good runner, hard worker, but appreciated everything he had."

Pablo Vigil, Larry Zaragoza, and others like them helped to
build the backbone of what Adams State was becoming, and it
was largely in the image of their coach. Many of Vigil's athletes
were bypassed by the big schools; they were Have-Nots among
college recruits. Their coach knew about Have-Nots and he welcomed their wide-eyed enthusiasm with open arms.

"I was blindly willing to do whatever he told me to do for
a workout because he was good and he motivated people," said
Bob Fink, a 4:23 high school miler who Vigil molded into a
three-time cross country All-American between 1976 and 1978.
And there were many others like Fink: Scott McMillen, a 4:24
high school miler, ran sub-4:00 for the mile at Adams State. Rod
Brown, barely a five-minute miler in high school, also ran sub-
4:00 for Vigil. And Pat Porter, who ran just under 10:00 for two
miles in high school, became a two-time NAIA cross country
champion and eight-time U.S. cross country champion, perhaps
the greatest cross country runner this country has ever seen.

"He couldn't recruit blue-chip athletes; Adams State didn't

have the money to get those types of runners," Fink said of Vigil. "So he'd recruit athletes that were good but not super-stars, and he developed them into these incredible athletes over time."

Vigil added: "Within a year or two, these kids would be beating those blue-chippers that went to other schools. And high school coaches began to realize this, so it became a little bit easier for me to recruit."

In 1970, Adams State's cross country team of mostly anonymous runners went to the University of New Mexico Invitational to compete against a field of NCAA Division I schools, including 1969 NCAA champion University of Texas-El Paso.

"Lo and behold, we won the meet," Vigil said. "They (UTEP) had a coach that they called the fastest mouth in the west—Wayne Vandenburg—and he came up to me and said, 'What are you paying those kids?' He'd never lost, or rarely, during that era."

"I said, 'What do you mean?'"

"He said, 'You're obviously paying them. They are great runners.' We were struggling at the time to run with the University of Colorado and others, but we won at UNM for some reason. Driving home that night, I got to thinking that we could be good if we happened to beat UTEP."

Behind Vigil's dynamic leadership and spirited efforts by his early athletes, the momentum in Alamosa built quickly. Vigil's 1976 cross country squad was the NAIA runner-up, with Fink, McMillen, and Ben Montoya earning All-American honors. Then in 1977, Adams State won the NAIA championship—the first in which Vigil was on hand to coach the team—with All-Americans Fink, McMillen, and Andy Montanez.

The cross country program was mostly filled with athletes from Colorado and New Mexico. Vigil was attracting good to average runners from Colorado who may have ordinarily chosen nationally ranked University of Colorado, or strong programs at Colorado State and the Air Force Academy. The New Mexico contingent generally was choosing Adams State over the University of New Mexico. It was a pride point in the late 1970s through the 1980s for the runners to identify themselves as the Colorado-New Mexico connection.

"In 1977, I had a work-study job where really what I was doing was spending time hanging out with Coach and helping him with whatever he needed to get done," said Fink, the first in a line of Adams State runners from Evergreen, Colorado, including future NAIA cross country champions Pat Porter and Craig Dickson. "And because I was working with him, I found out that he had all kinds of offers to go coach somewhere else. I remember New Mexico really wanted him, but it wasn't necessarily just big schools after him. One time, the national sport program in Colombia (South America) wanted him to go lead their program. He had some incredible offers, but he chose to remain at Adams State."

Vigil's track and field program had its share of early stars, too. Frank Gross, a monster of a man from Colorado Springs, was a five-time NAIA champion in the shot put, setting NAIA national records in winning the outdoor shot put and discus in 1978. His throw in the discus (198 feet, 5 inches) still stands as the Adams State school record. His record throw in the shot put (63 feet, 1 inch) was the best mark in the NAIA for 22 years. Gross was named the Most Outstanding Athlete at the NAIA national outdoor meet in 1978.

Gross also won three indoor national titles in the shot put (1976, 1977, and 1978), setting the NAIA record in 1977 at 61-3¾, which stood for 13 years. He was an 11-time All-American competing for Vigil from 1975 through 1978, then won several World Military Games titles as a post-collegian.

Let Me Tell You a Story

Joel Thompson, who competed for Adams State in the mid-1980s, was actually recruited by Joe Vigil in 1976.

"I was a senior at Evergreen High School in Colorado, and Coach Vigil called to ask if we could meet him at Stapleton Airport (in Denver)," Thompson remembers. "This was just shortly after the state cross country meet, where I had finished fourth and my longtime teammate Pat Porter finished 19th.

"My mom accompanied me to the airport, and Coach treated us to a cup of coffee while we chatted in the terminal. I was completely intimidated by the thought of meeting Coach Vigil, but when I saw him in person, his kindly eyes took away that fear immediately, and to this day everyone who has met Coach or listened to him talk can attest to the smile behind those eyes.

"Well, it was seven years after that airport meeting that I was finally able to go to college. Pat Porter, who by then had won several national titles and was tuning up for the Olympic Trials, came up to Evergreen to visit his parents and we hammered out a 20-mile run at six-minute pace. He told me that I needed to drop everything and go to Adams State. It's all I needed to make the jump and in a few months' time, I had moved to Alamosa to study and run.

"On the first day of cross country practice Coach came up to me, grabbed my hand and said, 'Thompson, you are seven years late.' Coach Vigil is the same person today.

I'm still running, in a manner of speaking, and his talks are still so reminiscent of the pre-workout meetings we had in Plachy Hall. I cherish every memory of Coach."

———— ▼ ————

But here's what Vigil remembers most about Gross: "He studied biology and chemistry at Adams State, then earned a master's degree in physiology and biomechanics at the University of Denver. Then he spent 20 years in the Air Force (1980 through 2000), where he earned the rank of lieutenant colonel."

Indeed, while Vigil was training athletes who seemingly had super-human abilities, he was equally adept at training super humans who also happened to be athletes.

Despite the program's success, the financial struggles were very real.

"One year, Myron Clayton (the college's business manager) called me and said, 'Coach, you can't go to track and field nationals this year. We have no money,'" Vigil recalled. "In the NAIA, you had to pay your own way. I didn't know what the hell to do. I had about 21 guys that qualified. So I sent out a couple letters. I was going to try to raise some money. The trip cost about 7,000 to 8,000 dollars.

"Then, I get this phone call from one of my former athletes, Tom Shockley, and he says, 'How much money do you need, Coach?' I told him what it was, and he says, 'You'll have a check in two days.' He sent me a check for the whole team. Seven grand. And that's because I was close to him."

Vigil tells the story that when Shockley first came to Adams State, the runner didn't get along with his dad. "But his dad would come to our meets, and he'd get up early like me at 4 a.m. and we'd go have a cup of coffee. I'd tell him about his son, and his attitude about his son changed. We've been close ever since."

Shockley was an All-American for Vigil in track and field, then joined the Adams State football team as a senior—and earned All-American honors in that sport, as well.

In 1975, Vigil took his team to the NAIA National Track and Field Championships in Arkadelphia, Arkansas. During a delay for a tornado warning, he ended up in a storm shelter next to a young coach from Malone College by the name of Jack Hazen.

"I ended up right beside Joe…How lucky was that?" Hazen said. "We sort of introduced ourselves and started asking each other questions and that's when I first met him. I was asking him questions about his training. Since that day, he's always told people we were good friends. I know he has become friends with so many people, so I'm honored that I'm one of them. I know I'm not the only one, but he made me feel like I'm the only one.

"It's amazing to me that we became such great friends," Hazen said, "because we live a thousand miles apart."

Vigil jokes: "That's probably why we became such good friends!"

"I was immediately struck by his friendliness and how willing he was to share," Hazen said. "But as I've grown to know him over the next 45 years, that's been his trademark. He wants to give back. He takes his time and spends it by making friends and helping people. He saw that I was eager to learn. I was a novice exercise physiologist myself, but I knew right away I was talking to a genius. We just sort of attached to each other at national meets and conventions. He would invite me to dinner or breakfast or coffee and I would end up taking notes on napkins. I would literally come home and I'd have a file full of Joe Vigil napkins, which eventually I'd put on real paper."

Vigil said his love for the sport, and the example that Fort

Hays coach Alex Francis set for him when he began coaching at Adams State, just naturally led him to want to meet and help coaches as much as he wanted to help athletes:

> All of my actions have been directed to inspire others to dream more, to learn more, to do more, and to become more. So as I talk about the qualities that athletes need to improve their event in track and field, we also threw in these actions on how to inspire them to do it. The danger for most of us in life is that our aim is too high and we miss it. But if it's too low and we reach it, then we quit.
>
> At Adams State, we chose to shoot high when establishing goals. We would have team and individual meetings on the goals for the year or the season. Individually, I'd get ahold of the athletes and establish goals for the individual. For any team or individual or organization, you must set goals. And once the goal is set, there has to be a trust that has to develop between you and the team, or you and the individual. This is one way to get into their mind or get into their heart. Because if they know you're interested in them, not only the individual but as a team, then you've got them captured. You've got them eating out of your hand.

Coming off his team's 1977 national championship in cross country, Vigil was expecting an even stronger team in 1978, with four of the seven runners returning and a strong incoming class. But for various reasons, Fink was the only one who returned from those that ran at nationals, and Vigil was left with a team of mostly freshmen.

107

"As far as a coaching miracle, that year was it," Fink said, "because he was basically starting our team from scratch and we managed to get back to nationals and place third. He was able to bring that new group around…it's one thing to have a really good team and do things with it, but it's another thing to develop a team that maybe is not considered all that good. I always think about that 1978 team…that really was coaching."

Fink and freshmen Frank Rivera and Tom White were All-Americans that season, which was highlighted by the debut of Adams State's signature lime-green singlets and green-and-gold striped shorts at the national meet. For Vigil, though, 1978 was more memorable for an entirely different reason.

"Out of the blue, Coach calls me out in Kansas where I was coaching and asks, 'Are you coming to the Air Force meet?'" remembers Norm Roberts, the former runner and graduate assistant for Vigil at Adams State, who was coaching at Colby Community College at the time.

"I said, 'Yeah, Coach, we're coming to run against Air Force's junior varsity.'"

"Well, we're running against Air Force's varsity. Can you bring Greta (Roberts' wife)?" Vigil said. "And can you guys plan to spend the night?"

"Well, sometimes you have to prod Coach, and so I ask him, 'What the hell is going on?'" Roberts said.

Vigil responded: "Well, I'm going to marry Caroline. Would you and Greta stand up with us?"

Vigil's soon-to-be wife had grown up in nearby Del Norte as Caroline Winfield. She earned a degree in English from Adams State, then began teaching part-time at the school. "The pay was part-time, but the job was full-time, actually," she said. "I had a lot of students."

Following a painful divorce, Caroline needed something

more to do. She enrolled in Vigil's evening running class for local residents and really enjoyed being around the runners. "Then I decided to get another degree in what was then called physical education," she said.

That led her to take several classes Vigil was teaching: kinesiology, exercise physiology, track and field, and several of the advanced physical education classes.

"I joke that I took 40 hours of Vigil," Caroline said. "It was like a minor in Vigil when I finally finished in several years.

"After I graduated, he took notice of me because he remembered I could write well. I was an English major, so I could write well on his tests, which were all essay questions. For his final in kinesiology, I wrote for six hours answering his questions, and it was almost like a thesis when I finally got through.

"I think he thought that was quite amazing, and he was very flattered that I would be that interested. That was how we met... accidentally. I was a student. We didn't get together until after I graduated."

Nearly two years later—and just a couple hours after Adams State outran the Air Force Academy on the cross country course—Vigil married Caroline in front of the Justice of the Peace in downtown Colorado Springs on October 14, 1978. Vigil, too, had been through a divorce a few years earlier, but he found happiness with his new partner.

"It was a beautiful fall day," Caroline remembers. "Really, just about perfect weather that day."

Norm and Greta Roberts brought a bottle of champagne, and after the 15-minute ceremony they popped the cork and all four drank a toast to a new beginning. Otherwise, there was no pomp and no circumstance. On Sunday, the happy couple returned home, and by Monday Vigil was back coaching his team.

"When we got back to Alamosa and the team found out we

had gotten married, they were absolutely stunned," Caroline said. "They all came over to our house in Alamosa, and that's when I got to know his team better. It was funny because they were really kind of angry we hadn't included them…They were like, 'Oh my gosh!'"

Joe and Caroline Vigil in 1978, about the time of their marriage.

While Vigil got back to the routine of coaching the Adams State cross country team, Caroline was finishing her student-teaching at Alamosa High School.

"I was fully intending to become a teacher, but then Coach said, 'Listen, if you'll travel with me, we can go a lot of places together,'" Caroline said. "He was traveling quite a bit and had hosted runners from many different countries who had come to train in Alamosa. Coach was planning to visit the Institutes of Culture and the physical education centers in those runners' countries. He said we could travel together, so I decided not to go into teaching."

Instead, Caroline became a coach herself. She enrolled in USA Track & Field's coaching education classes, which were designed and taught by her husband.

"It was very tough," Caroline said. "I went through Level I and Level II coaching education so I could help him with his team."

Through the 1980s, Caroline was a regular at Adams State practices, often helping to time mile repeats and one-lappers at Cole Park. She enjoyed Vigil's busy lifestyle as much as he did, and she was a popular figure among the athletes because of her cheerful, positive attitude. Their storybook beginning has now turned into a 42-year marriage—and counting—in which they've traveled to nearly every corner of the globe, watching the world's best track and field athletes in many of the greatest venues.

"We would take these trips mostly for Coach to study," she said. "But along the way, we got to see a lot of countries and a lot of world championships for cross country and track and field."

"I'm so fortunate that Caroline is such a strong, independent woman," said Vigil's daughter Peggy. "That's what my dad really needed because he wouldn't have been able to do all he has done without that support. Caroline has been with him every step of the way. Not every woman would do that."

By 1979, Adams State had developed something of a swagger. The program had finished in the top three at nationals for three consecutive years, and the 1979 edition returned most of the team that had placed third the year before. Another strong recruiting class had many in the program hopeful of continued national success.

Even so, team member Tim Terrill thought he and his mates needed an identity that expressed the Adams State Way; that is, something that labeled their deep-rooted loyalty to what their coach was teaching them, while honoring the athletes who had come before them and establishing the standard for those who would come later.

"We were a quiet bunch of guys who were committed to Coach and a very simple existence," Terrill said. "We ran, studied, and hung out together, and our focus when I arrived in January 1979 was to win cross country nationals that year. I felt we needed an identity that reflected the mindset of the distance crew we trained with, and the commitment we all had for Coach. We were vigilant, we were running mavericks, and Coach was the impetus behind our very existence as a team in Alamosa."

Terrill and a few others came up with the term Vigilante—pronounced with the Coach's name so that it reads, "Vee-hill-ahn-teh"—and developed a design with the word carved into the foothills of Mount Blanca, the 14,345-foot peak that is the signature symbol of the eastern end of the San Luis Valley.

"After drafting the logo, I took it to Coach and he liked it enough that he had a few shirts made, and from that point on we referred to ourselves as Vigilantes," Terrill said. "It was kind of our trademark. We joked that it gave us sort of a sinister, bad-boy identity, kind of like Pancho Villa, but not in a negative context because Vigil was in the name. It has been a source of pride ever since. It was a way to express the cohesiveness of our group as we trained together in 1979 with the eventual hope of making the national team, and I think it brought us together. And that year, we won the national meet…we Vigilantes."

Freshman Sam Montoya won the individual national title in 1979—the first-ever individual cross country champion coached by Vigil—and Porter was the runner-up. John Esquibel and White were All-Americans. That national title was the third for Adams State, leaving Vigil just one short of the record for most NAIA titles, held by Fort Hays and his good friend Alex Francis, and Emporia State. It was a door Vigil and his band of Vigilantes would soon crash through.

9

DECADE
OF DOMINANCE

The opening 1,000 meters of the championship course at the University of Wisconsin-Parkside in Kenosha is a brutal uphill start that quickly tests a cross country runner's fortitude. Halfway up the hill, the wide start is cut in the middle by a signature oak tree whose branches spectators and photographers were known to climb to get the best view of the start. (In 2017, the original tree was uprooted by wind and rain; a smaller tree has since been planted in the same spot.) When runners reached the oak tree, about 500 meters into the race, they get about a 50-meter respite from the uphill climb, before hitting another nasty slope.

It is a stretch where the meek need not apply.

The NAIA first held its national championship at Parkside in 1976 and, save for a one-year hiatus to Salina, Kansas, in 1980, took up home in Kenosha until 2002—or 26 out of 27 years. Annually, the historic course plays host to a college meet (named for Parkside coaching legend and course co-creator Vic Godfrey), as well as numerous local, conference, regional, and national races, including the U.S. national meet in 1992 and the Foot Locker Midwest Regional several times.

There may not have been a course anywhere that was better suited for Joe Vigil's blue-collar Adams State program than the one at Parkside. From 1976 through 1991—its final year in the NAIA—Adams State placed in the top two at the national meet 14 of 16 years, winning 11 national titles. The rugged opening stretch played to Adams State's strength of sprinting to the lead from the opening gun; very few teams were willing to bleed with the green and gold in the opening 1,000 meters. During their run of success, Adams State's mentality in Kenosha was to go as fast as they could to the top of the hill, positioning all seven runners in the top 10—*and then surge!* Their coach made each of his athletes believe that if they were in the top 10 at the top of the hill, they would leave the national meet as an All-American that day. And as a team, Adams State's runners were steadfast in their belief that the only way to win national championships was by running from the front.

It was, of course, easier said than done. Being able to race that way took a commitment to training that way...including demanding workouts at Alamosa's oxygen-deprived altitude so you could start *and* finish races in a flurry. It meant adhering to a sometimes hellish training program that was masterminded by their coach, who the runners believed without question was the smartest man on the planet when it came to preparing distance runners.

"You know that old saying, I'd run through a wall for that coach?" said Larry Zaragoza, Vigil's first national champion in 1971. "To this day, 50 years later, I'd still do it."

Day after day, Vigil preached to his team that they were doing more than any team in any division in the United States. He told them stories of great Olympians such as Frank Shorter and Billy Mills and George Young and Jim Ryun and many others who at one time trained in Alamosa. "None of those guys," he would say, "worked harder than you are working right now."

"What I remember is that his runners were tough, just tough," said John McDonnell, the legendary men's coach at the University of Arkansas from 1972 to 2008. McDonnell and Vigil struck up a friendship in the 1980s and had a series of close head-to-head battles from 1988 through 1991.

"Anytime you ran against his team, you better be ready to run," McDonnell said. "In a race, they didn't waste any time. They would run from the front and hammer."

◇◇◇

During the 1980 cross country season, Vigil's claim that his team worked harder than anybody was put to a stern test.

"Pat Porter never won a meet his first two years at Adams State," Vigil said. "One day, we are driving to Boulder for the Rocky Mountain Shootout and Pat pokes me on the shoulder and says, 'Coach, I'm going to win tomorrow.' I said to myself, 'Yeah, OK, you're going to win tomorrow, Pat.'

"Well, at the time, the University of Colorado had a runner by the name of Mark Scrutton, who broke the world junior record in high school, 13:43 for 5K. He was a college senior and had won eight Big 8 championships at the time. And there was another young man from Los Alamos, New Mexico, named Ric Rojas, who had just broken the American record for 15K.

"And Pat Porter, who has never won a college meet, is going to beat these guys?"

On race morning, Vigil was sitting in the hotel restaurant drinking coffee when Porter's dad, Jack, came down to join him. "How's the kid going to do today, Coach?"

"Well," Vigil said, "he tells me he's going to win."

"The race starts and they have two 5K loops. Rojas, Porter, and Scrutton are running together in the lead," Vigil recalled. "As the second loop starts, Scrutton takes off and builds about a 50-meter lead. Methodically and slowly, the other two catch him. Then Rojas takes off, but eventually the other two catch him. I was standing on a knoll at five miles, and Porter takes off. Well, the other two never caught him. He won the meet, and Adams State beat Colorado—that small school up north—for the first time ever."

Riding home, Vigil was still astounded at what he had witnessed.

"I said, 'Pat, what motivated you to win today?' Because whatever I did, I wanted to use it again the following year."

In Vigil's words, Porter told him: "Coach, you tell us that we work harder than anyone in the world, and I got to thinking that if that's the case, then we should be able to beat anyone in the world."

"He lined up on that starting line with the confidence and courage to go out there and beat those guys on that day," Vigil said.

Years of experience have helped Vigil make sense of Porter's breakthrough. "Cognitive awareness and neurophysiology are a large part of running," he said. "You have to coach that nine inches above the shoulder. You can be the best coach in the world physiologically—getting the body ready—but if it's not clicking up here..." He points to his head. "That's the hard part of coaching at the higher levels. I didn't know much about it then. With Porter, I must have said the right things. I don't know."

For the next 10 years, almost nobody beat Porter on the cross country course. He rolled to NAIA championships in 1980 and 1981, leading Adams State to the team titles—the fourth and fifth national championships for Adams State, vaulting them past Fort Hays and Emporia State for the most NAIA titles ever.

Porter—still training in Alamosa under Vigil's guidance—then went on to win eight consecutive U.S. men's cross country championships from 1982 to 1989, a record that stands today and is not likely to be broken.

"In one year, he was like right with us and the next year, we see pictures of him in *Sports Illustrated* wearing his Adams State uniform running with guys who we thought were our heroes… and he's ahead of them," said Tom White, a three-time cross country All-American at Adams State and a 4:02 miler on the track. "Alberto Salazar in his Athletics West jersey and Craig Virgin (a two-time world cross country champion) are behind him."

That race was the 1981 U.S. championships, and Porter did fall back to sixth place, but it was the last time in the 1980s that Salazar or Virgin or any other American beat Porter on a cross country course. The 1982 U.S. championships featured a rematch against Scrutton. Porter handed the Brit a 17-second defeat to win his first national title as a member of the Nike-sponsored Athletics West elite club.

Pat Porter (left) and his father, Jack, following one of Pat's eight victories at the U.S. Cross Country Championships. Joe Vigil and Jack Porter formed a great friendship during the younger Porter's dominance of U.S. cross country running in the 1980s.

Throughout his winning streak, everyone knew what Porter's race strategy was: sprint from the start, build a big lead early, and dare the field to come get him. That was Vigil's race strategy for his Adams State teams, and it was stamped firmly into Porter's DNA. The strategy worked year after year, but heading into the 1986 championships at Golden Gate Park in San Francisco, some of Porter's chief rivals were tired of it.

"Pat heard them talking the day before the race that they were going to let him get out to the fast start, but then they would work together and run him down," Vigil said.

The chatter irked Porter. He promptly announced to a small group of rivals that they could try to catch him on race day, but "you're going to have to bleed to do it."

The next morning, Porter ripped a 4:15 opening mile on the 6.43-mile course and, as expected, no one was even close. A small group gave chase. But Porter took his anger out on the course, building his lead to 500 meters halfway through the race. A couple runners closed the gap late, but he was never challenged en route to a 10-second victory over former marathon world record holder Steve Jones.

"There really wasn't any way for any of us to catch him," Jones told reporters afterward. "I feel like there's only one or two people in the world who can beat Pat."

That win marked Porter's fifth consecutive, and for the next three years, the competition remained humbled. Porter's eighth straight U.S. championship in 1989—again held at Golden Gate Park—broke Don Lash's previous record of seven straight. At the awards ceremony, his competitors gave Porter a standing ovation.

◈ ◈ ◈

Porter's ascension was validation for Vigil and the Adams State runners that they were training for success at a very high level. Yet, while Vigil may have kept a few secrets to himself, Adams State's training schedule was pretty well known, largely because Vigil was always willing to sit and talk with coaches, athletes, physiologists and...really, *anybody* about the team's training regimen.

"Joe was a great mentor of mine. He knew I didn't know very much, so he tried to help me in many ways," said Duane Vandenbusche (pronounced "Van-Den-Bush"), who coached at rival Western State College in Gunnison, Colorado, from 1971 to 2007, winning eight men's and four women's national cross country titles.

"In the mid-1980s or so, Joe made a special trip from Alamosa to Gunnison and stayed overnight at my house. We sat at the table, and Joe gave me all kinds of great information and I asked all kinds of questions. That's how I began to learn. That meeting lasted for about four hours; we started about six o'clock and ended about ten. Adams was always the standard we tried to get to; they were the pinnacle. I knew that if I could get to their level, we would start to win. And when we did get to their level, we did begin to win."

A dozen years earlier, Fort Hays's great coach, Alex Francis, had helped Vigil catch and surpass his program. Now Vigil was paying it back to the school just 120 miles to the northwest that threatened to dig into the Adams State legacy. Vigil's intentions could sound a bit suspicious to some, but Vandenbusche had no such misgivings.

"I'm a great gut-instinct person, and I can size people up in about five minutes," Vandenbusche said. "It didn't take me long to know that Joe was honest and sincerely wanting to help me. A lot of that is based on the fact that we both grew up in the same way. Even today—and Joe echoed this with me a lot of times—the people I trust the most and the people I identify with the most are the people who worked with their hands growing up—the plumbers, the electricians, the carpenters, the plasterers, and the farmers. Those are the people I trust. And Joe Vigil was one of those. There was never any element in me that said Joe wasn't trying to sincerely help me a lot, which he was.

"That's why we identify, because when I was growing up on my parents' farm, I picked potatoes in a wicker basket, bending over all day and putting them into a burlap sack. I could pick one quarter-mile of one row of potatoes a day. That's 440 yards, or what we called a forty. So Joe picked lettuce, and I picked potatoes. I milked cows by hand...he did all of that hard work, too. We both grew up with a great work ethic."

Consistency was the benchmark of Vigil's training program at Adams State. Each week brought the same rigorous lineup of workouts, albeit a gradual buildup in intensity over the course of the season. Today's coaches rarely follow the same day-by-day, week-by-week routine Vigil espoused during his time at Adams State. But years of study provided Vigil a scientific basis for everything he was giving his athletes. Nobody could argue with the results he was getting, not just from his teams but also from post-collegiate athletes like Porter and many others who routinely trained with the collegians.

Through the 1970s until the early 1990s, here's how it went:

Mondays: One-lappers at Cole Park

The park is a perfect 700-meter grass oval around the inside perimeter, with eight telephone poles located approximately 90 meters apart around the edge of the park. During the cross country season, Vigil's troops would do a fartlek-style workout of 16 laps, starting at 2 minutes per loop early in the season but progressing to 1:45–1:50 later on. The rest period was jogging two telephone poles, then a flying start into the next lap.

During the track and field season, distance runners would run 20 400s on Mondays at 65 seconds, one-to-one rest. Middle-distance runners would do a combination of 200s, 300s, and 400s faster than race pace.

Tuesdays: Hill work

This is the day of the notorious Rock Creek mountain runs, a rigorous 11-mile run entirely uphill and beginning at 8,000-feet elevation. The team would jump into a couple vans for the 30-minute drive from campus, hop out on a mountainous road, and begin the trek to nearly 11,000-foot altitude.

Later in the cross country season, Vigil's athletes would spend two to three weeks running resistance runs up the rolling mounds of the Great Sand Dunes National Monument. Then, for another three to four weeks, they would run up a steep, packed dirt road near Fort Garland (25 miles east of Alamosa), an incline Vigil called "All-American Hill" because it was eerily similar to the opening 1,000-meter stretch at the national championship course in Kenosha. Vigil tasked his cross country runners to charge up All-American Hill six times, surging 50 yards past the crest each time, before sending them off on a six- to eight-mile run across the nearby rolling hills.

Wednesdays: Recovery run

This was typically a 10-mile run at about 6:30–6:45 pace per mile, or at a heart rate of 150–170. Vigil would sometimes ride his bike along with the pack, stopping midway to take their heart rates and prod them either to slow down or speed up.

Thursdays: Mile repeats at Cole Park

Cole Park's outer rim is a tree-lined, asphalt-paved track that weaves its way past picnic tables and playgrounds and along the banks of the Rio Grande River. It forms two loops—one a little longer that snakes around a softball field, and a shorter loop that follows the outer edge of the grass loop. A mile repeat consists of one large loop and one short loop; Vigil adjusted the repeats for his team by slightly shortening the distance to represent the equivalent of a sea-level mile, giving him an indication of each athlete's potential fitness when they moved to late-season, national-meet form. The typical workout consisted of six one-mile repeats at a pace of 4:30 or faster for the quickest group, down to around 5:00 for those in the developmental group.

During its peaking phase, Adams State would run a two-mile time trial on the road, then jog two miles back to Cole Park for repeat miles—three repeats the first week, two repeats the second week, and one repeat about 10 days before the national meet. Many of the runners ran personal bests in the two-mile and mile during these workouts—sometimes as fast as 8:50 for two miles and sub-4:10 for the mile.

Fridays: Recovery run or pre-meet workout

Recovery runs were typically eight to 10 miles during cross country season. Pre-meet workouts consisted of a two- to four-mile warmup, followed by six to eight strides, and a two- to three-mile cooldown.

Saturdays: Race, or anaerobic threshold run

Many athletes joked they preferred to race on Saturdays because staying home was no picnic. The anaerobic threshold, or AT, run was a 10-mile out-and-back run to "The Barn," an old farmhouse located five miles from campus down a dusty country road. Many runners completed the AT run in less than 55 minutes, but it was typical for some of the stronger runners to complete the run in 51 to 53 minutes.

Sundays: Long run

Everyone was encouraged to run at their own pace, but the expectation was to run between 14 and 18 miles on Sundays. Vigil had a voluntary meet-up at Plachy Hall at 8 a.m. each Sunday. You didn't have to go, but if you didn't show, you darn well better get your run in before noon that day—doing the long run later didn't give you enough time to recover for Monday's one-lappers. Vigil would drive along in his truck and hand out water.

"Everything we did had a purpose," Vigil said. "Most people know they have to focus on the hard days, but then on the other days what a lot of these runners do is go out and play six rounds of grab-ass (Vigil's phrase for horsing around, or not concentrating on the task at hand). We were training all of the energy systems, and in order to do that, you have to be able to focus on the goal that you have established for that day."

Vigil's fervor to learn about training distance runners and track and field athletes stretched all the way back to 1956 when his high school star, Dale Pruett, asked how he could throw the shot put farther. "And I'm still learning more…to this day," the 90-year-old Vigil says. Vigil's family spent many summers away from Alamosa as he earned a doctoral degree at the University of New Mexico in Albuquerque, and did postdoctoral work at Louisiana Polytechnic Institute in Ruston and New Orleans, as well as at the University of Toledo in Ohio.

"The work I did in Louisiana was a combined program with Louisiana State University in which I studied at the Charity

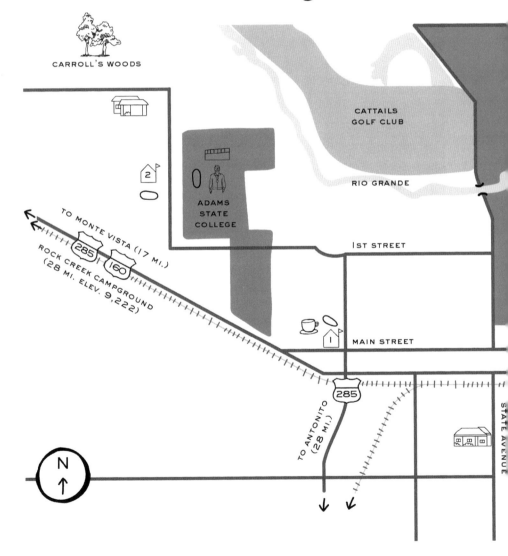

COACH VIGIL'S
Alamosa
(ELEV. 7,544)

CARROLL'S WOODS

CATTAILS
GOLF CLUB

2

ADAMS
STATE
COLLEGE

RIO GRANDE

TO MONTE VISTA (17 MI.)

285   160

ROCK CREEK CAMPGROUND
(28 MI. ELEV. 9,222)

1ST STREET

MAIN STREET

1

285

TO ANTONITO
(28 MI.)

STATE AVENUE

N
↑

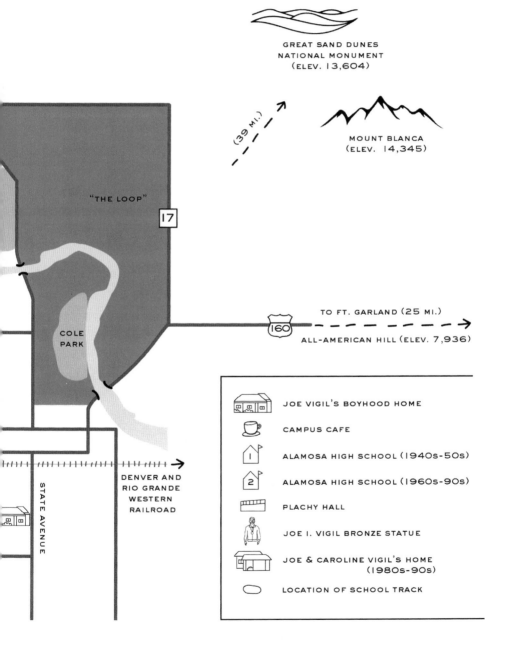

GREAT SAND DUNES
NATIONAL MONUMENT
(ELEV. 13,604)

(39 MI.)

MOUNT BLANCA
(ELEV. 14,345)

"THE LOOP"

17

TO FT. GARLAND (25 MI.)

160 ALL-AMERICAN HILL (ELEV. 7,936)

COLE
PARK

DENVER AND
RIO GRANDE
WESTERN
RAILROAD

STATE AVENUE

JOE VIGIL'S BOYHOOD HOME

CAMPUS CAFE

ALAMOSA HIGH SCHOOL (1940s-50s)

ALAMOSA HIGH SCHOOL (1960s-90s)

PLACHY HALL

JOE I. VIGIL BRONZE STATUE

JOE & CAROLINE VIGIL'S HOME
(1980s-90s)

LOCATION OF SCHOOL TRACK

Hospital in New Orleans," Vigil said. "They gave me a human brain in formaldehyde and I brought it back home with me in a glass jar so I could study parts of the brain."

Vigil traveled extensively, several times to Europe, where in the late 1970s and early 1980s he went to coaching schools or had individual meetings with many of the brightest thinkers of sport and human performance, including Frank Dick at the University of Loughborough in England; Carlos Perea in Lisbon, Portugal; Manuel Ballesteros in Madrid, Spain; and Denis Guilloteau in Terreno, Italy.

"I developed an interest in the lack of education American coaches had about running at the high school level, and probably at the collegiate level," Vigil said. "When I traveled, I was able to see what European coaches knew and how they focused their training."

Vigil also taught a summer class in which for many years he took a group of 15–20 students—many of them coaches or aspiring coaches—on a bike tour through parts of Europe. The trips included cultural experiences and occasional opportunities to meet the track and field stars of the day, such as England's Sebastian Coe and Steve Ovett, and Norway's Grete Waitz. He took a summer sabbatical from Adams State in 1980 to visit the track and field federation offices in numerous countries to ask them how they trained coaches in their countries. All those experiences afforded Vigil the chance to spend a lot of time absorbing knowledge and crafting his philosophy:

When I would go to conventions, me and some of the other coaches would talk about how poor coaches were; they didn't know anything. If you were working at a school and your son ran, they would hire you to coach cross country with no certification. As we talked, we decided to do something about it. I had a sabbatical coming at Adams State, so Caroline and I went to Europe, to 17 countries, and I went to the IAAF offices in 17 countries to find out what they did to provide certification for their coaches in Europe.

In 1980, I went to the AAU convention and met with my two buddies, Gary Winkler and Vern Gambetta. [At the time, Winkler was the women's track and field coach at the University of Illinois, and Gambetta was the women's track and field coach at the University of California, Berkeley].

We decided together that we were going to start a coaching education program for the United States in track and field, and that half of the instruction would be in the sciences and half of the instruction in training theory, because this is what I learned from my observations in Europe.

In late 1980, Vigil, Winkler, and Gambetta made a pact to meet in Alamosa to begin developing a coaching education program for USA Track & Field.

"It was probably one of the most amazing experiences of my life and my coaching career," Gambetta said. "Gary Winkler and I got on a little plane in Denver, I think it was a 12-seater, and flew to Alamosa to work with Coach Vigil. When we got there, he went through the entire training program he had for the Adams State distance people. We saw the park where they ran the 700s, where they ran at the Sand Dunes, and all of that. Honestly, I tell people still today that it was like visiting [coaching pioneers] Percy Cerutty in Australia or Arthur Lydiard in New Zealand."

Soon the work began. In a small Plachy Hall classroom on the Adams State campus, the three men hammered out the parameters for an education program that they hoped would raise the expertise of American high school and college coaches coast to coast. "We divided training theory into four areas: the throws, the jumps, the sprints, and the distances," Vigil said. "At conventions, we would tell other people what we were doing and several became interested. One guy was Al Beda, who was the coach at American River College in California. He was a very bright guy and he loved track. All of us had a passion for track."

Now a group of four, the men scheduled a second meeting in Long Beach, California, where they developed Level I and Level II coaching education programs in each of the four disciplines. They recruited coaches across the country who could help teach the program, and they made plans to offer coaching education schools in every region of the United States.

Eventually, they were ready to pitch the idea to the country's governing body for track and field.

"We were in Philadelphia at The Athletics Congress (TAC) convention and there's a tremendous amount of antagonism and opposition to the coaching education program among a vocal minority," Gambetta said. "They thought we had a hidden agenda. I was chairman of the committee and I was a lightning rod because I wasn't smart enough to keep my mouth shut.

"Well, it comes time for us to make our presentation. As I get up, someone puts a hand on my shoulder and it's Coach Vigil, and he says in my ear: 'Don't worry about the people who don't believe in this. There's a whole bunch of guys in this room who have had 30 experiences one time. You go up and go get them.' Then he slapped me on my ass and told me I knew more about this than anybody in the room."

Gambetta's presentation convinced the naysayers to support the deeper knowledge of formalized coaching education. Later,

USATF voted to provide $50,000 to fund the program, which was not a lot of money but enough to get it started.

"It was a reassurance that what we were doing was right and it wasn't meant to threaten anybody," Gambetta said.

Vigil served as the national chair for USATF's coaching education program from 1981 through 1989. As of March 2020, more than 40,000 coaches had completed at least Level I of USATF's coaching education program, according to figures from the organization.

Being a successful coach, Vigil said, "corresponds with education and becoming involved in what you're doing. I've often said: 'Eat as though you're a poor man, do endurance training daily, and don't let your mind go to seed.' What I mean by that is that coaches and athletes need to keep learning about themselves and what their potential is. They should ask, 'What is my potential and how long is it going to take to get there?' How long it takes depends on the physical preparation you did in advancing your physiology. Then, what we do as coaches is advance the athlete's neuroplasticity—the remapping of the brain. It goes hand in hand with physical preparation. These are things people may have done accidentally in the past, but they didn't know what they were doing. Now, because of coaching education, there's a plan."

While Vigil was helping to improve the sport on the national level, his team was getting better. Except for a blip in 1982 when Adams State finished eighth at the national meet, the 1980s belonged to the men from Alamosa.

In 1983, Adams State took back the national title with a 50-point win over Wisconsin-La Crosse, then backed it up with a 60-point win over La Crosse in 1984, and an 80-point win—again...La Crosse!—in 1985, with six All-Americans. Robbie Hipwood, the team's captain, won the individual title in 1985 and senior teammate Robert Ferguson was the runner-up. Adams State now had eight national titles, double what Alex Francis and Fort Hays won during their glory years.

The captain of the 1983 team was Dave Cuadrado, nicknamed Cuad (pronounced like "quad"), from Arvada West High School near Denver. Even among distance runners, Cuad (who stood 6-foot-4) was easily the thinnest guy in a crowd. He had been through the highs and lows of Adams State in the early 1980s, running on the NAIA championship team in 1981 prior to a disappointing eighth-place team finish in 1982.

For Cuad, the 1983 season was filled with both lows and highs. Early in the season, the trainer told him the pain in his foot was a stress fracture, which left the senior captain with an important decision—run through the pain and hope the foot held up, or step back and cheer his team from the sidelines.

He chose to fight through it.

"All season he struggled with that leg," Vigil said. "He was able to earn his spot on the team for nationals, and he made All-American and the team won. When he finished the race, he collapsed. He didn't want to let his team down. That's how strong the values were that we were teaching, through the leadership we had—not only from me, but also from the team members. They believed in Cuad and he didn't want to let them down."

In 1984, Adams State hired a 43-year-old student intern to be its sports information director (SID). Lloyd Engen—a 5-foot-5 Norwegian who was beloved on campus and in the community for his jolly nature—chronicled the college's athletics for more than two decades.

"I remember the first week I was on the job," Engen said. "I was sitting at my desk. Coach Vigil comes in and I was looking down at the time. I look up and he says, 'Are you the new SID?' I said, 'Yes, I am.' And I'll never forget what he said next: 'I'm Joe Vigil. I'm the head coach for cross country and track. You can forget about all of those other sports.'"

Engen responded: "Well, I don't think my boss would like it if I did that."

Vigil was blunt, but he was also realistic. He knew Engen had a job to do, but he wanted to impress upon the new guy the importance of cross country and track and field at Adams State. He then invited Engen for a ride in his pickup, and for the next several hours they drove around Alamosa so Vigil could show him the numerous trails where Adams State's runners trained, all the while showering him with stories of great Olympians who had trained on the very same paths.

Engen was smitten. From 1985 through the mid-2000s, he routinely traveled to the national meet with the cross country and track and field teams, logging tens of thousands of miles on his car and writing the unfolding story of the most decorated collegiate cross country and track and field program in the country.

His introduction to the sport was dramatic. He covered the 1986 NAIA cross country championships in Kenosha where the three-time defending champs found themselves in a tussle with conference rival Western State and their fiery coach, Duane Vandenbusche.

"In 1986, we went to the national meet at Parkside and Adams was ranked No. 1 and we were ranked either three or four," Vandenbusche said. "It was a great race, and after the meet, we went to the awards dinner at about two o'clock. Nobody knew who had won at that time; it was the tradition to announce the results at the awards dinner."

But Vigil and Vandenbusche suspected that something was shaking. Before the results were announced, Dave Socier, a reporter for Colorado newspaper *The Pueblo Chieftain* quietly asked Vigil and Vandenbusche for an interview. "Neither one of us knew why he wanted to talk to both of us," Vandenbusche said.

"Then the unbelievable happened. With 42 men's teams and 374 runners, they announced that Adams State and Western State had tied for the national championship. It was amazing."

Adams State's runners breathed a sigh of relief. Western's runners were ecstatic; it was their school's first-ever national title in cross country. The runners from both teams, though rivals on the course, respected each other off of it and they hugged and congratulated each other. Western State carted home the team trophy while Adams State brought back the 3x12-foot red banner that went to the NAIA champs. It was the first time a tie had occurred at a national meet, in any collegiate division, and it's happened only one other time since: in 1988, Edinboro and Mankato State shared the NCAA Division II title.

Things were much different in 1987. Spurred by their near-defeat the year before, Adams State roared to the front of the pack, taking six of the first eight positions at the top of Kenosha's opening hill, then hit the gas. Rick Robirds, who'd won the NAIA individual title the year before as a sophomore, successfully defended his title, and Adams State, for the first time ever, had seven All-Americans—all in the top 15 finishers over the 8K course. Adams State scored 21 points and won by 150 points over conference foe New Mexico Highlands.

The 21-point score was the lowest ever at the NAIA meet, a big difference from the school's first title in 1971, when they had the highest score ever at the NAIA nationals (196 points). The 150-point winning margin also was a record, in stark contrast to the smallest margin of victory—which, in essence, was the zero-point win with Western State the year before. In all, Adams State set seven NAIA records in 1987; it was also the first time any school had seven All-Americans in the same year. At the time, Engen dubbed the team the Fantastic Seven, writing about the accomplishment as though it would likely never be seen again at the national level.

Let Me Tell You a Story

James Seefeldt, who won the 1988 Rocky Mountain Athletic Conference individual cross country title in a driving snowstorm near Golden, Colorado, remembers how Joe Vigil could make his athletes feel important even in simple, everyday interactions.

"Coach Vigil motivated me in many ways when I was young and still to this day," Seefeldt said. "Specifically, his zest for learning, love of life, and his honest interest and compassion not only to his runners but to his community have always motivated me.

"But the one thing that stands out above all was his ability to make me feel that I was important, that I mattered not only to the team but in general—that I can have a positive impact on the people around me. It is hard to explain but I get that same feeling from him every time I see him. It is nothing he says directly but just the way he engages with me when I see him.

"It isn't just me though. He engages with most people in this way, which is why, I feel, people love to be around him."

Adams State won again in 1988 with six All-Americans (including national champion Craig Dickson), and in 1989 with five All-Americans (Robirds won for the third time), capping the decade with nine national titles in 10 years. Counting the 1979 team, Adams State actually had a run of 10 titles in 11 years. By now, the men's program—with 12 NAIA titles—had tripled what Fort Hays and Kansas State Teachers College in Emporia had accomplished in the 1950s and 1960s.

Adams State's collection of cross country individual national champs had grown to eight, including Montoya (1979), Porter (1980, 1981), Hipwood (1985), Robirds (1986, 1987, and 1989) and Dickson (1988).

"Sometimes," Vigil said, "I look at what we accomplished and I can't believe it myself."

10

A ROLLER-COASTER
RIDE

Success is rarely linear: not in athletics, business, relationships...and not in life. Adams State's dominating run in the 1980s was no exception. While racking up more than a dozen team national championships, nearly six dozen individual national champs, and more than 300 NAIA All-Americans, Joe Vigil's cross country and track and field teams experienced the highest of highs and lowest of lows, a roller coaster of emotions that can agonizingly characterize athletics.

The fact that Adams State emerged from the 1980s stronger than ever is a clear testament to their coach's resilience and dogged determination. At age 60 and having worked in public education for 36 years, he could have drawn a nice pension and lived a comfortable life in retirement with his loving wife. But Vigil wasn't finished coaching. He'd tell you he was just getting started and had a whole lot more to learn. Besides, beyond team championships and individual glory, Vigil simply loved to be around the runners of Adams State. Frankly, he lived for the challenge of helping young adults become All-American people and athletes.

"I would say there's people that influence us the most in our lives and that we spend the most time with and that we have the most invested in," said Tom White, a five-time All-American from 1978 to 1981 who is now a doctor in Buena Vista, Colorado. "In my life, I would order those people as being my wife, my parents, and my Coach."

White was an up-and-coming high school runner in New Mexico when Vigil first met him. As a senior in the late 1970s, White won a mile race on the track in Albuquerque against an all-star field of cross country champions from New Mexico and a few surrounding states. Vigil was in the stands watching.

"So I went up there and found him and talked to him. He told me, 'Tom, why don't you come to Adams State?'" White said. "My dad and I went to Alamosa to visit the campus and Coach took us around in his Jeep. Coach Vigil asked us what we wanted to see and my dad said that we wanted to see the library. Coach Vigil loved that. He always brought that up when he would tell a story about my dad. Coach and my dad really took to each other, although they never spent much time together. My dad had great admiration for Coach and mostly it was because Coach was so animated as he took us on a tour of the library. So I always felt a great kinship to Coach because he was such an academic."

Vigil is well known for waking up at 4 a.m. every day, even when he travels, to study and get his work done. As college kids might do, Vigil's runners often questioned if the legend of Vigil's early-morning work sessions was true.

"In 1980, Mike Maguire graduated from Adams State and was moving back to Nebraska," White said. "The day before he's leaving, he calls me up and says, 'Tommy, I want to find out if Coach really does get up at 4 a.m. I've got to leave really early in the morning; let's go for a run and let's stop by Coach's house.'

"So Mike and I get up at 3:30 in the morning, and we go for a run, and we get to Coach's house. We walk up to his front door, and we are afraid to push the doorbell—we don't want to wake Caroline up—but we push the doorbell. Nothing happens. We push the doorbell again, nothing happens. And we're thinking, I guess it's not true. We turn around and we're walking away. All of a sudden, the door just flies open. There's Coach. He's all dressed. He says: 'Hey, boys! I didn't hear you. Come on in. Come have some coffee.' He's got a pot of hot coffee. In his office, his books are all open on his desk. So we come in and we drink coffee. And we're thinking, 'Yeah, it's true.'"

White quickly added his name to Adams State's athletic lore as a freshman when he placed fifth at the NAIA national cross country meet in 1978, rebounding from a slow start that season due to a summer injury. His surprise finish was a big key to Adams State's impressive third-place finish that year, in which they beat conference champion University of Southern Colorado for the first time. It was also the only time that season when White ran as the team's first man.

He followed that up with a pair of All-American finishes in the 1979 and 1980 cross country seasons—both were championship years for Adams State—and a pair of All-American finishes in the mile during the indoor and outdoor track seasons. Heading into the 1981–1982 school year, his senior season, White was hyped for a thunderous encore, including a great shot at the individual national cross country title.

But this is where White's path to a happy ending takes a detour.

White spent his college summers near Rifle, in northwest Colorado, working as a beekeeper with his teammate and good friend Randy Cooper, whose family lived in that area. Each summer, the pair built a treehouse just off the Colorado River where they would sleep at night, trained early in the mornings, and worked the rest of the day. Pat Porter joined them in 1979, and White says it was the first summer that Porter realized he needed to train every day if he wanted to be successful at the college level.

White and Cooper headed to Rifle after the 1981 track and field season, intent on getting back to their summer routine. But on June 21, White was riding his motorcycle when a drunk driver crossed the center line. The truck's rear bumper caught White's left foot, nearly tearing it from his leg. Injured and alone, White assessed his situation and determined that he needed to apply a tourniquet to his badly injured limb, then asked a passerby to call for help. White instructed the Good Samaritan to apply a pressure point to his groin area until help arrived.

At the hospital, White begged doctors not to amputate his foot, explaining that he was a runner. Perhaps divine intervention was on his side, as the attending doctor and nurse had just received training that would help them to save the foot. Even so, the resulting skin grafts and rehabilitation were just not enough to rebuild the young running machine. White, a man who was revered among his teammates and who brought so much positive energy to the Adams State program, accepted the reality that his remarkable ascent to the top of NAIA distance running was over.

"After my accident, I spent the next 100 days in the hospital," White said. "I came back to school late that next fall, not knowing what it was going to be like making up classes and even getting around.

"But a couple things made it easier. First, Coach Vigil continued my track scholarship. Second, he gave me a job helping to coach the women's cross country team. It was an amazing thing he did for me. I don't understand why he would be as good to me as he has been, and I don't know why I deserve it, but I don't try to explain it, because it is what it is. And I think maybe that's what compassion is."

As if the gut punch of White's injury wasn't enough, the Adams State program was rocked again during the fall of 1981 when team member Dale Martinez was killed in a car accident.

"It left a void on our team and a huge hole in our hearts," said Dave Cuadrado, a sophomore on that year's team.

Yet the program bounced back. In fact, that year Adams State became the first NAIA school to sweep the men's and women's cross country national titles. Porter won his second consecutive NAIA title to lead the men, while Mary Jaqua won the women's individual title, leading four of her teammates who finished in the top 10—all seven crossed the finish line in the top 21. Adams State's women scored 25 points for the team win, an NAIA record that stood for 16 years and which still stands as the school's national-meet record.

The NAIA title capped the third season for the Adams State women's program. It was also the second year that the NAIA held a women's cross country championship. The team's head coach was 24-year-old Rock Light, a two-time All-American sprinter for Vigil in the late 1970s. Vigil, not wanting to spread himself too thin and believing in Light's ability as a young coach, advocated for the young man to be head coach for the women, despite the fact that Light was not a distance runner himself and had no head coaching experience. The women's title also came with NAIA Coach of the Year honors for Light, a native of Lamar, Colorado.

Largely because of Title IX requirements for schools to provide equal opportunity for female and male athletes, most schools in the Rocky Mountain Athletic Conference added women's track and field and cross country in the late 1970s or early 1980s. Adams State was an instant powerhouse in both sports. In 1982, Vigil—who was overseeing men's and women's programs while grooming Light—recruited a remarkable freshman class that hammered the rest of the league's schools.

"We started women's track and field at Western State in 1983," said Duane Vandenbusche, head coach at the school in nearby Gunnison. "Initially we had nine girls on the women's team. We went to Adams State for a dual meet and I remember telling our girls before the meet about an old Chinese proverb that reads: 'The longest journey begins with a single step.' And we were about to take it."

That day, Adams State's women beat Western State 93-6.

Adams State's talented women earned respect from schools at all levels. In 1985, Vigil took the team to the Kansas Relays, where he put his pack of young stars to the test against a strong field of NCAA Division I athletes.

"Coach was sitting in front of the coach from Villanova, Marty Stern; they called him Uncle Marty," said Jack Hazen, an NAIA Hall of Fame coach at Malone College in Ohio, who battled Vigil's Adams State teams for more than 20 years. "Well, Uncle Marty was talking about his great runner, Veronica McIntosh [the NCAA Division I indoor 800-meter champion in 1984], who Stern was certain would win the 800 that day. He happened to make the statement, 'I guess we know who's going to win this race.' Vigil heard him, and so he turned around and told Uncle Marty, 'I've got $20 that says she doesn't win.'"

"He and I had never met yet, and so it kind of pissed me off that he said that," Vigil said. "You've got to run the race, you know. So I wanted to let him know that."

One of Vigil's stars was Julie Jenkins, a powerful middle-distance runner yet lightly recruited high schooler who collected multiple Colorado state championships in Class A, the state's lowest classification. As a senior at Moffat High School, a small town in the northern San Luis Valley, Jenkins nearly won the team title by herself, scoring 38 points at the 1981 state meet for the third-place trophy.

At the Kansas Relays in 1985, Jenkins made good on her coach's bravado, running down McIntosh in the final stretch to win the race in a photo finish.

"A little later, the mile relay was coming up, and Uncle Marty asks Coach for a chance to win back his $20," Hazen said. In addition to McIntosh, Villanova had a great team that included four NCAA Division I All-Americans in events ranging from the 400-meter hurdles to the mile run. In 1984, Villanova's 4x400 relay placed fifth at the NCAA Division I Championships.

Adams State had a great 4x400 team, too. Jenkins was a 19-time All-American in three years at Adams State and was the 1987 NCAA Division I indoor 800-meter champion for Brigham Young University. The squad also featured 24-time NAIA All-American Lori Risenhoover, a jumper/hurdler/sprinter who is the most decorated athlete, regardless of sport, in the school's 100-year history. And in Connie Calkin and Brenda Jarvis they had a pair of 52-second quarter-milers.

So, of course, Vigil accepted Stern's bet. Then, a little over three minutes and twenty seconds later, he collected another $20 bill from Uncle Marty.

Adams State's women won the 1985 NAIA Indoor Track and Field Championship at Kansas City's Municipal Auditorium—the first-ever track and field national title for Adams State—with Jenkins and Risenhoover setting national records in the 800 (2:10.69) and long jump (19-8), respectively. It was also the first track and field national title—indoors or outdoors—for any men's or women's team from the Rocky Mountain Athletic Conference.

Vigil was not the head coach of the 1985 women's team. Again hoping to ease his workload, he asked the school's administration to appoint his graduate assistant Milan Donley as coach of the women's team. Donley, an accomplished hurdler in college at nearby University of Southern Colorado in Pueblo, had been at Adams State since 1981.

Donley later coached at Southwest Texas State, East Tennessee State, California, Illinois, and the University of Arkansas, and is now the Director of the Kansas Relays in Lawrence. He and Jenkins married in the early 1990s.

◊ ◊ ◊

By the mid-1980s, the legend of Joe I. Vigil was large in Alamosa and the region, and growing larger throughout the United States. Coaches at all levels understood quite well how good his men's and women's teams were, and his athletes realized the tremendous impact he had on them personally.

Let Me Tell You a Story

"Life-changing experiences come and go. Some great, some devastating. The truth of Adams State sticks with me most. The truth. The honesty. Unspoken bonds in a high-desert town. Listening to the advice from a rock-solid head coach who became something more than a head coach. Dreams achieved and yet to be fulfilled...."

—Dave Cuadrado, 1980–1984,
five-time NAIA All-American

"After I graduated from Adams State, I spent time in Boulder training with Frank Shorter, Ric Rojas, and many other great runners of the time," Pablo Vigil said. "I came back to Alamosa in the 1980s, and I wanted to do something for Coach Vigil to honor everything he had done for me, beginning with that letter he sent me when I was in high school, and helping me become the runner that I was.

"But it was more than that. I wanted to do something that honored Coach as a real human being and not just a coach, something that highlighted who he was as a man; you know, recognizing that he interacted with the janitor the same as he did with those who are high up in the sport. I came to realize that we should do something to honor Coach Vigil and all the respect that the local people in town had for him."

Pablo had been working on a term he intended to use to represent his own life's philosophy. Then, he realized "Vigilosophy" was better suited to his coach.

"In 1985, we put together a panel of several people who could talk about how much we learned at Adams State as runners under Coach Vigil and what we had gone on to do," Pablo said.

Porter was on the panel. So was Shirley Bervig, the Alamosa resident who took Vigil's class for stay-at-home moms in the 1970s. John Esquibel, a three-time national champion in the indoor mile from 1979 to 1981 who opened a local running store shortly after his college graduation, was part of the group.

"It was a tribute to Coach Vigil," Pablo said, "but we also wanted to show that what we learned as athletes for Coach Vigil translated to what we became later in our lives. It was his compassion, dedication, and commitment to us that made us better people. That's what Vigilosophy was all about."

Vigil liked the term. He had some T-shirts made that read, "Vigilosophy is the Pursuit of Excellence" that became a must-have item for athletes, friends, community members, and many others. Terry Gibbs, who with his wife owns Vigil's favorite restaurant, the Campus Cafe, routinely wears a Vigilosophy or Vigilante T-shirt as he tends the cash register each day.

"I told Coach, 'You know, there's a copyright on that word,'" said Pablo, with a laugh.

"I once told Coach that I think back to everything he went through when he was growing up, including the discrimination and racism in Alamosa, which was indicative of what was going on in a lot of places. I told him the fact that he had succeeded as a coach and as an academic makes him, in my mind, such an amazing and rare Latino."

According to Pablo, Joe Vigil responded: "I would prefer to be known as a human being."

"I told him, 'I know, I know, Coach, but it's beyond that. How many Latinos from that era that grew up with all of those odds against them were able to forge through the storm and do amazing things?' There have been a few, but Coach Vigil…I think we're all just blown away. There are many examples of kids on the south side of Alamosa who didn't forge through.

"That's why I think as educators or anybody else—whether you're a painter, a dancer, or a writer—we have incredible potential to say something positive, and to do something positive for the next generation," Pablo continued. "We owe it to them to give sound, realistic advice and not sugarcoat the facts; just tell it like it is. You know, you've got potential and it's not going to be easy, but you can do some great things should you decide to, and I'm willing to help you. It's kind of like when Coach Vigil told me many years ago that he wanted to help me develop my talent for running. When I read those words, it was like a lightning bolt going right through my body."

Thus, Vigilosophy came to represent not just the way Vigil

applied scientific principles to training distance runners, but also the Coach's set of ideals for living day to day: work hard, be honest, respect others, give your best to a cause, show compassion for humankind, and similar ethics. Vigilosophy came to represent the life that Vigil has been living ever since his mom, Melinda Medina, demanded he attend Sunday religion classes, and when, as a teen, he selflessly stood on a downtown corner to help strangers carry their packages across a busy street.

"I think Coach Vigil is one of those living legends that is a prime example of what can happen if you get people to believe in you and in a common cause," Pablo said. "The synergy of those types of groups is powerful stuff…deeply powerful, and that's what Coach Vigil has been all about."

The program Vigil had raised in Alamosa and at Adams State was highly visible—and highly sought. By 1985, Adams State may have been the only NAIA school that had a sponsorship contract with a major athletic company. Reebok hired Vigil as a coaching consultant, paying him $25,000 per year and agreeing to outfit his cross country and track and field teams—primarily providing uniforms, warmups, and shoes.

This was in the early days of large shoe companies' sponsorship of college athletic programs, and so the contract was exclusively for Vigil's teams. Reebok was under no obligation to support all of the school's athletic teams, and that caused some envy among others in the Adams State athletic department.

"I was asked by our athletic administration to go to Reebok and ask them to outfit all of our school's teams," Vigil said, "and I told them I would do that when those teams started winning."

Those close to Vigil knew he meant no disrespect to the other sports teams at the school, and certainly not to the college he truly loved. But he was a stickler about earning what you get; it's something that goes back to his childhood, when his family had nothing and whatever he and his brothers received, they had to work for. If Vigil wanted a bike, he'd have to work, buy the parts, build the bike. No free tickets.

But that approach rubbed some people wrong and as the years progressed, jealousy grew in the Adams State athletic department, usually among a small group of administrators and coaches. Vigil and his teams brought greater opportunities and attention to Adams State, much like the effect Tiger Woods had on professional golf in the 1990s. Most of the school's coaches and certainly the Alamosa community appreciated Vigil for his devotion. Still, the jealousy among a vocal few was something that Vigil dealt with in the 1980s through the end of his college coaching career.

Vigil's standards were also high for his athletes. In 1986, he coached sophomore Travis McKinley to the national title in the 400 meters—McKinley clocked 46.2 seconds at the NAIA national meet in Russellville, Arkansas. McKinley was a gazelle on the track, a picture of beauty around the oval. Nearly everyone on the track and field team—distance runners, jumpers, throwers, sprinters—looked forward to watching McKinley take the starting blocks at each meet.

But Vigil had a rule about being prompt to practice, meetings...and especially meets. In fact, if you didn't arrive five minutes early, you were late. If Vigil said the bus was leaving at eight o'clock, his athletes knew it would probably roll out of town at 7:58.

In 1987, Adams State boarded the bus for the national championships—again in Russellville—and all seemed well...except that McKinley, the defending national champion at 400 meters, had not arrived. Vigil didn't blink. He promptly told the bus driver to head out. Off went the squad without the athlete who appeared to be a solid contender for a national championship… and the 10 team points that went along with it.

McKinley arrived about five minutes late. The bus was gone. He didn't have a car, so driving to the meet was not an option. Unsure what he would do…*or could do…* he began walking back to his apartment off Alamosa's First Street.

The school's sports information director, Lloyd Engen, was leaving campus for the national meet in his own car when he spotted McKinley walking down the street. "Travis, what are you doing?" Engen said.

"Walking home," the soft-spoken McKinley said. "I missed the bus."

"Well, get on in," Engen said.

It was quite a sight, the 5-foot-5 Engen in his compact car driving along with the muscular 6-foot-4 McKinley. The talkative Engen and the quiet McKinley were on the road for 13 hours.

"That was the trip where we had to go through Tulsa, Oklahoma," Engen said. "We stopped at a restaurant to get some food and I remember the owner telling me I was welcome to come in, but Travis [who was African American] was not allowed to sit and eat. This was in 1987. I was shocked. I promptly told the restaurant owner he would not be getting any of our business."

The two made it to Russellville and McKinley finished as the national runner-up in the 400. But it was the last meet McKinley ever ran for Adams State. On December 18, following the fall semester, McKinley and two of his high school classmates were driving home to Denver late one night for Christmas break. Along Interstate 25, near Colorado Springs, their car's taillights failed. A semi-trailer rammed the car from behind, sending it rolling into a nearby ditch. According to news reports, the truck driver never saw the car until it was too late. McKinley and one of his classmates died; one survived.

Heartbreak again had hit the Adams State program. The following spring, Adams State's outdoor track and field meet was renamed the Travis McKinley Memorial. That season, every athlete on the Adams State team—cross country and track and field—wore a black ribbon on their jersey to honor their friend. Vigil helped to set up a fund that would raise money for McKinley's one-year-old daughter so that, one day, she might be able to go to college.

Back on the track, better times were ahead for Adams State. But there were still some bumps in the road. Maurice "Mo" Smith, a transfer from the University of Kansas, strung together indoor and outdoor championships in the mile run and 1500 meters. Smith is the only Adams State athlete ever to go undefeated in national competition, winning five individual championships and an indoor title in the distance medley relay. Smith, who won the indoor mile national title in 1987, continued Adams State's dominance in that event, beginning with John Esquibel (1979, 1980, and 1981), Peter Graham (1983 and 1984), and Mark Steward (1985 and 1986). Dan Maas also won the indoor mile in 1990.

All of the Adams State milers were solid 4-minute-flat runners or faster. Smith clocked 3:59.70 to set the school's indoor mile record. Outdoors, Maas nabbed the school's 1500-meter record with a solid time of 3:39.64 (the equivalent of a 3:55 mile). Both marks still stand at Adams State.

Smith likely would have won the indoor mile in 1988, but literally hours before Adams State boarded the bus for the NAIA championships, they received a call that one of their triple jumpers had been competing illegally. The NAIA ruled all members of the team ineligible to compete in the 1988 indoor championships.

Vigil wasn't the head track and field coach at the time, but many of the school's qualifiers were his distance runners. The February 25, 1988, edition of the Alamosa *Valley Courier* summed up how abruptly the decision descended on the team:

> *A phone call to the NAIA's director of administration, Wallace Schwartz of Kansas City, Mo., confirming the team's ineligibility was particularly devastating, since head track and field coach Dr. Tom Lionvale said the vans were loaded and motors idling while the 15 national-qualifying track athletes prepared to depart for Kansas City, Mo., to enter the national tournament.*

At the same time his teams were succeeding, Vigil's coaching tree was blooming. Among dozens of others coaching at the high school and college levels, Jim Bevan, an all-conference jumper and Vigil's graduate assistant in 1985, was hired at Rice University. (He completed his 35th year there in 2020.) Rock Light was a hot commodity at NCAA powerhouses Oregon, Louisiana State, and Texas Tech before returning as head coach of the Adams State men's and women's track and field program in 2013. Ben Montoya, a cross country All-American in 1978, was leading a powerhouse track and field program at Fountain-Fort Carson High School near Colorado Springs. Larry Jeffryes, who starred for Vigil at Alamosa High School and Adams State, had a nationally ranked high school cross country program in Los Alamos, New Mexico. And Larry Zaragoza, Vigil's first national champion in 1971, built two championship programs—first at Centauri High School in nearby La Jara from 1976 to 1983, and then for the next 36 years at Alamosa High School.

"I'll always remember one of the best things Coach ever said to me: 'As a coach, your style is a little rough, Zamagoza. It's going to get you in trouble sometimes,'" Zaragoza said. "I told him, 'Yeah, I know, Coach, I know.'"

"But dammit, Zamagoza, you've got to be your own man," Vigil said.

"And that's what I've tried to be," said Zaragoza, who is the first coach in Colorado to win boys' and girls' state championships in cross country and track and field, completing the cycle when his 1985 Alamosa boys' track and field team scored a one-point win. At the time, it was just the second boys' track and field state title at Alamosa, dating back to Vigil's 1963 championship team.

Vigil was pretty confident in his abilities as a coach, as well. He tells a story of recruiting Maas, a high school star from Santa Fe, New Mexico:

> In 1987, I went to Santa Fe to try and recruit Dan Maas, who had won the southwest regional in cross country his senior year. I had written to him and called him, but I was going to be in Santa Fe and wanted to stop by and meet his folks. His dad graduated from Duke, which had already offered him a full ride.
>
> I sat down with them and I'll never forget Fred Maas, at the end of our conversation, says, 'What have you got to offer my son?' You know, parents want to know about money. So I told him, 'How about a million dollars… worth of coaching?'
>
> I guess that impressed him, because Danny came to Adams State.

Maas racked up six NAIA individual titles and 12 All-American honors, ran on two national championship cross country teams, and made the 1500-meter finals at the U.S. Olympic Trials in 1992.

◇◇◇

In 1988, Vigil faced his own personal ordeal. Earlier that year, he had been named the head coach for men's and women's distance runners on the U.S. Olympic track and field team, an appointment that would take him away from the Adams State men's team for most of the fall cross country season.

A few months before the Olympics, he was interviewed by a reporter who wondered why black athletes in the United States were not strong distance runners. Vigil's mind turned toward science and history, leading him to a now-well-known fact that the reason many runners from African nations emerged as dominant distance runners was because by the time they were 18 years old, they had approximately 10,000 more miles on their legs than the average 18-year-old in the United States.

Vigil knew that training for distance success had to be intentional. It took years and years of preparation, something that was not specific to any ethnicity but rather to all human beings. It was

Joe Vigil around the time he was selected to be head coach of the U.S. distance runners at the 1988 Olympics in Seoul, South Korea.

just not a sport many African-American athletes in the United States had pursued to that point in time. So his response to the reporter's question was general: "They just haven't put in the work yet."

The reporter's translation of Vigil's comment was that black athletes were not *capable* of putting in the work, a misrepresentation that got Vigil in hot water with USA Track & Field. During the U.S. Olympic Trials in June—two months before the Olympics—USA Track & Field held a meeting to discuss whether to remove Vigil as an Olympic coach.

"Three African-American athletes stood up for me," Vigil said. "One of them was Edwin Moses [the 1976 and 1984 Olympic champion in the 400-meter hurdles and owner of an almost-incomprehensible, decade-long 122-race winning streak]. I had visited with him in the past, and I had patted him on the back at various meets for a job well done.

"Anyway, Moses got up there and he said, 'This guy has worked all his life and he can't be treated that way. I didn't hear the conversation, but he has never shown any prejudice toward African Americans.' And it caught fire. A couple other guys came up and spoke up on my behalf. So the people who were conducting the meeting said that's good enough and they dropped the matter. I was relieved."

Vigil's next move that summer was to name Damon Martin the interim coach for Adams State's men while he was at the Olympics in Seoul, South Korea, in September and early October. Martin had spent the previous two years as a graduate assistant with the women's cross country and track and field programs. As a junior at the University of Arkansas-Monticello, Martin had edged Adams State's Peter Graham for the 1983 NAIA championship in the 1500 meters, and had also been training the previous year with Vigil's men's squad. In fact, he had earned a sponsorship from Reebok when he clocked 13:49 for 5000 meters during the 1987 track and field season.

Before leaving for his Olympic duties, Vigil met with Martin and Scott Slade, the graduate assistant for the men's program, for what the two men thought would be Vigil's training plan while he was away.

"I set aside a big chunk of time," Slade said. "I had a notebook which I was ready to fill with pages and pages of wisdom and daily workouts for the weeks to come. I sat there eagerly and then Coach spoke: 'You guys understand training well enough, so I'll leave that up to you. But the number one thing to remember while I am gone is to maintain team unity.' That was it. No wisdom. No daily training plans. Maintain team unity. To me, that showed how strongly he felt about the importance of the team over the individual."

Let Me Tell You a Story

Scott Slade came to Adams State in 1987 as a graduate assistant for Joe Vigil's cross country program, though he was a solid middle-distance runner who still had hopes of competing post-collegiately.

In 2019, Slade—who has coached collegiate athletes since 1991—wrote a heartfelt letter to Vigil remembering what it meant to be accepted into the Adams State program. An excerpt of Slade's letter is below:

"I thought I worked hard in college; when I showed up in Alamosa, I really learned the concept of hard work," Slade wrote. "You raised my standards. You inspired me not to settle for mediocrity. At the same time, you taught me a simplistic approach to happiness and success: eat like a poor man, train daily, and don't let your mind go to seed...You taught me that the way to fulfillment once you have reached the top is to serve the strata below you. The value of anything is multiplied when it is shared.

"You continue to give of yourself. You have created value in my life and have motivated me to create value in other people's lives."

But Vigil did leave Martin with a stern piece of advice: "Dammit, Martin, I'm giving you an undefeated and untied team, one of the best programs in the country. Don't screw it up."

While Vigil was away, Martin led Adams State to four team wins in four races. Vigil returned in early October, at which time Martin gave the ol' Coach a taste of his own humor: "Coach Vigil, I'm giving you an undefeated and untied team, one of the best programs in the country, where it needs to be at this point in the season. Dammit, don't screw it up."

A week later, Adams State traveled to the University of Arkansas to run against the two-time defending NCAA Division I champions on their home course. "And then we lost by three points," Vigil said.

It was Adams State's only loss of the season, which ended with another NAIA title for Vigil's men's team. Martin was later named head coach for the women's cross country program, and in 1989, the two men led their teams to a sweep of the NAIA titles.

"I remember when we won and Coach tells me, 'Dammit, Martin, you won your first national title as a head coach; I'm going to buy you a dinner,'" Martin said. "For the NAIA championships, we always flew through Chicago and after the meet, we'd let the kids go out on their own. After the meet that year, he took me to this place called the Szechuan Inn; it was a five-star place, and he bought me the most incredible meal. It was just an awesome experience. It is surreal to think about that now. I didn't even know what the hell I was doing. I was just having fun and learning and working hard."

Earlier in the 1989 season, Adams State's men went to Malone College in Canton, Ohio, to run against one of their chief competitors that year, coached by Vigil's friend, Jack Hazen.

Let Me Tell You a Story

In 1986, Joe Vigil and former UCLA cross country coach Bob Larsen were at the World Cross Country Championships in Neuchâtel, Switzerland. As he was known to do, Vigil wanted to spend a day at that country's high-altitude performance center, which was a few hours' drive from their hotel.

"Joe tells the story that he and Bob got up at 2 or 3 in the morning to drive to the center," said longtime coaching friend Jack Hazen from Malone College in Ohio. "It's pitch-dark and Joe is driving and Larsen is sleeping. They get to the spot in the road that goes through a mountain and the road is closed."

There is a train that is transporting cars through the mountain. Vigil drives the car onto the train and off they go through a dark tunnel.

"About that time," Hazen says, "Bob wakes up and he asks Joe, 'Where are we?'"

Hazen then delivers the punch line: "Oh Bob," Vigil tells Larsen, "we've been in a terrible accident. We're on the way to heaven."

"I told Joe I would try to help him with the money to get out here," Hazen said. "He said he could speak at the local hospital, or do a clinic. So I put him to work and we raised the money to bring his team out. He always kidded me that he never worked so hard in his life because I had him going here and there.

"I remember he went down to the local hospital and talked to doctors at an in-service and he did a fabulous job talking about things like membrane exchange, osmosis, and enzymes. And then they started asking him questions about umbilical cords, and I said, 'Oh-oh, we are in trouble here.' But he answered every question. He just blew me away and blew all of them away, knowing all the answers to all this stuff."

Joe Vigil (center) with fellow coaching legends Jack Hazen of Malone College (left) and Bob Larsen of UCLA.

Malone beat Adams State at their home meet, but a month or so later, Adams State beat Malone 39-53 for the NAIA title.

"At the time, the NAIA gave the winning coach the award for Coach of the Year, a big silver bowl," Hazen said. "After Joe received that award and everybody applauded, he called me up on stage. So I went up…and he gave it to me."

"What are you doing?" Hazen said.

"I'm giving you this because you did a better job with your team than I did with my team this year," Vigil told Hazen.

Hazen told Vigil that he couldn't take the award, but Vigil insisted: "It's yours. I'm giving it to you. You're Coach of the Year."

No one knew it at the time, but it would be the last time Vigil was actually named NAIA Coach of the Year...and he gave the award away. The official record from that meet even lists Hazen as the recipient of the award.

Throughout the 1980s, Adams State's success was boosted by the fact that the college's athletes were training alongside a half-dozen or more post-collegiate runners. Olympian Pat Porter, who was on his dominating run of eight consecutive U.S. cross country championships, was the best-known member of the group training in Alamosa.

Others who routinely trained with the college team were Pablo Vigil, John Esquibel, Robbie Hipwood (1985 NAIA cross country champ), Robert Ferguson (1986 NAIA 5000-meter champ), Chuck Smead (a former world champion in mountain running who pushed Pablo toward that discipline), Damon Martin, and numerous others who came to Alamosa to train with Vigil and his now widely respected program.

The influx of post-collegiate runners training in Alamosa, many of them Adams State alumni, led the way to an annual clash between current and past team members. The Alumni Run, a highlight of each season, was held during the "off" week between the Rocky Mountain Athletic Conference Championships (where Adams State had to finish in the top three to qualify for nationals) and the NAIA national meet. Those three races typically took place the first three weekends of November.

Most years, the Alumni Run offered Alamosa residents their only chance to watch the green and gold run during the peaking season, so the crowd that cheered as athletes past and present went head to head was typically large and loud. Vigil would often convince a half-dozen members of the school's band to load up in the back of his pickup, and they'd play lively music as

Vigil drove in front of the lead pack. The local newspaper covered the Alumni Run as though the exhibition race was the real deal. The alumni, often donning singlets that read "Vigilante" across the chest, would proclaim that the college team was No. 1 in the country, "but No. 2 in the San Luis Valley." The current team members, in their game-day green and gold uniforms, would counter by questioning how the "old guys" (some just a couple years older than them) were still able to stand without assistance.

Once the gamesmanship subsided, it was blood-and-guts racing for five miles around "The Loop," the same paved road course that once hosted the 1968 U.S. Olympic Trials marathon. Vigil would tally up the scores by hand and the winning team would promptly rub salt in the wounds of the losers. Normally, the current team would win the Alumni Run because of its depth; the "old guys" rarely could put together more than three runners able to outrun the Adams State squad.

In 1992, however, the team battle became a side note when Vigil learned that Tom White would be returning to run...*yes, run!*... the Alumni Run. For more than a decade, White had limped through medical school and the early part of a medical career. He had recently taken a position to coach cross country at Buena Vista High School, about two hours north of Alamosa where White also had a medical practice, and he was pushing himself to learn to run again on a crooked leg. "His wife calls me up and says, 'Don't tell anyone, Coach, but Tom is coming to Alamosa to run the Alumni Run,'" Vigil said.

White recalled a meet 12 years earlier in which the Air Force Academy came to Alamosa to take on Adams State on "The Loop." The road course finishes with a nearly three-quarter-mile stretch down Alamosa's First Street.

"I remember distinctly coming onto First Street and you had

that long stretch…and this will give you nightmares…I come around that corner and I see in front of me, one Adams State runner, two Adams State runner, three Adams State runner, four Adams State runner—and then me," White said. "On this shoulder right here I've got Bret Hyde, who made the Olympic Trials in the steeplechase that year, and on the other shoulder another strong Air Force runner. If I can beat these two guys, we get a perfect score. Now that is scary. It's a big responsibility. I don't want to be the guy that let my teammates down."

White won the fight that day, and Adams State got its perfect score at the home meet in 1980. But the 1992 Alumni Run was more dramatic. Porter won the race, and the alumni ran well, mixed in with a wave of green-and-gold Adams State varsity runners.

"That was a year when we only had four alumni, and Tom White was the fifth man, so he had to finish for the alumni to get a team score," Vigil said.

Normally, the 8K (4.96 miles) race is done in a little over 30 minutes, but on this day, the crowd didn't disperse when it appeared that all the runners had finished. Everyone…*everyone*…was waiting for Tom White, who was plugging along at about a 10-minute-per-mile clip. At first sight of White hobbling down First Street, the crowd and runners exploded. Instead of fighting off runners from the Air Force Academy, White was fighting off the searing pain in his left leg. Many tears fell as one of the most courageous runners in the program's history willed himself to the finish line in last place.

"You know, to be honest with you, I did not want the attention," White said. "I was happy just to be there. For me it was symbolic to be able to do that, to be running again. It is funny that I went from being a collegiate, front-of-the-pack person to being at the very back of the pack, but I always just wanted to be part of the group. That is what was most important to me. If there was not a dry eye in the house, well, I don't know. I started running again because I didn't want to get left behind. I wanted to be able to be part of the group because the most fun I ever had was running with my teammates. That's why I wanted to run after my injury."

Vigil figured out the team scores. White's finish mattered, as the alumni's top-end strength was enough to win. Without White, the alumni would not have scored. On that day, the Adams State alumni were No. 1 in the San Luis Valley.

11

A PERFECT DAY

Steady rains pummeled Slippery Rock, Pennsylvania, for four days leading up to the 1992 NCAA Division II men's and women's cross country championships, turning the already-challenging course into a sloppy mess. The forecast was for more rain and temperatures hovering near freezing on race day. However, the beating Slippery Rock was absorbing paled in comparison to the storm that had been brewing in Alamosa, Colorado, for the previous few months.

Joe Vigil and his Adams State men's team had heard the whispers. They were a great NAIA program, the greatest ever, but they were heading into unfamiliar territory in the 1992 season: the NCAA. Adams State's move to the NCAA was largely based on money; the NAIA could not afford to help pay for schools to travel to national meets, while the NCAA could. Most of the schools in the Rocky Mountain Athletic Conference made the jump the same year. At Adams State, it was purely an administrative choice to move, Vigil said; coaches weren't involved in the final decision.

Before the 1992 season began, Adams State was hearing that

schools such as Edinboro, South Dakota State, and Cal Poly San Luis Obispo—which had dominated Division II cross country for much of the previous decade—and a few other squads were ready to give Adams State a rude introduction to the big leagues.

"I can't remember anything specific, but I think it was a combination of us hearing one or two things, and then us blowing it up a bit," said Damon Martin, who was in his fourth year of coaching Adams State's women. "I think Coach had talked to one of his Division I buddies who told him there were a few teams that were going to show us how to run, something like that."

Initially, the tough talk didn't faze Adams State or Western State, two schools that were quite familiar with high-level competition. In fact, at Adams State, many thought that moving to NCAA Division II was a step down for its men's cross country team. For starters, Adams State no longer had to contend with Lubbock Christian (LCU) and its five-Kenyan juggernaut, which had beaten the Indians for the 1990 and 1991 NAIA titles, the first two of LCU's record eight consecutive championships.

In those days, the best NAIA schools regularly beat Division II competition, and sometimes they beat the top Division I competition.

"Coach Vigil fashioned a schedule that fit us," said Jason Mohr, a 10-time All-American at Adams State who broke Kregg Einspahr's NAIA record in winning the 1992 steeplechase title in a time of 8:43. "He wanted to run against good teams. We went to the Roy Griak Invitational at the University of Minnesota and raced Division I schools, Wisconsin and Iowa State and those types.

"I loved racing D-I programs and beating them. I kept track of every team we beat...Wisconsin and Iowa State and a lot of Big Ten and Big Eight and Pac-10 teams. We raced Arkansas, and they kicked our butt, but they raced us; that's the other thing, I have a huge respect for Arkansas, because they raced us. (Arkansas coach) John McDonnell had a lot of respect for Coach Vigil, and he was willing to put his team up against us."

Throughout the 1980s, Adams State never lost to a Division II or Division III school, traveling coast to coast to run against teams from all three NCAA divisions. In 1988, Adams State lost to two-time defending NCAA Division I champion University of Arkansas by three points on the Razorbacks' home course, the first of three straight years in which the two schools would run against one another. In 1992, two weeks after Lubbock Christian beat Arkansas (which would go on to win the Division I championship that same year), Adams State beat Lubbock Christian at a meet in Albuquerque. At the Roy Griak Invitational in 1992, Adams State placed five runners in the top 10 and won the Gold Division by 30 points over the University of Wisconsin, which was the NCAA Division I runner-up later that season.

A little closer to home, the University of Colorado—a perennial top-five team in NCAA Division I—hosted a large meet known as the Rocky Mountain Shootout throughout the 1980s. From the time Pat Porter led an upset win over the Buffaloes in 1980, Adams State did not lose to the University of Colorado at the Rocky Mountain Shootout for the entire decade.

The point? In the minds of the Vigilantes from Adams State, the power in U.S. collegiate cross country was in the NCAA Division I and the NAIA. Yet, somehow, the success that Adams State and Western State had as NAIA schools got lost on many of the Division II coaches and athletes.

Western State's coach, Duane Vandenbusche, also was surprised at the animosity his team was sensing from Division II schools.

"Joe competed against Division I teams all the time. We did, too," Vandenbusche said. "We went to the University of Minnesota meet a couple of times, and we did so well that after a while they divided the divisions up into I and II and they wouldn't let us run against Division I because we beat Wisconsin and Iowa State and Michigan and Michigan State. They didn't like that, but it didn't mean anything to us because we were better than they were."

Vigil admits he didn't really know what to expect in his team's inaugural NCAA season. He had not spent the time to study Division II teams. "I had my own team to get ready," he said.

The pollsters were paying attention, however. Adams State's men's squad spent much of the 1992 season with the No. 1 ranking in Division II, while Western State was No. 2. Still, they received an icy reception when they arrived for the Northcentral Regional meet in Omaha, Nebraska, in early November.

"Joe and I went to the coaches meeting the night before and I had to calm Joe down because it was really hostile," Vandenbusche said. "Nobody would really talk to us and you could just tell that they were either jealous or they figured that we were not as good as the NAIA thought we were. I had the feeling that everybody in the NCAA felt that Adams and Western were big-time in the NAIA, but now they're in the NCAA and they're not going to do what they did in the NAIA."

Ironically, Adams State and Western State became allies as the two schools ventured into the NCAA postseason. They were bonded by a common cause: to show the country's best Division II schools not only that they belonged, but that there was a new sheriff in town—and he was a two-headed, not-so-sleepy giant from the Rocky Mountains of Colorado.

Buddying up was not the way it had always been with these two schools. Despite their coaches' great friendship off the course, they were fierce rivals on it. From 1985 through 2015, there was Adams State and Western State in the Rocky Mountain

Athletic Conference...and no one else. The two schools finished 1-2 in the conference meet nearly every year for three decades. Much of the country only saw the two rivals duke it out at the national meet each year, but the conference meet also was a bloodbath.

"It really was," Vandenbusche said. "I burned to beat Joe Vigil, because I knew if I beat him, I beat the best in the world. And I know Joe did not like to lose. He might have been friendly to me, but he did everything he could to beat Western, and most of the time he did. I don't know if I've ever met a better competitor."

The rivalry may have cooled just a bit in recent years, but from 1979 through 2009, Adams State versus Western State was the greatest rivalry in collegiate cross country...and *maybe* in all of collegiate athletics. No two schools in any division of collegiate cross country can match what the men's and women's programs from schools located 120 miles apart were able to accomplish during that time.

Since 1979, Adams State and Western State have combined to win 57 national cross country titles (men and women), and finished 1-2 at the national championships an astounding 24 times, including a tie by the men's squads in 1986. Adams State's men had winning streaks of seven in the NAIA and six in the NCAA, while Western State's men won six of seven NCAA titles between 1999 and 2005 (interrupted by Adams State in 2003). Adams State's women won eight consecutive NCAA titles from 1992 through 1999, a streak snapped by Western State, which went on its own winning streak from 2000 through 2002. Then Adams State's women won seven more in a row.

Though they came to the NCAA Division II party 34 years late, the Adams State (13 NCAA championships) and Western State (eight) men's programs are No. 1 and No. 2 in Division II titles won. The Adams State women, coached by Vigil's former graduate assistant Damon Martin for all of their NCAA history, are No. 1 in that same category, with 18 NCAA Division II championships. The Adams State women won 15 of 18 Division II titles from 1992 to 2009; Western State's women won the other three during that span.

Let Me Tell You a Story

It is not easy to follow a legendary coach, but over 31 years, Damon Martin has managed to surpass the wild success Joe Vigil had at Adams State.

"I just look at it as though it's my turn at the wheel," Martin said. "Coach was always good about giving the credit to the kids. We would have meetings and he would praise people about their efforts and their contributions. I've always tried to take that to heart and realize, OK, this is just my short time at the wheel and hopefully there will be somebody else after me.

"When you love Adams State and you love the program, I think you need to have special people that understand the totality of the whole thing. Very rarely do I think it goes from one person to another; I was allowed to do that because I hope that I have the right love of the community and the people here at Adams State and I'm doing things the right way. But I also think that I was a willing student of Coach Vigil. I like to think that I learned and paid attention to not only the physiology but the other details about getting the most out of kids."

*Joe Vigil with Damon Martin (right). The two men have
led the Adams State cross country and track and field
programs to 56 national titles in 52 years.*

But in 1992, there were no crystal balls to forecast the wild
success of the two programs, and the existing teams in NCAA
Division II were blind to the tsunami that was about to hit them.

The first wave came at the Northcentral Regional cross
country championships in Omaha on the first Saturday of
November. Adams State's men, feeling confident that they could
move on as one of the four qualifying teams, lined up with just
four of the runners who would eventually make the top seven to
run at the national meet two weeks later.

That may sound a bit pretentious, and certainly risky. For
most programs, it would be. But Vigil's 1992 team was loaded,
and the fill-ins for regionals included junior Martin Johns—a
4:01 miler who would later represent his native New Zealand
at the 1996 Olympic Games—and sophomore Daniel Caulfield,
a gritty runner from Ireland who still holds the Adams State
record for the indoor 800 meters (1:48.94).

"That year," Johns said, "we had an extremely deep team.
We could have taken 14 kids to nationals and our second team
would have done quite well. We'd be doing mile repeats at Cole

Park and we'd run 5x4:20 per mile and we would have a pack of 10 or 12 of us doing that."

At the regional meet, as expected, Adams State shot out from the start, with Mohr, Caulfield, and Shane Healy in front of a chase pack of a dozen pursuers. They led the field through the first mile of the 10K race in 4:40.

"Joe (Vigil) and I were at the mile mark of the race and the first 10 runners that came through were from Adams and Western," Vandenbusche said. "We just blew them away, and after that they began to realize they were in big trouble—that everything we had done in the NAIA was going to translate to the NCAA."

Mohr, the Indians' team captain, went on to win the race, but Western State—led by freshmen Philip Spratley and Matt Titcombe—pulled together a much better pack and the Mountaineers beat Adams State by two points for the regional title.

It was the only win for Mohr that season, and in fact the only time he was the team's first man during the year. But he remembers the meet for another telling moment: "I remember somebody from an existing D-II team saying: 'Ah yeah, these Adams State guys think they're so great, but they can't even win regionals.' I never liked losing to Western State, but I always had a lot of respect for them. It didn't make a lot of sense to me, this guy saying that, because both of our teams had just steamrolled every other D-II school in that region."

Mohr set the tone for Adams State earlier that season when he approached Vigil in September, concerned that something was missing.

"I'll never forget the night Jason Mohr comes to my house, and he says, 'Coach, we've got to start running for something,'" Vigil said. "I thought all along we were running for something, but sometimes teachers and coaches take things for granted. I didn't really know what he meant. So I told him, 'Jason, you're the captain. Tomorrow when we have our meeting, you take over and tell the team exactly what you're thinking.'

"The next day, I call him up there and he starts talking about the team and he tells them: 'From now on I want seven guys to be able to touch each other in every workout, whether we're doing a 10-mile run, or repeat miles, or whatever. We need to touch each other.'

"And they bought into it," Vigil said.

Mohr, who stands 6-foot-5, tended to get his team's attention, and not just because of stature. He had a calm demeanor and strong work ethic his teammates respected, and a national title on the track to back it all up. He came from Cañon City, Colorado, and was coached his senior year by Lori Risenhoover, the 24-time track and field All-American from Adams State. He also looked up to a former Vigilante, Ken Woodard, an All-American and national runner-up in the steeplechase at Adams State who also came from Cañon City.

"What I remember is that team unity was drilled into my head from my freshman year onward," Mohr said. "Ken Woodard was an assistant coach when I started. I remember always thinking, 'Touch your teammate, touch your teammate, touch your teammate.' We'd do one-lappers at Cole Park…finish together. Mile repeats…finish together.

"It did seem though that in 1992 we had so much talent and we were running so fast that we had the chance for something more. What I remember thinking from running mile repeats and one-lappers all together was that maybe we could do a race where we could come across literally able to touch a teammate. It was sort of aspirational, but it just kind of seemed like maybe we could do this."

The week leading up to the NCAA Division II national meet was fraught with turmoil, however.

"There was some churn," Mohr said. "In the couple weeks

before nationals, guys were getting a little snippy with each other. You're with them all the time and you're fighting tooth and nail to make that top seven. This year was no different."

There was a good deal of debate about who should actually be in the top seven. Caulfield, seventh at regionals and third at the conference meet, was on a tear, but Vigil had a well-defined set of criteria that took into account early-season performance, a time when Caulfield was not at his best. He had run almost a minute faster than Adams State's seventh runner late in the season, but was left off the team for nationals. "Sure, I was definitely bitter at the time," Caulfield said.

Let Me Tell You a Story

Four-time NCAA Division II champion and 10-time All-American Dan Caulfield is the only runner in Adams State history to have competed for all three coaches in the program's history: Joe Vigil, John Kernan, and Damon Martin. He earned All-American honors under each coach's tutelage, competing from 1992 to 1996.

However, when the young Irishman was recruited by Vigil, he was instantly mesmerized.

"Coach Vigil's looks, eloquence, and showmanship are what drew me in, but it was his unconquerable passion and certainty for *everything* that made me an unworthy disciple," Caulfield says. "Nowadays, as a collegiate coach (at California University of Pennsylvania), I am perpetually motivated by him, so I am simply joyful when I get to see or speak with him."

Johns, too, was left off the national team, but he admits it was his own doing. "There was a Saturday-night drinking incident, and Coach did what he had to do, which I truly respect," Johns said. "As I recall that story, I would say a coach with lesser convictions would have taken me to nationals because it would have been about winning, and that would not have been the right thing to do, in my opinion. I think it's a testament to Coach Vigil's character that he did the right thing."

Damon Martin notes: "For the men, there was a lot of controversy going into that national meet. There was an arrest on the team. Another kid got caught drinking beer. And there was controversy among the guys about who was selected to run at nationals.

"And for the first time ever, I witnessed Coach cry in a team meeting. You know, I saw a few tears. He said he had always held his kids and his program to a higher standard, and he realized at that moment that they weren't upholding the standard. With all of that going on, and the fact that we all thought we had to prove ourselves being in the NCAA and the stress involved with that, I think there were a lot of kids who were supremely motivated to do something special. They wanted, as best they could, to rectify the situation and bring something positive."

Adams State was dealt another blow on the Monday before the national meet when sophomore Phil Castillo, from the Pueblo of Acoma, received a call from his mother to let him know that his maternal grandmother was dying. He rushed home to Grants, New Mexico, (a 4½-hour drive) to be with his grandmother, with whom he was close, and was at her bedside when she passed away on Tuesday. With almost no sleep for two days, he returned to Alamosa on Wednesday—less than 72 hours before the national meet—to board a plane with his teammates to Pennsylvania.

By now, the reception from other Division II coaches and athletes was more restrained. In the hotel lobby, Vigil saw Brooks Johnson, the former Stanford coach who was coaching at Cal Poly San Luis Obispo. Vigil and Johnson had been friends for many years, both having been active in USA Track & Field for more than two decades.

"How's your team looking this year," Johnson asked Vigil.

"Ah, we're not worth a shit," Vigil said, playing his cards close to the vest.

"Well, you know," Vigil said years later, "I really didn't know how we were going to do."

On the morning of the race, Vigil gathered his team in a hotel room for one final talk. Lloyd Engen, the school's sports information director, was invited to join the group.

"You may be the best team in the history of Adams State College," Vigil said. "Today, you will have to run as a team. Put aside your individual desires. I want you to pack together so tightly as a team that you can touch each other. And remember this: win or lose, you are the greatest team in America."

The team members took turns sharing their own words of encouragement. Castillo said he was dedicating his race that day to his grandmother. There was a moment of silence, and then the men gathered their bags, boarded vans, and headed for the race course.

"I was never really nervous or overconfident going into a race, because it was out of my hands at that point," Vigil said. "I always asked myself, 'What kind of job did you do, Vigil, of getting them ready mentally and physically?' Was I able to get the message across? I was always hoping no one would get hurt, hoping everyone would have a good day, and if everybody had a good day, then good things were possible. But you never hope for the win, or I never did. I just wanted them to do a good job, and if that good job was good enough for a win, fine. It's an amazing thing when it all works out."

November 21, 1992, was a nasty morning in Slippery Rock. The course was sloppy. Engen joked that he had not seen many rocks, but he saw plenty of slippery. And the rain seemed to be coming down harder on race day than it had all week.

"The entire course was just a couple inches of mud," Mohr said. "It was the only time I ever ran a race where I think I had either ⅝-inch or ¾-inch spikes in my racing shoes. We had humongous spikes. The cold weather was another story of the day, and that might have been why Abilene Christian, which had some good African runners, just kind of melted away on that day."

It did seem that the conditions were tailor-made for Adams State and Western State. Over the years, the two schools had gone head-to-head in nearly every type of weather. There was the year in the late 1980s when they ran the Rocky Mountain Athletic Conference Championships on a sloped hillside near Golden, Colorado, in a foot of fresh snow. There was the dual in Kenosha, Wisconsin, for the 1987 national championship when temperatures challenged 10 degrees below zero. And there was a late 1970s battle for the RMAC title in Las Vegas, New Mexico, when a flash flood washed out part of the course and runners literally had to wade across a gully during one section of the course.

There's also the fact that the two schools' hometowns—Alamosa and Gunnison—routinely battle for the dubious title of coldest spot in the United States each winter. Winters in both locales can be brutal, with windchills regularly reaching 20 or 30 degrees below zero.

"For me, or anyone who has run at Adams State, with all the weather we've had to deal with, [the weather at the 1992 national meet] was invigorating," Mohr said. "I think we were confident, and then to see the weather like that just brought out our warrior spirit. We all had our different reasons for running. Phil (Castillo) was the true Native warrior of all of us. It was kind of a deep, primal, pretty basic instinct…just put one foot in front of the other, running through the elements. That was pure cross country and I think we all embraced it."

At the starting gun, Adams State and Western State shot out as expected. At the first mile, Adams State had six runners and Western State had four in the top 10. Mohr, Healy, and David Brooks led the pack. The one-mile split was 5:20…slow on a normal day, but fast in the conditions.

"It was one of those days where it was all about position," Mohr said. "We used to have a joke that Coach would say go out hard, surge in the middle, and finish with a flurry. Coach always wanted you at the front. It really wasn't an option in my mind."

By two miles, Healy had dropped off, but Castillo, Peter DeLaCerda, and Paul Stoneham were methodically catching up to Mohr and Brooks. Western State's Spratley and Titcombe were in the lead pack. Castillo's prescription glasses fogged up in the rain, and he tossed them to Vigil as they passed the two-mile mark. "Then it was like a blackout," Castillo said. "I couldn't see at all, but I could tell where my teammates were all around me… we were so close to each other."

Halfway through the 10K course, at 3.1 miles, Adams State's top five and Western State's top two had left the rest of the field. Spratley was the only one breaking up Adams State's top five, but the pack was so tight it was still anyone's race for the individual title. Adams State was clearly dominating the team chase, as Western State's third through fifth runners were well back. No other team was even close.

Vigil stood on a hill near the five-mile mark with Milt Place, a member of the 1971 Adams State national championship team. Place coached at Medina (Ohio) High School, where he regularly invited Vigil to come talk to his athletes and coworkers.

"I was with Coach Vigil and as the runners neared five miles, he told me, 'We're going to get a perfect score today,'" Place said.

It was said matter-of-factly, but neither man thought it could really happen.

In cross country, a perfect score is 15 points, usually as the result of placing your five scoring runners in the first through fifth spots. A team can actually score 15 points without finishing in the top five individual spots, because competitors who qualified as individuals without a full team of five runners don't count in the team scoring.

"I don't think our guys ever thought about the conditions because they were used to adverse weather," Vigil said. "It wasn't a negative thought in their minds and they stuck to the belief that they could run together, and they did. Coming off that hill at five miles when they started catching each other was just unbelievable."

"I remember just kind of being in the zone," Mohr said. "I remember the five of us and Phil (Spratley) just running along. But with 1K to go, I snapped out of the zone. I lost concentration and drifted off the back. Spratley got between us. Coach's criticism of me was that I would go to sleep late or in the middle of races, and I did. I did go to sleep. But then—and I remember this like yesterday—there was some guy, I think in a Missouri Southern jacket, and he saw me dropping off, and I remember looking at the four in front and me behind, then looking at his eyes and he said, 'Get up there! Get up there with your teammates.' I remember thinking 16 points is good, but 15—that would be pretty great. That motivated me to just kind of get as close as I could to those guys."

Down a final hill heading into the finishing stretch, Mohr caught and passed Spratley. Engen was standing on a bridge near Vigil.

"You could see them all coming in running together and I'll never forget Engen saying, 'Holy shit...they're coming in together!'" Vigil said.

Engen scrambled to get closer to the finish line. He passed two NCAA photographers whose job it was to get pictures of the race winner coming in.

"One of them was standing up high on a truss and the other was down below," Engen said. "When the runners came around the bend, I heard the photographer up high say, 'Oh, shit, what should I do? What should I do?' The other photographer told him, 'Just shoot, shoot, shoot...'"

Adams State's 1992 NCAA Division II cross country champions in the middle of their perfect-score race—the only time the feat has been done at a collegiate championship meet. From left, the runners are Phil Castillo, Peter DeLaCerda, David Brooks (partially hidden), Jason Mohr, and Paul Stoneham.

Adams State's five men came splish-splashing through mud and ankle-deep rain puddles. Spratley was 10 meters back. The most incredible finish in the history of U.S. cross country was unfolding. Engen shot picture after picture. Vigil shot picture after picture. The NCAA photographers shot picture after picture.

And Phil Castillo—probably not the best sprinter in the bunch—was edging just slightly ahead of DeLaCerda, with Brooks, Stoneham, and Mohr nipping at their ankles. The Adams State men could reach out and...*gasp!*...actually touch each other.

Days later, Engen would write of that moment: "If one runner had faltered or slipped in the mud, the next runner would have been the individual national champion. So, in that respect, this is a tale of five national champions carving out a story that will become the folklore of the NCAA, as well as Adams State College."

At the finish line, it was Phil Castillo, 32:24; Peter DeLaCerda, 32:25; David Brooks, 32:26; Paul Stoneham, 32:27; and Jason Mohr, 32:28.

Left to right, Mohr, Stoneham, Castillo, Brooks, and DeLaCerda sloshing to the finish of the 1992 NCAA Division II Cross Country Championships, in which they recorded a four-second pack time.

Over 10,000 meters—6.2 miles—of sloppy cross country agony, Adams State's men posted a four-second pack time and the first-ever perfect score at a national collegiate cross country meet. Only the University of Texas at El Paso (UTEP) in 1981, which scored 17 points to win the Division I title, had ever accomplished anything close to what Vigil's men had done.

"Brooks Johnson finds me after the race and he calls me a lying sack of shit," Vigil said. "He says, 'I thought you told me you weren't very good.' Then I tell him, 'Well, we're really not. We just didn't run against anybody today.' Oh, how I laughed. But he was pretty pissed off."

Western State's Spratley and Titcombe were sixth and seventh overall. Adams State's Healy was 11th and the squad's seventh man, Kevin Schaefer, was 30th. For the second time in school history, all seven of Adams State's runners earned All-American honors at the national meet. Western State's men placed second in the meet, nearly 50 points ahead of the third-place team.

In the finish area, there were the expected hoots and hollers of joy and happiness for Adams State. At one point, Vigil nudged Engen and told him, "Look at that guy, he is crying," pointing to one of the runners.

"Then I look at Coach Vigil," Engen said, "and he's crying too."

"I remember feeling pretty happy about it," Mohr said. "That's not too descriptive, I know, but just being happy. There was a lot of joy. The finality of it all was big. Phil (Castillo) had an emotional ride to get there, with his grandma passing. Me? I felt relief. I didn't want to be the guy who finished sixth, so I was a bit relieved.

"I know Coach was happy, and that never gets old. He had a megawatt smile he'd get when you did something beyond what you thought you could do. I saw that a couple times in my career, and that was one of those times. We were huggers, so there was some of that. And then our goofy cheers and a lot of whoopin' and hollerin'."

There was, however, another race to be run. The women's championship race was just minutes away, and Adams State's women—who had won two of the past three NAIA titles—had their eyes on trying to break the 10-year stranglehold Cal Poly San Luis Obispo held on the Division II women's national championship.

"During the men's race, I remember being with our women and trying to keep them calm," Martin said. "We had a great challenge as well. I told the women, 'If you're not willing to run as hard as the men ran, then go sit in the van. Let's have fun, but this is it.' I think they were inspired by the men's effort."

Adams State's women proceeded to capture their own convincing victory, scoring 64 points to Western State's 99. Cal Poly San Luis Obispo, the program Lance Harter built before moving on to coach women at the University of Arkansas, was third with 101. Western State's women were ecstatic. They had finished fifth at the regional meet two weeks earlier (one place short of qualifying for nationals), but were chosen for an at-large bid into the national meet.

"I suspect Joe Vigil and maybe even Damon Martin had advocated for our women's team to get into nationals because of our strength of schedule," Vandenbusche said. "We weren't even supposed to be there, and then two weeks later, we're the national runner-up."

Adams State's women had their own story of overcoming adversity. The squad won despite losing one runner to injury during the race. Two others—All-Americans Amy Giblin and Kristin Shern—were at less than their best due to injuries suffered earlier in the season.

Once the running was done, the party began for the two NAIA powerhouses who had just pulled off a pair of 1-2 team finishes at their baptism into the NCAA Division II National Championships.

"After the women's race, Joe and I gathered both teams, men and women together—I'd never do this again, but we were just angry at how we were treated—and then right at the finish line, Joe and I led 15 cheers: 'Hip-hip-hooray for the NAIA, hip-hip-hooray for the NAIA, hip-hip-hooray for the NAIA...'" Vandenbusche said.

"We kind of stuck it in their rear, so to speak, because we weren't treated well. Now, we would never do that again, but at the time it seemed to be appropriate."

Recalling that day, Martin turns introspective.

"I remember as the women's coach being proud of the men's team for getting through a lot of adversity," he said. "People look back and think, 'Ah, it must have been a magical season and everything was perfect.' Well, nah, it wasn't perfect. It was hard work. It was dedication. It was overcoming obstacles. It was people forgiving each other and moving on. I think sometimes people look at a program like ours that has won so much, or a perfect-score team, and they think everything is perfect. But one of the lessons I learned that year is that things are not ever perfect. Finding a way to overcome adversity and not make excuses and do it in spite of something is the only good option."

Mohr adds: "The 1992 team scored a perfect score, but we weren't a bunch of 'perfect' people. We had academic, social, training, and other personal challenges. We all made mistakes. I remember getting warned for nearly failing calculus, and breaking team rules made me almost miss a trip to nationals. But it all came together, and that 'perfection for a day' I believe is a reflection of not just the five of us, but our team that season and the program for nearly three decades."

Once all the hip-hip-hoorays died away, the trophies were awarded, and the race gear was packed, Castillo found a phone to call his mother.

"I told her we had won," he said. "Then I paused for a long time and told her that her son was a national champion. She started to cry...and I guess I did, too."

12

END
OF AN ERA

The headline of the Alamosa *Valley Courier* screamed "SIMPLY PERFECT" in big, bold type across the top of its front page, celebrating the hometown heroes' return from the NCAA Division II Cross Country Championships. The accompanying photograph, stretching nearly the width of the page, showed DeLaCerda, Stoneham, and Castillo, rain-soaked and muddied, running together early in the race, each with "Adams State" across their chest, running as one. Engen's recap and photos from the national meet filled two pages in that day's sports section, giving equal play to the Adams State women's remarkable win.

The team members were greeted at the Alamosa airport by a couple dozen community members and several of their teammates, who erupted in cheers as the runners exited the plane. There were hugs and laughs and smiles and more cheers as they waited for a couple cardboard boxes, each standing about three feet tall, to come around the luggage turnstile. When the boxes arrived, the crowd tore off the top and lifted out two trophies, each one proclaiming "NCAA Champions." Hip-hip-hooray...

The national champions received a perfectly worded front-page treatment when they returned home from the 1992 national meet.

The new hardware, some said, would look nice next to the 15 trophies that read "NAIA Champions" back at Adams State's Plachy Hall.

The week stretched into a few more well-deserved public celebrations for the men's and women's teams: recognition at halftime of a home basketball game, an editorial in the local newspaper, and a city proclamation honoring the champs, among other honors.

All of that was nice and appreciated, Mohr said, but he and his mates didn't believe they had cemented some sort of legacy with a single win.

"Honestly, I have never really talked with Coach about the 1992 season," Mohr said. "Being a college distance runner is not like being in most of the other sports. You have a cross country season, you're done, you may get some awards, a couple weeks off, maybe have the ol' college beer, and then you're back to indoors (track and field)...then to outdoors...and then you're building the base for next fall's cross country season.

"For us, it was a continuum. It was thrilling to be part of. I kind of got the sense from Coach that it was thrilling for him, too. He loved telling the stories about that team, but he didn't believe in resting on your laurels. If he could have figured out a way to score 14, he probably would have. He always said you're only as good as your last race, and the next race is coming up."

Not everyone was so thrilled with the team's success, however. There was still a rub inside the Adams State athletic department toward Vigil's programs, and it began to rear its ugly head in the midst of the magical 1992 season.

"We had that great cross country team in 1992, and that's when the NCAA started paying for us to go to nationals," Vigil said. "So I went to our athletic administration and I said, 'Jay Birmingham (the graduate assistant coach) has done a great job; can you get money to buy an air ticket for him? He can sleep with me in the hotel room.'

"The athletic director says, 'No. The NCAA only allows one ticket for coaches.'

"So I say, 'OK, he can have my ticket,'" Vigil said. "I called Reebok, and they paid for my way to go. As great a team as we had, they could send two coaches. There were little things like that they did to try to discourage me."

"It wasn't Adams State. It wasn't Alamosa. It wasn't the San Luis Valley...there were three people in that athletic department that were so jealous of him and his team's success that they almost wanted to see him fail," said Norm Roberts, the Alamosa businessman who was Vigil's former runner and best man at his wedding.

In the college's new NCAA-governed environment, where every move was scrutinized by the compliance staff, Vigil felt continually squeezed as he adjusted from the more lax ways of the NAIA. The college was overzealous in their enforcement of those rules but, frankly, some of the NCAA's rules verge on the silly.

"One of my runners from our 1992 cross country team came into my office one day, and I could tell something was wrong with him. He wasn't himself," Vigil said. "So, I told him, go get in my pickup and we'll go have a cup of coffee and talk. That's innocent. When I get in the pickup, he starts crying and he says, 'Coach, I just got word that my parents are getting a divorce.'

"He needed someone to talk to. Who else was there but me? So we went and had a cup of coffee at the Sands Restaurant. We must have spent an hour in there; I think he ended up having a cup of hot chocolate and I had coffee. I pay the bill and it was, what, maybe 50 cents, a dollar? By the time I get back to the office, there's a note in my box that reads, 'You broke two NCAA rules and I wrote you up.'"

The note was from the school's athletic director. By the strict letter of the NCAA law, coaches cannot buy food or drink for athletes, and they cannot transport athletes in personal vehicles.

"She didn't even bother to talk to me about what I was doing," Vigil said. "There's always a reason for everything. And that really pissed me off."

Vigil suspected there was more at play than just a cup of hot chocolate and a one-mile ride to downtown Alamosa.

"There was a jealousy that got built up, and they resented the success of the cross country and track and field programs," he said. "And all along what we had accomplished was for the school, you know."

The NCAA and Vigil's deep love for his athletes were never going to make a great marriage. Vigil fully invested himself in his team, from having deep discussions over coffee to cooking up bratwurst at his house. During the school year, Vigil was available to his athletes every…single…day; clearly, he was willing to pour his time, energy, and soul into their daily well-being. Many are the stories from his athletes of Coach Vigil pulling up beside them in his pickup while they hammered a 10-miler or grinded out the Sunday long run. Or runners chasing Vigil down South River Road in Alamosa as he pedaled along on his bike. Seven days a week, rain, snow, or shine, Vigil was there to support his athletes. And they treasured every precious minute they spent with him.

"When we moved to the NCAA, we had to file a report every week on when we ran," Vigil said. "I couldn't show up one day a week, on purpose, because the NCAA had a rule that limited you to six days a week that a coach could be at practice with the athletes. We were following the rules, but our athletic director at the time would meet my runners in the hall, and she'd ask, 'How many days did you run this week?' Those are the little things they were doing that are so childish."

Vigil's program, in other words, was under a microscope. The message he was getting was this: We're watching you… closely. Don't mess up, but if you do, we're gonna get you.

"One time we met at the Campus Cafe and he brings the NCAA bylaws," said Larry Zaragoza, Vigil's former athlete and graduate assistant who by this time was leading the Alamosa High School cross country and track and field programs. "We start talking, and he says, 'I think I'm out of here, Zamagoza.' And I ask, 'Why, Coach?'

"He says, 'The college doesn't back me and I don't like these bylaws.' He slams them down on the table. 'I can't even take you guys to breakfast. I can't give you a ride anywhere. What kind of bullshit is that?' He was very frustrated at the time."

Vigil was not shy about making known his displeasure with the NCAA's nitpicking ways. "At the time, I felt that if this is

187

what coaching in college at the NCAA level is all about, then it's not for me," he said. "That's when I started thinking about retiring; not from coaching, just from Adams State."

Actually, Vigil had already retired from teaching at Adams State in 1986. He was drawing a retirement income and getting a coaching salary from Reebok, so he didn't need a coaching paycheck from Adams State.

"I coached the distance squad for seven years with no pay," Vigil said. "I was just donating my time, taking all that abuse. But I used to enjoy the kids."

Vigil's athletes were shielded from the tumultuous relationship he had with the three colleagues in the athletic department. To his runners, he was their sturdy leader, a spirited motivator who provided them the edge they needed to challenge the best collegiate runners in America. Whatever was going on with the older adults was none of their business, and so away from the noise in Plachy Hall's administrative offices, Vigil made sure the athletes were not cheated in their growth as solid citizens and runners.

Coming off the perfect-score team of 1992, Vigil had another strong group in 1993, including Castillo, DeLaCerda, and Brooks—the top three finishers at the national meet the year before. Also returning was Shane Healy (11th the year before) and Daniel Caulfield, who was running as the team's third man late in 1992 but didn't get a spot on the team that ran at nationals. Healy and Caulfield were the group's speedsters, clocking sub-1:50 for 800 meters and just a few seconds above 4:00 for the mile.

That group ran every bit to its ability. The regional meet in 1993 was held in Hays, Kansas, and Vigil watched the men's race from atop a hill with one of his most treasured mentors—Alex Francis, who had retired 13 years earlier as coach at Fort Hays

State. The two friends watched as Adams State dismantled the field, nearly racking up a perfect score.

Two weeks later at the NCAA Division II National Championships in Riverside, California, they dominated the field again; some might say it was more convincing than the 1992 team's victory because they won by nearly 80 points over 1990 champion Edinboro. Healy out-kicked Castillo to win the national title and become the seventh individual to win a national cross country title for Vigil's Adams State program. Caulfield was the team's third man, in fifth place. Adams State had six All-Americans, including the five key returners and newcomer Hector Hernandez.

"We scored 25 points to win in 1993," Vigil said. "So, in two years, we scored 40 points at the national meet. That has to be some kind of record, doesn't it?"

Adams State's women won the Division II title in 1993 as well, scoring a 31-point victory over Cal Poly San Luis Obispo. Alamosa celebrated the sweep again, though this time with a bit more restraint. No one doubted anymore that Adams State's success in the NAIA certainly did translate to the NCAA, and perhaps the two programs' greatest foe in this new division was complacency.

Joe Vigil holding NAIA and NCAA Division II championship trophies near the end of his incredible run of success at Adams State.

But the 1993 cross country season turned out to be Vigil's last at Adams State. He stepped away from coaching duties at the school, hoping to continue his work with numerous international federations that wanted to bring their teams to train in Alamosa. Vigil was a master organizer for these groups. While they chose the San Luis Valley to capitalize on the benefits of altitude running, he would help them acclimate to the community and the region, often arranging transportation, lodging, and meals for the groups.

"I would help to get them housing on the Adams State campus," Vigil said. "They had money and could pay for whatever they needed, but needed someone to help them make their arrangements. And Adams State was good about getting them a place to stay."

One time, a group of Japanese runners came to Alamosa to train. Vigil thought they would like to have Japanese food to eat.

"Coach Vigil called my mother," said Larry Fujimoto, who ran track and field for Vigil at Alamosa High School from 1955 to 1958. "He asked her if she could put together a Japanese dinner for them."

Fujimoto's mother, Shizuye (pronounced "Sheez-Away"), was more than happy to do it. She had grown to love and respect Vigil as much as his athletes did.

"I was in Alamosa to visit Coach Vigil one time and I brought my mother with me," Fujimoto said. "After we talked for a little while, Coach tells me, 'Larry, why don't you wait over there in the corner. I want to spend some time just talking with your mother.'

"They talked for about a half hour and as we were driving back home, she was higher than a kite. She told me, 'You were so lucky to have him as a coach, and I can see why you admire your coach so much.' I feel the same thing every time I see Coach Vigil."

When Vigil stepped down as cross country coach, however, the athletic administration saw its opportunity to move on from the popular leader. Vigil asked for a modest office in Plachy Hall so he could continue to work with visiting federations and a handful of post-collegians. The college was willing to give him an office…just not in Plachy Hall. He was offered space in the education building, an area that had no athletic facilities and was not at all conducive to working with elite athletes.

Instead of taking the college's offer, Vigil chose to continue his work from his house on Carroll Street, a two-story flat-top in northwest Alamosa. He would use his home office, and on most days he could meet his runners at Cole Park, or occasionally at his home. It wasn't ideal, but he believed it was the best option given the circumstances.

"When they chose to move him out of Plachy Hall, he was so shocked," said Vigil's wife, Caroline. "And I'm not sure why it happened; I think there was a lot going on behind the scenes in Plachy Hall. Coach was having a lot of success with his teams, and a lot of fun with those federations that were coming in. He was trying to incorporate them into Adams State because they would bring in money for the college also.

"And I'd say it was very hurtful because of the way it happened and how they would not entertain any ideas of growth in terms of what we thought was growth for the college. You never know what people are thinking except that all of this happened and Coach became very depressed about it and I did too because we thought we'd always be there. We wanted to be in Alamosa. We had started traveling, and he knew some things that would help. I'm surprised they didn't use him that way. It feels like you have no friends at all when you're kind of ousted like that. And we had no idea what was going on."

Adams State's president at the time, William Fulkerson, had been appointed by the State's Board of Trustees to a dual role as president of Metro State College in Denver, and was rarely in Alamosa. Tom Gilmore, dean of the business school, was serving as president in Fulkerson's absence. With Adams State's upper administration in flux, the athletic administration had much more authority to wield its hammer. And those in charge chose to use that authority to push Vigil away from his beloved alma mater.

"The problems I had," Vigil said, "were not with Adams State as a college. There were three people in Plachy Hall who wanted to see me gone. And I guess they got their way."

Vigil was left to pick up his life after serving the school he loved for nearly 30 years. From the time he was a young child, riding his bike on Alamosa's south side, serving his community as a loyal Boy Scout, he had so treasured his hometown and the people in it. Now, at the height of his professional success, Vigil felt betrayed by some of those who he loved...and who he thought loved him.

"It was a tough time because a guy that I looked up to, my mentor, was struggling with the way he was being treated, or the way that things ended up," said Damon Martin. "I think he resented that; he was angry about that. It's a shame that it couldn't have been done a different way or it didn't go down a different way.

"It was also hard during that time for me because I was on a tenure-track position, and the people in charge...well, I don't think they were good to me, either. I would hear things like, 'Ah, he's another little Coach Vigil...we don't really want that anymore.' So, for me, it was difficult because Coach was not happy and then I didn't think people were overly fair with me. It was a tough time."

Let Me Tell You a Story

Joe Vigil's youngest daughter, Peggy, recalled her father's abrupt departure from Adams State:

"It's unfortunate that happened, but I think there's always going to be petty jealousies when people are successful," Peggy said. "But to be honest with you, I think that is probably one of the best things that could have happened to my dad because he moved on to greater things.

"The reason I believe he stayed in Alamosa was actually twofold: my grandmother was still there and he wanted to be near her, and he was successful there. Things weren't broken. Once they became broken, then it was time to move on. That's what he did. Unfortunately, the way that it played out, it's too bad, but I think my dad came out being the winner.

"He's still very loyal. He still goes back to Alamosa. I think that shows his character. He's always going to be loyal to the college he went to and where he had success, and some of his friends are still coaching there. But he's also loyal to Alamosa and San Luis Valley. And he's very proud of that. He's one of the reasons why Alamosa, the San Luis Valley, and Adams State are on the map."

She adds: "I think life is too short to have anger and resentment. That doesn't get you anywhere. I think favor comes to him because he is constantly paying it forward, helping people, and in turn great things happen to him. I keep seeing that over and over. He's a great example of what it means to pay it forward."

In 1994, Adams State's athletic department appointed John Kernan—who had led Adams State's men to the 1992 NAIA indoor track and field national championship—as the school's new cross country coach. Kernan, a good coach who had worked extensively with the U.S. Paralympic team, almost immediately sought to distance the program and its runners—all of whom were drawn to Adams State by Vigil—from their former coach's massive influence.

"There was a lot of tension in Plachy Hall, and I remember that John Kernan called a meeting of all the runners," said Lloyd Engen, the sports information director. "I was close to a lot of the runners and I could feel the tension they were feeling. So I decided I would go to that meeting.

"The door to the meeting room was open when I arrived and Kernan was talking to the team. And one of the things he said sticks with me to this day: 'The Joe Vigil era is over.' I don't think it had quite the effect he was hoping for because as I was standing by that open door, I watched many of the runners come out and the looks on their faces were both anger and sadness."

Phil Castillo, the 1992 national champion and 1993 runner-up, decided to forego his senior year, instead choosing to join Vigil's team of post-collegiate runners. Kernan implemented drastic changes that many of the runners resisted, such as no more workouts at Cole Park. The season was tension-filled, though Adams State went to the NCAA Division II championships in November 1994 and defeated rival Western State for the national title, notching seven All-Americans.

Shortly after that meet, the mass exodus occurred.

Hector Hernandez, a two-time cross country All-American, announced soon after the 1994 season that he was transferring to Western State. Many others followed him out the door, some also heading to Gunnison to run for Vandenbusche and others

choosing different schools. By the time the 1995 cross country season arrived, the Adams State program had been gutted,
and for the first time in the program's 30-year history, Adams
State's men failed to qualify for the national meet. Western State,
already a strong program, was a beneficiary, winning the 1995
NCAA Division II championship, the first of seven titles they
would win over the next 10 years.

Indeed, the Joe Vigil era was over...and nobody was happy
about it, least of all the coach who had built the powerhouse in
the first place.

"I would get up with Coach at four in the morning to sit
and talk with him because he was depressed," Caroline said. "I
have never in my life seen him depressed and he's never been
depressed since.

"But how he got over it was he started writing his book. I
think it pulled him out of that because suddenly we had so much
to do with the book, and it kind of gave us an idea that maybe
we could be all right."

Vigil's book, published in 1995, is called *Road to the Top:
A Systematic Approach to Training Distance Runners* and has
sold 27,000 copies in 24 years. The cover is printed in Adams
State green and gold colors and features the remarkable picture
of Castillo, DeLaCerda, Brooks, Stoneham, and Mohr running
side by side at the 1992 NCAA Division II championships. Vigil
worked with Todd Cotton, son of former Adams State coaching
colleague Jack "Doc" Cotton, to get the book on computer and
off to a publisher.

The book is something of a bible for training runners, aimed
primarily at helping coaches build workouts for their teams.
Vigil talks about the training programs he used at Adams State
and the concepts that led to success. Because Vigil presents concepts—rather than specific schedules—the book is intended to

be a resource coaches at any level can use with adaptations in mileage and intensity to help their own runners.

Up to that point, many coaches relied on guidelines published by noted exercise physiologist Jack Daniels in his book *Daniels' Running Formula* to plan workouts that fit their athletes' ability levels. Similarly, Vigil published numerous tables in *Road to the Top* that incorporate the science he'd learned for nearly a half century, neatly interpreted for coaches looking to build their own training programs.

The book is available to order online, but don't get roped into buying it from one of the big companies, where the cost of the book is three or four times what Vigil sells it for out of his garage. That's right...*he sells the book out of his garage.* Since the first press run in 1995, Vigil has primarily sold his book one by one, based on a good-faith deal with the purchaser that if they send him an email or a letter with $29.95, he'll send them a book through the U.S. Postal Service.

A simple post on the runner's discussion board LetsRun.com lists Vigil's mailing address for book orders. One poster noted he was apprehensive about sending money in the mail to what he interpreted as a home address, but he took the chance anyway: "Within a week, I received my copy of the book, signed by Joe Vigil."

Another wrote that he, too, sent Vigil a letter asking for a copy, along with 40 dollars to cover the cost. "A week later, I received an autographed copy of the book...and a 10-dollar bill!"

That instance again speaks to Vigil's stubbornness in sticking to his life's values. Asked why he chose to send back the 10 dollars, when it's likely the buyer seemed happy to part with that money, Vigil said, "Honesty is the best policy."

"Most days," Caroline said, "Coach is off to the post office, mailing off a couple more books."

As Vigil rebounded from the abrupt departure from his alma mater, he had a solid group of post-collegiate runners training in Alamosa. In 1996, he agreed to take on a relative unknown named Deena Drossin, who had just completed a solid, though not spectacular, career at the University of Arkansas. And he was working with a group of men who had their sights on running at an elite level.

One of those men was Marco Ochoa, a naturalized U.S. citizen born in Mexico who came with his family to southern California when he was a teenager. Ochoa spent a couple years as an above-average community college runner in California, then transferred to Adams State after a friend told him about a great coach by the name of Joe Vigil at that school.

Ochoa's outgoing personality, as much as his running ability, quickly endeared him to teammates. In 1987, he finished in the top 10 at the NAIA Cross Country Championships as the third man on the team that scored a then-record 21 points for the national title. He was a three-time All-American at Adams State in two years.

Ochoa launched a string of top-five finishes for athletes coached by Vigil in the U.S. Olympic Marathon Trials. In 1996, he entered that race with the 72nd best time in the country, but with just under five miles to go, he was leading the breakaway pack. He eventually finished in fifth place, running a personal best time of 2:14:37.

Four years later, it was Peter DeLaCerda, the NCAA Division II runner-up on the 1992 Adams State team, who nearly stole headlines at the Olympic Marathon Trials. DeLaCerda lingered in anonymity for much of the 26.2-mile race, watching one contender after another succumb to the hot, humid conditions. DeLaCerda then pounced and finished second in 2:16:18.

However, DeLaCerda had not met the Olympic standard, so despite placing second at the Trials, he didn't get a spot on the U.S. Olympic team. That year, the United States had just one representative in the Olympic Marathon in Sydney, Australia: Rod DeHaven, who had finished ahead of DeLaCerda.

That race was something of an eye-opener for USA Track & Field. How could the world's greatest track and field team qualify just one marathoner for the Olympics? It was painfully evident that despite all of USA Track & Field's success, it had been nearly 20 years since U.S. distance runners had contributed much on the Olympic stage.

Meanwhile, Vigil's personal life took another unexpected turn. In 1999, he and Caroline were at the U.S. Embassy in Madrid, Spain, on their way to watch Drossin compete at a meet in Monaco, when they received a call that Caroline's father had died from a heart attack. Caroline had recently helped her mother and father move from Arkansas to Monte Vista, 17 miles west of Alamosa, so she could help provide care as they aged.

In 38 hours, the Vigils were back in Alamosa to make funeral arrangements for Caroline's father. "It was a really hard time," Caroline said. "We were planning to move to Green Valley, Arizona, and take them with us; we had bought a house for them, as well as one for us. But my dad never made it."

Within the year, the 70-year-old Vigil finalized plans to sell his house in Alamosa and move his wife and his life to southern Arizona. He rented two large moving trucks for the 10-hour trip from Alamosa to Green Valley, which is located about 20 miles south of Tucson. He had a couple old pals from Alamosa's south side, Boogie Romero and Gene Herrera, help him drive the trucks and keep him company.

"Coach and I would drive one truck, and Gene would drive the other," Romero said. "It took us a couple days to get there, because we would stay overnight on the first day. We'd take off at four o'clock in the morning, stop somewhere to get breakfast and eat it on the way because he wanted to keep going. We had some great conversations."

The three men made the 20-hour, round-trip journey twice in order to move everything from Vigil's house and his mother-in-law's house. "I tell you," Romero said, "I would do anything I could to help that man. To me, I will always think of Coach Vigil as my father. He was a good man and still is a good man."

After nearly seven decades living in Alamosa, Vigil put that rich chapter of his life behind him. However, a new one was just beginning: two weeks after moving into his cozy Green Valley home, he was hired to coach Team USA California in Mammoth Lakes, a high-altitude training group that aimed to put America's distance-running struggles in the rear-view mirror, as well.

13

THE
UNDERDOGS

*W*hat are the odds that a group of elite U.S. distance runners would leave their current training environment and gamble their future to chase Olympic medals alongside some of their rivals with a new set of coaches in a remote mountain community in northern California?

Not very good, right?

That was essentially the challenge Joe Vigil and former UCLA coach Bob Larsen took on when they agreed to coach Team USA California in Mammoth Lakes, a secluded town located at 7,881 feet in elevation. The club formed in 2001 with an ambitious goal to heal American distance running, which had mostly suffered on the Olympic stage for nearly three decades.

From 1972 to 2000—a period of seven Olympiads (the United States boycotted the 1980 Olympics in the former Soviet Union)—American distance runners won just five medals, including golds in the marathon by Frank Shorter (1972) and Joan Benoit-Samuelson (1984) that spurred a boom among recreational runners. However, during that time, 171 Olympic medals were awarded to men and women in distance races from

1500 meters or longer, which means U.S. runners garnered just 2.9 percent of the loot.

The group of professional runners Vigil and Larsen assembled in 2001 was not going to save U.S. distance running completely, but they could be part of the solution. Not long after the Mammoth Track Club began, a few other training groups began forming around the country. American distance running was beginning to show a united front in hopes of climbing back to significance on the world stage.

The approach did seem to work. In four Olympiads since (through 2016), American distance runners won 12 medals, including at least one in every men's and women's event from the 1500 meters to the marathon (except for the women's 5000). During that time, there were 120 medals awarded in distance events, which means that Americans increased their medal haul to a respectable 10 percent for those 16 years.

At Mammoth Lakes, Larsen and Vigil had the credentials to draw elite runners to the ambitious new approach.

Larsen had recently retired as head coach of cross country and track and field at UCLA, where he led the Bruins to NCAA Division I Outdoor Track and Field championships in 1987 and 1988 and a runner-up finish in 1995. He revived the cross country program at UCLA, taking that program to the national championship meet six times. Like Vigil, Larsen received numerous awards during 50-plus years of coaching, including most recently the 2019 Legend Coach award from USA Track & Field.

Vigil's coaching success also was widely recognized by this time, and he was celebrated as the country's greatest scientific mind on how to train distance runners at high altitude, making him the perfect fit for Mammoth Lakes. "Ninety-five percent of the Olympic medals in distance running are won by runners who either live or train at high altitudes," Vigil said. Almost effortlessly, Vigil can list 21 variables affected by altitude, things like an increase in red blood cell mass, and a boost in the body's oxygen-carrying capacity, which produces aerobic energy.

Joe Vigil with Bob Larsen (left) in front of an American flag during the 2004 Olympics in Athens, Greece. Vigil and Larsen formed Team USA California in Mammoth Lakes in 2001.

The United States Olympic Committee established the James "Doc" Counsilman Science Award in 2004 to recognize a coach who utilizes scientific techniques and equipment as part of their coaching methods or creates innovative ways to use sport science. As validation of Vigil's contributions to the science of running, he was the first-ever recipient of that award.

However, what may have made Vigil an even greater choice to help lead U.S. distance running's new path was a lifetime of playing the role of the underdog. Seventy years of living with fewer resources than many others had forged a steely resolve that fed the fire in his gut, an undying belief that he had much more to achieve in his sport. He believed he was always the chaser, never the one being chased. Vigil, a small-town boy and a small-college coach, was a king of underdogs, a man who always believed he had to prove himself.

"I learned a long time ago that whatever I was doing, I had to represent my daughters; you know, I was their dad," Vigil said. "And anytime we went to run a conference meet, I was the coach at Adams State, and being Latino I didn't want anybody to say anything bad about the people I represent. So I watched my p's and q's. I never drank, I never smoked in front of people, and I always did what I was supposed to do.

"When I became a national coach, I did the same thing. I'm representing the country, the sport, the national team. I can't screw up. I never had an excuse not to do the best job I knew how to do. I lived the part."

Vigil's Adams State teams overflowed with underdog stories. That may sound like a strange claim because much of America identifies the small school from southern Colorado with college running excellence. Yet, before Vigil's runners became powerful running machines, they were often the athletes pushed to the curb, the ones who rarely got a sniff from major college programs. Vigil believed in them, though.

One of those was Martin Johns, an aspiring rugby player in his native New Zealand who came to the United States in spring 1988 as part of a track and field tour group from his country. He competed at Colorado meets in Alamosa and Pueblo, plus one in Tempe, Arizona, and a couple others.

"I had the chance to meet Coach Vigil while we were in Alamosa," Johns said. "I thought he was a small guy…in height, at least. But right away what I got from him was a caring attitude. Had I known who he was, I wouldn't have been shocked if he was telling me about all he's accomplished. But that's not him; it's not about the accolades or the recognition."

By that summer, Vigil had offered Johns a partial scholarship and the young man had decided to come to America to try his hand at running.

"I got to Alamosa two weeks early and I was extremely homesick because there was nobody there yet," Johns said. "I come from a tight family and I was just 18 at the time. The first event we ran was the First National Bank 10K (a local road race that Vigil scheduled as an intrasquad meet for his team) and I think I still hold the record for the slowest 10K ever run by a college runner. By the time I finished, they had already eaten all the watermelon."

Damon Martin was the interim coach that fall as Vigil served as head coach for the U.S. Olympic distance runners in Seoul, South Korea. "At one point, I think Damon told Coach, 'I don't know about that Johns fellow. I don't think he's going to make it,'" Johns said.

But by the time Johns graduated from Adams State in 1993, the longshot rugby player from New Zealand had amassed 15 NAIA All-American honors, including five national championships in indoor track and field.

"Martin Johns came to me as a quarter-miler, but by the time he completed his senior year in college he wanted to run the mile," Vigil said. "He ran the half mile and on relays, but he wanted to be a miler. I told him he had to run with the cross country team and do as much as he could. He wasn't a cross country runner; he wouldn't complete the workouts, or he wouldn't do the laps at the park like some others would, but he tried to do some of them.

"I found a hill for him at Fort Garland (Adams State's Tuesday workouts), about 400 meters high. I told him, 'Martin, every time we come to Fort Garland, you're going to run this hill 10 times. And if your heart rate isn't at max at the very top, I'm going to add one more on.' So he tried to run as hard as he could to the top so he'd achieve a max heart rate. He went through the fall season and never worked out on a track once.

"Around Christmas time, after cross country nationals, I called Marty Liquori, who was the director of the Miami Road Mile, and told him I had a young man who would like to run the road mile. He said, 'Fine, Coach, what can he run?'

"He's never run a mile," Vigil answered, "so I can't give you a time."

According to Vigil, Liquori then laughed and said, "You want me to pay his way out here and he's never run a mile? You've got to be kidding."

"I know what your record is; it's 4:01.7," Vigil said. "If this kid doesn't break 4:10, I'll pay his way."

"Anyway, we got him out there, and he runs 4:04 in his first mile ever," Vigil said. "After that, he got motivated, and later that year he was third at the Prefontaine Classic open mile in Eugene, Oregon, in a time of 3:54.1…in his first year running the mile."

Johns's college career overlapped with another runner who came to Adams State in anonymity. Irish-born Shane Healy's hardscrabble story began when his mother bundled up his sister, Lorraine, in the middle of the night to escape an unsuccessful marriage, leaving behind four-year-old Shane, one brother, and the children's father while they slept.

Within a year, Healy's father had taken his brother to England and sent Healy to an orphanage near Dublin. Healy then spent several years in a series of schools. He regularly skipped classes and ultimately dropped out of school altogether at age 13.

On his second try at making a life in the United States, Healy talked his way into Contra Costa Community College in Martinez, California. The track and field coach saw him one day and, thinking that Healy looked and sounded a lot like a young Eamonn Coghlan (an Irish legend in the indoor mile), offered him $50 to see how fast he could run a mile. Healy had never been a runner, but in beat-up tennis shoes he clocked 4:52—fast enough to get a spot on the track and field team.

Two years later, with a college best of 4:17, he begged Vigil to let him come to Alamosa to run his final two years for Adams State. Vigil, though reluctant, gave Healy a chance.

"Within a year, I was running a four-minute mile," Healy said. "Coach Vigil got the best out of his athletes. He was all about positivity. He always said, 'Don't hang around negative people.' But listen, we trained really hard. Really, really hard."

In two years, Healy was a seven-time All-American at Adams State, with four individual national titles and two more with the indoor distance medley relay. His titles ranged from the outdoor 1500 meters to the 1993 Division II cross country championship (10,000 meters).

In 1996, Healy completed an amazing journey from an Irish orphanage to the pinnacle of track and field. He clocked 3:36.8 for 1500 meters at a meet in Madrid, Spain, to earn the third spot on the Irish Olympic team. That year in Atlanta, he and Johns, competing for New Zealand, ran the same heat in the opening round of the 1500 meters. Johns was unable to move on, while Healy advanced to the semifinals, falling just one race short of the Olympic final.

◇◇◇

For downtrodden runners, Vigil may have been the perfect medicine. His long-held religious values made him believe every person had something good in them.

"I used to tell my athletes, 'You're one of God's children, and God loves you. And God gave every one of his children a talent. It's up to you to find that talent and develop a passion for it, and work toward that passion,'" Vigil said. "And they started believing that concept. That was a big thing for me. When they believed it, they followed through. And they improved."

The group of runners at Mammoth Lakes were not really underdogs in the traditional sense. Most of them were at the top of the U.S. rankings or had won U.S. national titles. Some were already Olympians. But the fact that they were among a group of U.S. runners being looked at to help turn around a generation-long miserable record by U.S. runners at the Olympics was a monumental challenge in itself. Nobody was giving American distance runners very good odds at Olympic glory in the 1990s and early 2000s.

It helped the Mammoth Lakes program that Larsen brought with him Meb Keflezighi, a star at UCLA who won four NCAA Division I championships on the track. Vigil brought his own star in 28-year-old Deena Kastor, who already had a pair of World Championship finals in the 10,000-meter run to her credit, was the country's top female at that distance, and had a nice shoe contract from ASICS, which is still her sponsor today.

Just five years earlier, Kastor (then known as Deena Drossin) was a running nomad, wandering aimlessly after wrapping up a solid career at the University of Arkansas. She had no one to coach her after college, nowhere to go, and, really, no plans to continue training and racing.

*Meb Keflezighi (left) and Deena Kastor training
at Mammoth Lakes, California, in preparation
for the 2004 Olympic marathon in Athens, where
Keflezighi earned a silver medal and Kastor a bronze.*

"I guess I just had a really complicated relationship with talent and being told I was talented since I was a young girl, age 11, in the sport," Kastor said. "Hearing for so long that I was talented, I subconsciously thought I didn't have to work hard. I thought talent was innate and not something I could work for to get better. I used to think the two hours of the day that I spent in my running shoes was a focused two hours and then I could do whatever I wanted to in the day, not realizing that every choice I made in the day was either going to steer me closer to my running goals or farther away."

The grind of a college career had Kastor thinking the bakery business sounded pretty good, yet she was holding onto slim hopes of continuing to run after college. That's when Milan Donley, an assistant coach at the University of Arkansas, suggested she call Joe Vigil.

In her 2018 book, *Let Your Mind Run: A Memoir of Thinking My Way to Victory*, Kastor said she talked with Vigil by phone for five minutes. Vigil didn't promise to coach her, but left the door open just enough that Kastor loaded all of her belongings and a glimmer of hope into her car. She made the 12-hour trek from Fayetteville to Alamosa.

"Coach Vigil energized me in a sport that I was ready to walk away from," Kastor said in an interview for this book. "He re-energized me in such a short amount of time on the phone, and when you're face to face with him, you feel that tenfold."

After she arrived in Alamosa in 1996, Vigil agreed to let Kastor join a group of post-collegiate men he was training. He was very clear to her that he would not tolerate any nonsense. There were no second chances.

"It was really immediately that I tidied up and really focused and dedicated 100 percent of my day to making running work, and making sure I was making the best decisions for running," she said.

"I went to Alamosa really wanting to understand and be open to his teaching, but I realized once I was under his coaching hand that there was so much I misunderstood about myself, about talent, about working hard, about discipline," Kastor said. "In just a very short amount of time, he taught me so much, and I needed to be open to that crash course in learning."

As Kastor managed her life around training, she got better. And better. And better. By 1999, she had risen to No. 1 in the 10,000 meters among U.S. women, and No. 2 in the 5000 meters. She was a terror on the roads. She won U.S. cross country championships in 1997, 1999, and 2000. And she earned a spot on the 2000 U.S. Olympic team in the 10,000-meter run.

But her finish at that year's Olympics fell well short of her expectations. Kastor failed to make it out of the semifinals, officially placing 18th.

◇◇◇

With Vigil now gone from Alamosa, it was an easy decision for Kastor to follow him to Mammoth Lakes in 2001. There, she could train with great female athletes such as Amy Rudolph (a two-time Olympian in the 5000 meters), Colleen De Reuck (a four-time Olympian in the 10,000 meters and marathon), Jennifer Rhines (a three-time Olympian in the 5000 and 10,000 meters and the marathon), Milena Glusac (a U.S. national champion for the half-marathon and 20K), and Elva Dryer (a two-time Olympian at 5000 and 10,000 meters).

Training at Mammoth Lakes, that group of six women managed to sweep all the team spots for the 2002 World Championships in cross country. Just one year after the U.S. team finished last at the same meet, they pulled off a stunning silver medal—edging Kenya by three points. Kastor and De Reuck led the way, placing second and third individually.

The U.S. women's national team coached by Joe Vigil that won the silver medal at the 2002 World Cross Country Championships. Pictured left to right are: Amy Rudolph, Colleen De Reuck, Deena Kastor, Jennifer Rhines, Milena Glusac, and Elva Dryer.

It was a shining moment for U.S. distance running—two individual medals and a team medal at a major international meet—and an early indication that the club model was doing what USA Track & Field hoped it would.

"I have the lab tests on every international runner I've ever coached, including their lactate analysis at velocity, their heart rate, their VO_2 max (a measure of the maximum amount of oxygen a person can utilize during exercise), and more," Vigil said. "The average American has a VO_2 max of 27 mL; good high school runners between 40 and 50; collegiate runners 60; and international runners between 70 and 80. We would build distance runners up anaerobically by training at the right volume at the right intensity to increase their VO_2 max. So there's a method to my madness...a scientific madness.

"What I learned is that to maintain a fast pace longer, you need to run at 90 percent of your vVO_2 (velocity at maximum oxygen intake) and build up volume. The more you build the volume up, the longer you can sustain it. And that becomes the marathon pace. That's why I was successful with marathon runners."

In 2001, Keflezighi set the American record for 10,000 meters after Vigil convinced him he could run much faster than his previous best of 27:51.

"I showed him his lab report and workouts he had done and told him that he was capable of 27:12," Vigil said. "I said, 'If you go out at a pace of 4:23 a mile, you will run 27:12.'"

Keflezighi did as Vigil suggested and finished in 27:13.98, an American record that stood for nine years.

"I did the same thing with Deena [Kastor] the next year," Vigil said. "I told her that her potential was 30:40, and she had to run a certain pace, and she ran 30:50.8. She was off 10 seconds.

"Then we went to the Gate River Run in Jacksonville for the

15K national championships. I said, 'Deena, you're capable of a 5:01 pace per mile for 9.4 miles.'"

Vigil said Kastor told him: "Coach, I'm not that fast."

"She used to like to argue with me, and she didn't care about numbers. I said, 'Do me a favor, Deena. Go out at 5:01 pace and maintain it as long as you can.' That's simple.

"Well, there's a long bridge about a mile and a quarter before the finish at Jacksonville. She was on world-record pace, but the bridge took a little bit out of Deena because she's not as muscular. But she won and broke the American record by a minute and fourteen seconds. At the banquet that night, I told Deena, 'Let's play a little game of mental gymnastics.' We figured out that she averaged 5:01.7 per mile.

"After that, she started believing in everything I told her."

In 2003, Kastor again finished second at the World Championships in cross country, then set her sights on the marathon for the 2004 Olympics in Athens, Greece. Keflezighi also qualified for the Olympics in the marathon. Vigil charted a course around Mammoth Lakes to simulate the course in Athens. Then, he devised a training plan that would prepare the two American stars physiologically for the course's rigors, and mentally for its geography.

"Every day in practice, Coach would shoot his arm out the window of the van, and he'd say, 'This is just like Athens!'" Kastor said. "And I would look around and kind of chuckle because it looks nothing like Athens in Mammoth Lakes, California. But it would really put into my head that the purpose of that day's run wasn't just charging up this mountain to get in a good workout. I was charging up this mountain because I had really high goals ahead of me.

"One of my most intimate moments leading up to the Games was when Coach and Caroline and my husband, Andrew, and I were with the Olympic track and field team on the island of Crete for the month before the Games, adapting to the time zone and the climate. It was the night before I was going into Athens for the race itself, and I said…" Kastor pauses as she checks her emotions.

"I told Coach, 'You know, I realize we've been working hard for this, but the medal almost doesn't matter anymore because I feel like you all have elevated me in such a way that I never could have duplicated that.' The reinforcement of the journey is so valuable, not just the prize or medal hanging around your neck. And we had such a special time pursuing that together.

"For me," she said, "Athens was special before the race even happened."

The men's and women's marathon drew upon the ancient origins of the race, beginning in Marathon, Greece, and ending at Panathenaic Stadium, the site of the very first modern Olympics in 1896. The women's race, held during the Olympics' first weekend, began with temperatures topping 95 degrees Fahrenheit (35 degrees Celsius), an absolute nightmare for distance runners.

Kastor's plan was to run conservatively, allowing the top contenders to lead while she saved her energy for a late push. It worked. Great Britain's Paula Radcliffe set a fast early pace that gradually wore down the lead pack. As one runner after another fell off the pace, including Radcliffe, Kastor picked them off… one by one. Just before entering the stadium, Kastor mistakenly thought she was in fourth place, disappointed that she was so close to winning an Olympic medal. As she hit the track for the final 500 meters of the race, she heard the public address announcer call her name…in third place.

Tears streamed down her face. No one was close enough to catch her at that point. Kastor realized she was one lap around the track from winning the bronze medal. She held her arms up high as she crossed the finish line, becoming just the second American woman to win an Olympic medal in that event.

"When I finished, I looked up in the stands for Coach," Kastor said. "My jaw dropped when I made eye contact with him and I yelled, 'We did it!'"

"We sure did, baby," Vigil yelled back. "We sure did."

The following week in Athens, Keflezighi made history for the U.S. men as well, winning the silver medal. It was the first medal for the United States in the men's marathon since Frank Shorter won gold in 1972 and silver in 1976. The two Mammoth Lakes runners won the only two distance medals for the United States in Athens, doubling the number of distance medals won by the Stars and Stripes in the previous four Olympics combined.

Thus, in its first major test, the Mammoth Lakes program provided a proverbial shot in the arm for U.S. distance running.

Vigil, naturally, was energized by the program's success, but it had taken its toll. In order to coach Team USA California, he was away from his wife for months at a time. Caroline was in Green Valley, Arizona, taking care of her mother, whose health had been declining.

"My mother had broken her hip, which required a lot more care," Caroline said. "I was taking care of two houses as well as my mother. Coach was very supportive. He loved my mother and she loved him. When Coach would come home, as often as he could, he would visit with her and we'd do fine, then he'd leave again and I'd go back to working on the house and doing all that. That's how it went."

Not long after the Athens Olympics, Vigil decided he wasn't going to put his wife through that any longer. He resigned his position with Team USA California and moved back permanently to Green Valley.

"I was so happy for him because I feel like he gave to me for so many years, just giving, giving, giving…and never complaining," said Kastor, who under Vigil's guidance made 19 U.S. national teams, won 18 U.S. titles, earned two silver medals at the World Cross Country Championships, and scored an Olympic bronze. "He was living here in Mammoth getting me ready while his wife was the rock, living in Green Valley holding down the fort. He was with us for months out of the year training with me and the Mammoth group.

"It was such a time burden, but he gave so generously during that time, just continuing to teach and learn. Even when he retold a story for the fifth time, I would listen with big eyes as if it was the first time he was telling it, because he would tell it in a slightly different way, or use a little bit different language. I would just eat it up when he would tell his little anecdotal stories. It was those days that he gave so much to me that I felt the Olympic race was the only thing I could do to give back to him."

Vigil may have gone home to be with his wife, but he wasn't finished coaching. He continued advising the Mammoth Track Club and took on a few elite runners. He was employed by ASICS, which he joined in the late 1990s, and traveled across the country giving coaching clinics.

One of his elite runners was Mexican-born Diego Estrada, who ran the 10,000 meters for his native country in the 2012 London Olympics. In 2016, Estrada—now a U.S. citizen—was running the finals of the 10,000 meters at the Olympic Trials. He was not feeling well and dropped out 6,000 meters into the race.

"I told him, 'Diego, if you ever drop out of another race, get yourself another coach,'" Vigil said. He was serious.

Then, in 2017, Estrada was running the Chicago Marathon when he stepped on a water bottle at the second water station and sprained his ankle.

"He remembered what I had told him, so he got up and started running," Vigil said. "His ankle was this big (Vigil holds his hands about a half foot apart) when he finished. He was the highest-finishing American, fourth overall, and made $87,000.

"When I got to him about 20 minutes later," Vigil said, "the therapist was working on him in a wheelchair and he says, 'Why didn't you drop out? That's a bad ankle sprain.'"

"I didn't want to lose my coach!" Estrada said.

"I come walking up about that time and I say, 'Here comes that mean coach,'" Vigil said, laughing.

In 2010, Brenda Martinez finished her college career at the University of California-Riverside, where she was a three-time NCAA Division I All-American. That spring, she was the national runner-up in the 1500 meters and appeared to be one of the top female middle-distance runners coming out of college. The problem was, she couldn't find anyone to coach her.

"I kind of butted heads with my college coach, so I knew I didn't want to be coached by him post-collegiately, and he didn't like that very much," Martinez said.

Martinez tried to catch on with an elite group in California, but before making the move, the group's coach not so politely asked her to not show up. Then she and her husband, Carlos Handler, moved to Colorado Springs, where they thought they had found a coach who would work with her.

"We had signed a lease for an apartment and tried to meet

up with the coach," Martinez said. "Then, we got a call from the coach who said they had just gotten off the phone with my college coach and it wouldn't be a good situation for them."

Rejected. Twice. Martinez had no coach, no training partners, and no options. She had run 2:00 for 800 meters and 4:09 for 1500 meters and yet was being cast as a renegade child.

"My husband had been coached by Marco Ochoa in junior college," Martinez said. Ochoa was an All-American at Adams State who had finished fourth at the 1996 U.S. Olympic Marathon Trials, training under Vigil. "Marco always talked about Coach Vigil. I wasn't too familiar with Coach, but my husband said Coach Vigil is the best in the world and he's going to help us out, or at least get us in the right direction. We were under the assumption that he wasn't coaching anyone, or maybe not coaching at all."

On Ochoa's urging, Martinez made a call to Vigil and described her situation and her desire to run professionally.

"I remember getting off the phone with him," she said, "and all he said was let me figure something out for you guys and I'll call you back in two days. So we waited for his phone call, and finally he called us back."

"Before I'm a coach, I'm a man," Vigil said, "and when two people ask me for help, I'm going to try to help. It seems like you need my help. So I'm going to coach you."

"We said, 'Oh my God, Coach. Thank you, thank you!'" Martinez said. "We were shocked. We just thought he was going to send us to one of his former athletes. But he told us, 'If you mess up, I'm going to get rid of you.' I said, 'OK, Coach, I'm not going to let you down.' That's how our relationship started."

Vigil told Martinez to move to Big Bear Lake, California, where she could live and train at high altitude. Vigil would map out workouts from his home in Green Valley, and Handler

Let Me Tell You a Story

Tim Sall, who competed for Joe Vigil's Adams State teams from 1974 to 1977, remembers how his former coach had a knack for getting the best out of his athletes—no matter what level they came to him.

"Coach was able to get you to believe in your own ability, when you really didn't believe it yourself," Sall said. "His tough-minded motivational attitude really rubbed off on you. When I was at Adams State, the team nicknamed him 'Bulldog Joe' and we had a T-shirt made for him with that nickname on the back. He loved that shirt and always seemed to have it on at practice.

"He was such a giving, helpful person. When I was coaching a high school cross country and track team in California, I contacted him to get help for our program. When we started to dominate and win state championships, he was adamant that we teach our program to other coaches. He was such an educator.

"Another time, he was in San Diego at the Olympic training facility, an hour away from our school, and he came to talk to our kids. He even brought Deena (Kastor), Meb (Keflezighi), and Ryan (Hall) with him. One time, he invited me to bring a couple of kids to the Olympic training center. He left such an impression on the kids. I was amazed at the interest he had in our program and all the calls and talks I had with him."

would be his eyes and ears, putting Brenda through workouts and reporting regularly to Vigil.

"Big Bear Lake is about an hour from my family, and we can drop down to sea level in about 50 minutes," Martinez said. "So it's a perfect situation for me. That one phone call changed my life."

The unusual coaching arrangement worked. Martinez won a silver medal in the 800 at the 2013 World Championships, and in 2014 ran on U.S. teams that won gold in the 4x800 and silver in the 4x1500 at the IAAF World Relays.

Joe Vigil checking the heart rate of Brenda Martinez during a track workout.

In 2016, Martinez entered the U.S. Olympic Trials at the University of Oregon's Hayward Field as the top-ranked woman in the 800-meter run. She cruised through the first two rounds, and most saw her as a strong favorite to win the finals.

Through 600 meters, Martinez was in position to strike. "I was coming off the last turn ready to slingshot and make my move," Martinez said. As the women fought for position, another runner clipped the back of Martinez's foot and she went down. The field sped away, and along with them Martinez's best shot at the U.S. Olympic team.

"In that moment, I couldn't believe it was happening," Martinez said. "I was in shock. It went from me about to make the team to it not even being a thing anymore."

Crestfallen, Martinez got up and jogged to the finish, right past a teammate with his own connection to Vigil who was about to experience a very different emotion. Boris Berian was lining up for the men's 800. A national champion in the outdoor 800 meters as a freshman at Adams State before dropping out of school, Berian was working at a McDonald's in Colorado Springs when Vigil invited him to try running again. He was later contacted on social media by one of the athletes at Big Bear Lake, and Handler agreed to coach him. Within a year, Berian won a gold medal in the 800-meter run at the World Indoor Track and Field Championships, and then minutes after Martinez's heartbreak, he won the Olympic Trials and a spot on the 2016 U.S. Olympic team.

While there was joy on the track for members of the Big Bear team, there were tears in the media room.

"I remember going to the interviews and I kind of cried, but I remember thinking I don't want to cry and feel sorry for myself because that's the worst thing I can do," Martinez said.

"I remember giving interviews and thinking about how Coach would react during adversity. When he'd talk with me, he'd say, 'You can toughen up; you're tougher than you think.' And I believed that in the moment. I remember doing the interviews and saying, 'You know what? It happened. I can't blame anyone. I have a 1500 to wind up, so I'm just going to get ready for that.' I wasn't going to pout about it; it was already over. The team's already been selected.

"I think people were surprised I reacted that way. It reminded me that I have a bunch of little girls and even adults looking up to me and I don't want them to see me react in a bad way. That's something Coach Vigil taught me. You have a reputation to uphold and there's a lot of kids who look up to you. I was always keeping that in mind."

After the interviews, Martinez reunited with Vigil and her husband on the track. "I could tell that they had cried and had tried stopping the tears because, honestly, I don't think they knew how to console me," Martinez said. "It was sad to see Coach Vigil kind of cry, and I remember thinking, 'Can you stop it, because it's going to make me cry...'"

It was Vigil who, in 2013, told Martinez it was her responsibility to give back to the sport that was giving her so many opportunities. So she started the Big Bear High Altitude Training Camp for girls. Each year, dozens of girls send letters of application for Martinez's summer camp, and she selects 10 to 12 to attend, all expenses paid. New Balance, her sponsor, provides a couple pairs of shoes, outfits, and accessories to each girl. The camp is four days long.

Through 2019, Martinez has hosted 65 girls who come to run, make friends, and learn about healthy behaviors, self-confidence, and mental toughness.

"It took me some time to realize what impact having a camp could have," Martinez said. "Some of these girls will come to camp, and I find out while they're here that they had wanted to kill themselves. I would have never gotten that from reading their letters, but it has helped me understand that I need to keep doing this because there are a lot of girls who need help. More than ever, there are kids that have more anxiety and depression, and I want to do my part through running."

That healthy dose of perspective helped Martinez overcome her heartbreak in the finals of the 800 meters. In the days that followed, she wrote in her journal and prepared her mind to get through the qualifying rounds of the 1500 meters. She fought through the first round, winning her heat. She fought through the second round, again winning the heat. Then, in the finals, she attached herself to prerace favorites Jenny Simpson and Shannon Rowbury as the lead pack motored through the first 1,200 meters.

Martinez clung to Simpson's shoulder coming off the last turn, the same spot where a week earlier she fell in the 800-meter finals. But this time, Martinez stayed upright. Five women charged down the final stretch with three Olympic spots on the line.

Joe Vigil (foreground, with back to camera) getting a hug from U.S. Olympian Brenda Martinez after the finals of the 1500-meter run at the 2016 U.S. Olympic Trials. Martinez grabbed the third qualifying spot for the Olympics, and afterward sought out Vigil during a victory lap at Hayward Field in Eugene, Oregon.

"I remember the last 100 meters, the crowd was insanely loud," Martinez said. "I don't think I've ever heard Hayward Field get so loud in all my life for someone who wasn't from the University of Oregon."

Simpson surged ahead to win in 4:04.74. Rowbury was next in 4:05.39. Martinez and Amanda Eccleston forged a small gap on Morgan Uceny before lunging at the finish line for the final spot. "I thought I got fourth," Martinez said.

"I remember them calling off Jenny and then Shannon and there was a long pause…and then I think they said my name. It got crazy loud and I still didn't know if I made the team. It wasn't until Jenny ran up to me and said, 'You did it! I'm so proud of you!' that I knew I made it."

Martinez, whose time was 4:06.16, earned her spot on the Olympic team by three-hundredths of a second over Eccleston.

A few minutes later, Simpson, Rowbury, and Martinez took the customary victory lap. On the last stretch, 100 meters from the finish line, Martinez spotted Vigil standing all by himself.

"I saw him on the fence, just crying," she said. A bystander snapped a picture of the two as they hugged.

"And then I told him: 'I'm glad these are happy tears now.'"

14

COACHING
WITH HEART

*I*n 2008, Larry Fujimoto invited Vigil to attend the 50th reunion of the Alamosa High School class of 1958. Fujimoto, remember, was a freshman the year Vigil began teaching at the school, so the members of that graduating class were the first students Vigil had taught and coached throughout their high school years.

Fujimoto's heartbreaking fall in the 180-meter hurdles at the state meet his senior year cost him and his team the championship, but he earned a greater reward that day: the lifelong friendship and compassion of Joe I. Vigil. Fujimoto never forgot that. He knew that many of his classmates still felt a great affection for their science teacher, coach, and friend, so he hoped Vigil could make the 10-hour trek from Green Valley, Arizona, to Alamosa for the reunion.

Vigil, however, was the head coach for U.S. distance runners going to the 2008 Olympics in Beijing, China, and he just could not fit the trip into his busy summer schedule. Instead, he wrote a letter to the class that Fujimoto presented for him:

Dear Larry,

I enjoyed our visit the other night. It was uplifting to visit with you as we spoke about your upcoming reunion. So many thoughts come to mind.

One, I cannot believe that it is the 50th reunion of your high school graduation. Where has the time gone?

Two, I cannot believe I have been teaching and coaching for 54 years. I still have a strong passion for what I am doing and can't see an end in sight. I am particularly enjoying my international experiences giving clinics, coaching and teaching.

Three, chronologically I am 78 years old but my spirit and my enthusiasm for studying and learning, and my identity, is that of a person that is just starting out. At times, I think I have died and gone to heaven.

I am grateful for having been born in the San Luis Valley. My education, in part, and my values were formed by all of those wonderful people I have come into contact with. My teachers, coaches, laborers all were a vital part of my development and I love that the San Luis Valley is the greatest.

I sit in my office at home and reminisce about the wonderful class of 1958. You had it all. Active, bright and engaging. Students with a world of potential and dreams about the future. I have to be honest with you: their enthusiasm and spirit did more for me than any other group I have ever been associated with. The beginning of my career as a teacher and coach made a genesis with the class of 1958. Much of what I accomplished, I owe to that group. They helped to mold my vision, my aspiration and my desire to grow professionally.

As I shared by phone, I remember so many experiences that occurred with that class. Some students I knew better

*than others, but I loved them all, and my door was open
to them all. I remember the class plays, the music, the aca-
demics and the individual conversations I've had with so
many. Wow, they were all great.*

*As I travel the country, I occasionally cross paths with
my former students. I am totally impressed with what they
are doing and how they are giving of themselves to create a
better world for all.*

*I could go on forever, but please, do me a favor. Convey
to the class that they were special in my life. They energized me to do what I have become. Their spirit remains
in my heart and in my mind. They touched me in a way
no other class or group has. Thanks to all.*

*I would certainly like to be there to enjoy the reunion
with all of you, but my appointment as an Olympic coach
will keep me busy. To all, enjoy this special moment in time.*

Your friend, coach and former teacher,

Coach Vigil

If this story were simply about Joe I. Vigil the coach and his pursuit of excellence, you could point to his winning percentage of
.942 and 19 national team titles in 28 years as a college coach. Or
you could highlight the 22 Olympians he has helped guide to the
world's biggest track and field stage. Both accomplishments are
exceptional.

"I followed his coaching career, which was fantastic. He had
much success," said John McDonnell, the legendary University of
Arkansas coach whose cross country and track and field teams
won 40 NCAA Division I championships between 1972 and
2008. "I have no doubt that Adams State could have won championships at the Division I level. They were a very disciplined

team and they paid the price. The difference between their program and ours is that they didn't have the budgets Division I teams had. It was really good to see a guy like that competing against and beating Division I schools who had the benefit of money on their side."

History is likely to place Vigil on par with the most successful track and field and cross country coaches of all time, guys like McDonnell, Bill Bowerman of Oregon (who coached 22 individual NCAA champions and 31 Olympians), and Jumbo Elliott of Villanova (who coached 82 individual NCAA champions and 28 Olympians).

"I say to people that I have *helped* to develop Olympians, because I was not the only one involved," Vigil said. "There were people who helped those athletes with their biomechanics, sports psychologists, and other coaches they had before me that brought them along quite well. But I helped them in their final preparations…22 of them who had a dream of becoming an Olympian."

There are track and field coaches in the United States who have built sterling reputations as great leaders, great exercise physiologists, or great educators. It's difficult to think of many who are excellent in all three areas, but Vigil checks all the boxes.

As an educator, he led the creation of the U.S. coaching education program and was its national director for the first nine years. As of spring 2020, USA Track & Field's coaching education program has trained more than 40,000 coaches in the nearly 40 years since Vigil and three coaching colleagues hammered out the curriculum in an Adams State classroom. Vigil has recruited hundreds of coaches and scientists to teach the courses in every region of the United States. He has lectured on the topics of physiology and training on six continents and traveled tirelessly; in 2019, just shy of turning 89 years old, he made 24 trips across the United States to teach and coach.

"I start talking at a clinic and sometimes I talk for two or three hours without any notes, and the coaches are just amazed," Vigil said. "They ask, 'How in the world can you do that?' And I say, 'You can too by dedicating yourself to your field. Don't be happy with getting a degree and never learning any more, just looking forward to going home at night. Plan your day so you can grow a little every day professionally in whatever you're teaching or whatever you're doing.' The big thing is commitment to a cause."

In 1984, Vigil was head coach for the U.S. team at the World Cross Country Championships at the Meadowlands in New Jersey. Milan Donley, currently director of the Kansas Relays, was in his third year as a graduate assistant with Vigil.

"He invited me to come along as a gofer for the team," Donley said. "We get to the Meadowlands and there are all these teams and coaches from around the world. The U.S. team walks in and people start migrating toward us; I wasn't a distance person and knew very little, so I thought, 'Wow, all of these people want to see our distance runners.'"

In minutes, Donley said, a group of 30 to 40 coaches and administrators from various countries had encircled Vigil.

"This didn't happen just that one day; it happened every time we went over to the Meadowlands," Donley said. "Or at the hotel…I shared the hotel room with him and someone was calling him all the time wanting to set up a meeting.

"The interesting thing was that he could converse with a lot of them in their native language. If a coach from Italy came up and spoke to him, he would talk Italian. Of course, if a coach from Mexico talked to him, he'd talk in Spanish. Over time, you realized this was the norm for Coach no matter where he went in the world of track and field or cross country. People sought him out. If they knew he was there, people would find him."

On the plane ride home, Donley asked Vigil how he came to know so many people.

Let Me Tell You a Story

Dan Green remembers taking his team to Alamosa one summer to train and meet Joe Vigil.

"I was so excited because Coach was going to talk to my team," Green says. "One of my guys was coming down to the meeting, and he was literally eating a Twinkie. Coach runs into him and says: 'What the hell are you eating?'"

The runner's response: "Well, Coach, it's a Twinkie."

"What are you putting that crap in your body for?" Vigil asks.

"What?" the runner responds.

"Aren't you a runner?" Vigil says.

"Yeah, Coach," the young man responds, "but I don't run for a couple of hours."

Vigil says: "I don't care when you run. Why are you putting that stuff in your body?"

Green finishes the story: "Our kids get into the classroom and Coach is talking to them. He says: 'How many of you guys are getting to bed on time?' A couple of them raise their hand and Coach tells them that he doesn't coach anybody who is out past twelve o'clock on a Saturday night, that he's not wasting his time with those people. It set a tone for our whole team."

"By 1984, he'd already had a lot of experiences worldwide and met many great coaches and scientists," Donley said. "He'd get back home and he was always writing back to them, calling them, and talking to them. He was sharing information with them, but they were also sharing information with him. That's how he developed all these friendships and respect."

"I think what has impressed me for so long—and it seems like it's on refrain in my mind any time I'm with him or in the lobby of the hotel and he's holding court with a bunch of people around him—is that he has spent his life studying the physiology and psychology of this sport," Deena Kastor said. "And yet he shares what he knows within a second of meeting somebody. That is so beautiful to me because a lot of people who put that time and discipline into creating a sport philosophy hold their cards tight to their chest so only they and their athletes can benefit from it.

"Coach Vigil, in his ultimate generosity, in the first second of meeting someone, would give away information that took him years to get his doctorate for, or his continuing education. He continues to read every day, even at the age of 90, to learn more about the sport."

In the mid-1980s, Vigil gave a clinic at the University of Houston where a fiery coach from The Woodlands High School was in the audience.

"I'm not making this up," said Danny Green, who at that time had led his team to three of the previous four Texas state cross country titles. "I was so motivated when I heard this guy talk that I just wanted to go down to the nearest tattoo parlor, rip off my shirt, and have them tattoo 'Coach' across my chest!

"It was one of the first times in my life that I came across somebody that was extrinsically vocal about his passion for coaching and the significance of that job. I knew when I heard him speak that day that it was a job I wanted to know more about. I wanted to hear him talk every chance I could, and over the next several years, that's what I did."

Green's program went on to win 15 Class 6A Texas cross country championships and one track and field title during his 30-plus years as a high school coach.

Vigil recognized that Green was an eager student. By the mid-1990s, Vigil had invited him to begin teaching Level I and Level II coaching education courses, a gig in which Green had the opportunity to travel and present alongside Vigil and U.S. high school coaching legend Joe Newton.

Newton was the head coach for boys cross country at York High School in Elmhurst, Illinois, from 1956 to 2016, during which time he won 28 state championships and finished in the top three 44 times. Vigil and Newton had been friends since the 1970s, and when Vigil was named head coach for the U.S. Olympic distance runners in 1988, he brought along Newton as an assistant—the first high school coach ever to be selected for a U.S. Olympic track and field staff.

Newton was named the National High School Cross Country Coach of the Year four times, and in the years before there were actual competitions to settle the debate on the course, his high school teams were often regarded as the best in the country. He was known to shake hands with each of his runners and address them by name—*more than 120 of them*—every day after practice. Newton also was known for his ability to show just as much empathy for the slowest runners on the team as he did for the faster ones.

Through much of the 1990s and 2000s, Vigil and Newton were sheer electricity on the coaching education circuit. Poor Danny Green…having to talk to audiences after those two guys went to work. Newton was Vigil's equal when it came to motivating coaches, athletes, and even the common man.

"I was such a blessed guy to be in the presence of such excellence," Green said. "To be on a panel with those guys and to listen to them and glean little things that were going to help me be a better person as well as a better coach is just incredible.

"What made them so great in everything they did is the fact that they coached people. Those guys would be successful coaching pinochle. They just would. They knew how to get people to do what they needed to do to improve themselves and to perform in a manner that maybe those people never thought they'd be able to do."

Like Vigil, you would almost never hear a negative word from Newton's mouth. After a full day of lectures at a coaching clinic in Kansas City in 2008, the three men went to dinner that evening at a remote barbecue joint.

"This," Newton proclaimed as he sipped his drink, "is the best lemonade I have ever had."

The pre-dinner conversation was filled with jokes and laughter and a few rounds of Vigil and Newton throwing friendly barbs at each other. Then dinner arrived.

"This," Newton said, taking the first bite of his smoked chicken sandwich, "is the best barbecue I have ever had."

In 2014, Vigil traveled to Elmhurst to talk to Newton's team about commitment to a greater cause.

"He's the No. 1 distance coach of all time in the United States...although I say he's No. 1 in the world," Newton said as he introduced Vigil. "I met him 40 years ago and he's like my brother. He's 85, I'm 85½—so I got him by half a year. He's the most dynamic speaker I have ever heard in my life. You know what he's charging me today? Zip! All I have to do is put him at my house to sleep and take him to the airport tomorrow."

For the next 25 minutes, Vigil captivated the group of 15- to

233

18-year-olds—more than 100 of them crammed into a modest classroom:

> *It's actually my pleasure to be here, and I'll tell you why. There's no high school in America that has a greater running culture than York High School. You guys have it all. What you do with it is something else.*
>
> *I was standing on the shores of Cadiz, Spain, one year—that's the old capital of Spain where Christopher Columbus set sail for the New World—and I was reminded at that moment that Columbus said he didn't know where he was going. When he got there he didn't know where he was at. And when he got back, he didn't know where he had been.*
>
> *That's the way many of us live our lives. I heard a couple comments now about accountability and knowing what you're doing. You have to focus on the task at hand, whether it's a workout or a competition or getting ready for a state meet, or getting ready for an exam. You have to focus.*
>
> *I tell my people that there is a difference between training and deep training. I used to coach and I didn't know much. My runners would go out for a long run and they would play six rounds of grab-ass. They didn't have any objective for what they were doing.*
>
> *Listen carefully. Whatever you do in life, think about it until it goes from the conscious to the subconscious. When it does that, you myelinate your neuron (activate it to resist fear), the lining of the neurilemma (nerve fiber in the peripheral nervous system), and the next time that impulse comes through there, it comes through with greater amplitude and speed. And that's called deep*

thinking about your training. You focus on what you're doing. How else are you going to know how the body feels in a 5:00 flat mile in competition if you don't pay attention to your body? You have to concentrate on what you're doing every moment of the workout...

We live in a country where we have a lot of freedom. You have the freedom to do whatever you want. You could be playing football or some other sport, but you have the right to choose cross country. That's a great freedom, people. You also have the freedom to choose how good you want to be. Think about that for just a minute. Do you want to be poor, mediocre, or do you want to be good? Do you want to add to the history of York cross country?

I used to tell my people, you don't come out for cross country to run for the coach or for yourself. You come out to have an impact for the program. I don't care how much you suffer as individuals in training and how hard it is and how many sacrifices you have to make. You have to make a sacrifice for the team. What exactly are you doing for your team? Are you a leader of some kind? You don't have to be No. 1 to be a leader. You can encourage people that are not having a good day. You can encourage them by being there all the time and being supportive of the progress the team is making and sharing in their victories or defeats...

So my challenge to you today is to ask, what kind of impact are you going to have on your program? I think you have to ask yourself, 'What am I doing to help the team?' It's not about you. It's about York cross country— that's bigger than all of us. I don't want my people to run for me when I'm coaching the national team; I want them to run for the USA to help their team out, or run for their parents...dedicate their race to someone or something that's bigger than them.

It's hard to do, living in America, when you're narcissistic. We have a narcissistic culture; all we think about is ourselves. Forget about yourself and think about York cross country. When you come to practice every day, what can I do for the team?

I will conclude with this: what other human endeavor can match the healthy ego satisfaction and the moral self-discipline supplied by mental courage, bodily endurance, and muscular strength, those incomparable instruments for living most and serving best? You want to be a good son, good team member, good classmate, good church member? The more strength, courage, and endurance that you develop, the better you are going to be able to serve your team. Do it to the maximum.

Among hundreds of clinics he's given worldwide, Vigil has given three clinics in Tokyo for the Japanese Athletic Federation.

"The first time I went," he said, "I had about 150 physiologists out there and the only way I knew they were introducing me was because I heard my name. I sort of got scared. They can't speak a word of English and I can't speak a word of Japanese, and I'm supposed to teach them something today?

"They provided a coach and a physiologist who could interpret for me. So, as I walked around the stage and I started talking about the physiology of training at high altitude, I'd make one statement at a time and they would translate. It took me four hours to deliver a one-hour lecture, because I got some questions, too.

"Ultimately it was successful. I got letters from a lot of them."

Vigil planned to stay a couple days after the clinic, so organizers asked him what he would like to do.

"They asked me if I'd like to play golf," Vigil said. "They love golf in Japan, but I have never golfed in my life. Golf is an interruption of a good walk. It's three hours of recreation frustration."

Instead, Vigil said he wanted to see where Japan's great marathoner Toshihiko Seko trained. Seko was a two-time Olympian who won major marathons in Fukuoka (Japan), London, Boston, and Chicago. In 1981, he set world records for 25,000 meters (approximately 15.5 miles) and 30,000 meters (18.6 miles), which stood until 2011.

"They took me to this park in downtown Tokyo," Vigil said. "Imagine one of the largest cities in the world and there is a park where more than one million people pass through every day. Seko used to run 50 kilometers there—31 miles. They explained to me that he would just run in and around the people. That's how he got used to running in and getting out of congestion."

As an exercise physiologist, Vigil's stature matches or exceeds some of the greatest experts in running physiology, including Jack Daniels, Bruno Balke, and Dave Costill. Those three men were in Alamosa around 1968 when many members of the U.S. Olympic track and field, wrestling, and basketball teams were training there in preparation for the summer Olympics in Mexico City. Their early work inspired Vigil to dedicate his life to a greater understanding of how the human body functions.

In 1988, as head coach for the U.S. Olympic distance runners, Vigil was asked by USA Track & Field executive director Ollan Cassell to come up with a plan that would give America's athletes the best chance of success in Seoul, South Korea. Vigil hatched an idea to send U.S. athletes to Tokyo—which was within a few hours' plane trip to Seoul—well in advance of the Olympic Games.

"I told them we had to get there two weeks before the Olympics start because it takes one day to adapt your circadian rhythms for each time zone, mentally and physically," Vigil said. "For athletes living on the East Coast, the difference was 14 time zones by the time they got to Tokyo. However, at that time the Olympic Committee only funded athletes to arrive three days prior to the Games.

"Ollan Cassell calls me and says, 'Your plan is great, but we don't have the money or finances to send the team for 14 days.' I told him that he merely asked me for a program and I gave it to him. Then I explained it to him based on science. He flew to Tokyo and met with the Japanese Athletic Federation and they established a warmup meet between England, Japan, and America. Our share of the take was $274,000, which was enough to cover our expenses for 14 days.

"By knowing a little science," Vigil continued, "I was in a position to offer that idea. They bought it and that's why we were there two weeks ahead of time. Over the years, I've used science not to impress people with how much I know, but for practical application that helps athletes succeed."

That year, the U.S. team eventually set up camp at the Nihon Aerobic Center in Chiba, Japan, which is about 60 miles north of Tokyo. Shortly after the team's arrival, Vigil was in the hotel lobby talking with the front-desk staff.

"This guy comes out from the back and it's Yoshi Kobayashi," Vigil said. "He and I got our PhDs together at the University of New Mexico in 1971. He was in charge of that center in Chiba. So for the rest of the two weeks that we were there, I had it made. He called his sister and she took my wife, Caroline, all over Japan in the bullet train. Caroline got to see things I didn't get to see because I was working my ass off getting our team ready."

In 1988, the U.S. Olympic Track and Field team won 13 gold medals, seven silver, and six bronze. The 26 medals were 22 percent of all Olympic track and field medals awarded that year.

Vigil's life is filled with similar experiences, which he concedes sometimes seems unreal.

"So many things have happened to me in my life that are boggling," Vigil said. "I start talking to coaches about it, and they think I'm lying. It's just so fantastic."

Vigil's story, though, is not only about coaching athletes to stardom and his own dreamlike events. It is rooted in such concrete traits as compassion, kindness, self-sacrifice, a mad thirst for knowledge, and service to humankind—all of which partially explain why he writes letters to former students a half century after they last attended his classes. It is a story of how a boy born with below-average means grew to help average people believe in their own unique gifts, prodding each one to excellence and encouraging them to share their talent with others. If track and field and cross country provided Joe Vigil's canvas in life, then his passion for excellence and his love for people were his two favorite paintbrushes, the tools he used to create his story.

"When you spend time with him, what hasn't been cool, really?" Donley said. "I've never had a bad moment with him... ever. That's why people look forward to seeing him so much. People wonder about his legacy or whatever, but to me his legacy is that nobody has ever had a bad moment with him."

Vigil inspired his Adams State program to be the best the NAIA has ever seen, but he loved the beauty of human performance just as much as he loved his team. When Vigil saw a great race or effort, the color of the athlete's uniform was not important to him.

"I wasn't even on his team, and he cared about my success," said Juan Diaz, a four-time cross country All-American and three-time track and field champion for Adams State's rival, Western State College.

In the mid-1980s, Western State's coach, Duane Vandenbusche, built a recruiting pipeline to Venezuela, drawing several strong runners including Diaz, Eduardo Navas, Jose Rojas, and Frank Oropeza to his team. Just as Vigil helped Vandenbusche learn about training distance runners, he was equally gracious with the Western State athletes, especially the "Venezuelan Connection," with whom he always spoke Spanish. It spawned a great rivalry and helped both programs grow stronger.

"In my four years running for Western State, Coach Vigil was a respectful person and really professional in his treatment of other teams," Diaz said. "He meant a lot to me, and in fact I felt that part of my improvement as an athlete happened thanks to him, because he was always there to give great advice. He had a lot of knowledge as a coach...he motivated me to train every day to achieve the level of his great middle- and long-distance team. The races against him and his warriors were true battles each week, but each of those battles was friendly, respectful, and rewarding."

In 1987, Vigil was the coach of the U.S. team competing at the Pan American Games in Indianapolis. By that time, Diaz and Navas—who was burning up the track in the NAIA on his way to five national titles—were among the best runners from their native Venezuela, yet they did not receive a spot in the Pan Am Games.

This perplexed Vigil. He talked with the president of the Venezuelan track and field federation to ask why Diaz and Navas were not on that country's team.

"When I saw Coach Vigil that fall, he told me the answer

he got really surprised him," Diaz said. "He said they (Venezuelan track and field officials) didn't know us and that we must be Mexican athletes."

Diaz and Navas were not Mexican, and Vigil pointing out they were Venezuelan did not solve the problem. Nonetheless, Vigil's concern impressed Diaz: "He paid attention to us even knowing we weren't on his team."

Navas first met Vigil at an indoor track and field meet at the University of Colorado in 1985.

"I was racing two miles that day and shortly before my warmup, coach Vandenbusche introduced me to Coach Vigil," Navas said. "He was dressed in the (Adams State) green warm-ups that during my whole college career I respected and admired for what they represented. Then, knowing that I was Venezuelan, he put his hand on my shoulder and spoke to me in Spanish in a very fluid and warm accent:

Es un honor conocerte. Eduardo, te deseo buena suerte en tu competencia de hoy, así como en todas las venideras, estoy seguro de que serás muy exitoso durante el tiempo que permanezcas en tu universidad y en tu vida como corredor. Así como para cuando llegue el tiempo de que regreses a tu país, lo haras con honor y mucho profesionalismo. Eso es mas importante que cualquier otra cosa.

In English, what Vigil said was:

It is an honor to meet you. Eduardo, I wish you good luck in your race today and in the future while you are at your university. I am sure you will have a successful career as an athlete and when it comes time to return to your country, you will do it with the highest of honors and with professionalism. That is more important than anything.

One of Vigil's coaching pals also credited Vigil's kind heart for boosting his career.

"Back in 1992, I was at the USA Track & Field convention and Joe told me that I've got to come to this meeting in one of the rooms, that I needed to get involved and meet people," said Jack Hazen, who has coached 325 All-Americans and won five national cross country championships at Malone College in Ohio. "We were in the room with about 12 or 15 people, and they said, 'We are going to select the coach for the U.S. men's team for the World Cross Country Championships.' Joe nominated me. Nobody else knew me, but they all voted for me because Joe nominated me."

For Vigil, the gesture was simply paying it forward. Nearly 25 years earlier, Fort Hays coach Alex Francis nominated the relatively unknown Vigil for a spot on the U.S. Olympic Committee, paving the way for more than 50 years of international assignments. Similarly, Hazen went on to serve U.S. teams at the Junior Pan American Games, the Pan American Games, and the World Cross Country Championships a second time.

"I also coached the men's distance team at the London Olympics in 2012," Hazen said. "That was totally Joe Vigil. The long-distance running committee had a big say in who got that, and they all so much respected Joe that I got in on his coattails. He's been instrumental in much of the success I've had as a coach."

In 2012, Kim McConnell, a coach for Peak to Peak Charter School in Lafayette, Colorado, attended a summer USA Track & Field Level II coaching school in Las Vegas at which Vigil presented. McConnell knew a little bit about Vigil; she had run collegiately 22 years earlier at Rice University, where Vigil's former graduate assistant Jim Bevan was her coach.

"At one point, Coach said something to the effect that he coaches a few non-elite types," McConnell said. "I just sort of stored that in my mind, and actually had been praying about it. I coached kids, and I coached adults, and I thought, 'I wish I had a coach.'"

Let Me Tell You a Story

The Rev. Alan Stahlecker, a two-time All-American decathlete at Adams State between 1977 and 1981, remembers how Joe Vigil made him feel important beyond the athletic field.

"I remember one instance after my eligibility was completed that speaks to me of Coach's commitment to his athletes' total being—not just as an athlete," Stahlecker said. "In early May, as my last year was wrapping up and I was heading off to Denver to take the CPA exam, I stopped by the park where Coach was watching the distance runners' workout. We talked for a couple of minutes and then as the runners came by, he stopped them so they could all wish me the best on the exam. I was fired up to take a 2½-day test!

"While I had done the hard work of preparation with a lot of studying, Coach's inspiration contributed to me becoming the first Adams State accounting student to pass the entire CPA exam on his first sitting. He wanted me to succeed in everything that I encountered."

McConnell was 44 years old at the time, which for track and field athletes can mark a new lease on a career as a master's athlete. "I got back home and I thought, 'What would it hurt if I emailed Coach and asked him to coach me,'" McConnell said. "The worst that could happen is he'd say no. He had a connection to Colorado, and he liked that I lived at altitude. So he called me, and to my shock, he said, 'Yeah, I'll coach you.'"

According to McConnell, Vigil told her: "The cost will be $50 a month."

"Fifty dollars a month? I would pay you $500!" McConnell responded.

For the next three years, Vigil wrote out and mailed a monthly training plan to McConnell. She was responsible for doing the workouts and reporting back. Vigil would routinely call her to check in.

"I was super concerned at first because the workouts were incredibly difficult," McConnell said. "I wasn't sure I could do the work he's giving. He would just say, 'Do your best. Do what you can do.' He wasn't going to tolerate me saying that I didn't do it. But he certainly also wasn't going to say, 'I can't believe you didn't hit your times.' When we would talk on the phone, I would be waiting for him to ask about my workout times, but what he would ask is: 'How's your husband? How are your children? How are you doing in life?'

"He's a lot less concerned about whether I'm hitting my times than he is about me as a person. Obviously, that stood out a lot."

Beginning in 2016, McConnell was hit with a series of life-shaking events. First, on September 15, Brandon Reis, the captain of the Peak to Peak boys cross country team, collapsed near the three-mile mark of a 5K race and later died. Doctors determined the cause of death to be a heart arrhythmia.

Within days, Vigil was on the phone to console McConnell.

"It was just a lot of good listening on the phone. Telling me to keep my chin up. There was a strength born out of having that relationship with him," McConnell said.

Two weeks later, Peak to Peak competed at the Desert Twilight Classic in Casa Grande, Arizona, about a 90-minute drive from Vigil's home in Green Valley.

"We raced at nine o'clock at night, and so on his own dime he drove to Casa Grande to hang out with our team," McConnell said. "He gave Brandon's parents a hug. I think he liked talking with Brandon's mom, looking her in the eyes, giving her a hug. I think he said, 'You're strong. It's going to be okay.' Those were really the messages he was giving to Brandon's family and our team: 'This world is tough, but you're tougher and you're going to make it.'"

About 15 months later, McConnell's husband, Ed, collapsed and died while on a run in the family's neighborhood. And a few months after that, Kim McConnell grieved the deaths of her father, and then her mother-in-law.

"It's been kind of rough," she said. "But Coach, he was always there for me. He would say, 'I'm so sorry and you're going to make it. I will be here for you. You're strong and you can get through this.' He wasn't saying *strong* like a coach does when he's pushing you. It was more like, 'I know who you are, Kim, and you're going to make it through this.' He always said, 'Just call me whenever you want to and we'll talk.'

"It still astounds me that Coach Vigil is in my life. It's a gift of God. This should not have happened. I'm too average. It just should not have happened. How did I get connected to someone like that? There is a real sense of gift in my life. Also, we both know that in this busy world, it's not easy to find people who are like he is. It's almost like there is a sense of stability there for me; he's like a little rock that I have. For me, he is an ongoing thread of constancy. And I know he really cares about me, even though I've only known him seven years."

If you live as long as Vigil has, dealing with heartbreak becomes a fact of life. Travis McKinley died in the tragic accident in 1987. Joe Newton passed away in 2017. Pat Porter died along with his son and a friend in an airplane accident in 2012. National-champion miler Dan Maas and his wife were killed in a car accident in 2016.

On November 3, 2007, during the U.S. Olympic Marathon Trials in New York City, Ryan Shay collapsed just past the five-mile mark and died shortly after being rushed to a nearby hospital. Vigil, who had coached Shay for the previous five years, was heartbroken.

"I'll never forget Ryan speaking to the York High School cross country team," Vigil said. "He made a statement that has just stuck with me: 'Whenever you're faced with fear, anxiety, or a lack of confidence, one has to dig down deep to find that golden grain of steel called *will*. If you will yourself to do something that's possible, you'll do it, or you'll succumb to your own mental weakness. Don't be weak mentally; this is a tough life. You have it made here in high school, here at York and in Chicago. It's a great place. The rest of the world is suffering. You are lucky you're not there. You made a choice to run cross country. It's a freedom and I want you to run well.'"

If that sounds a lot like Vigil, it's probably because Shay really was a lot like his coach. For Vigil, losing Shay was like losing a son. Instead of flying back to Arizona the next day, Vigil instead flew to Ypsilanti, Michigan, to comfort Shay's parents and to help with funeral arrangements. He called Caroline to let her know he would be gone an extra week.

"I still get tears when I think about it," Vigil said. "The hardest thing for me was to give his eulogy." Quoted in a story that appeared in *The Denver Post*, Vigil honored Shay during the funeral by saying: "You choose to be poor, average, or excellent at what you do. We all knew Ryan chose to be excellent."

Two weeks after returning home from Shay's funeral, Vigil received a phone call from Tom White, the former runner who nearly lost his foot in an accident the summer before the start of his senior year at Adams State.

In the 26 years since his accident, White had taught himself to run again, though his crooked leg created a noticeable limp in his gait. White was operating a successful medical practice in Buena Vista, Colorado, where he also landed the job as head coach of the high school cross country team.

"Coach, I need your advice," White said as Vigil answered the phone. White then went into the story of how his leg hurt constantly and he was no longer able to jog with his team.

"Tom, I know what you're thinking," Vigil said. "Visit with your wife and call me back in a week."

White called Vigil back a week later and he says, "Coach, I've decided to amputate my leg so I can run again."

Weeks later, after a surgeon in Denver took White's lower left limb, he sat in his hospital bed and looked through catalogs of prosthetic legs. Scores of his former teammates at Adams State and athletes from his high school team showed up to be with him. *The Denver Post* learned of his story and sent a reporter. NBC Dateline sent a camera crew. His journey was being documented by a reporter from *Runner's World*.

"When the TV crew showed up, they were feeling sorry for him," Vigil said. "But Tom was motivating them. He said, 'Don't feel sorry for me. Don't you guys understand that I'll be able to run again.' Tom White was dying to run the way he used to run."

It took nearly a year for White to adjust to his new running leg, a blade runner made of titanium. But once he did, he was eager to go.

"After my amputation, I got fast again," White said. "I won the Colorado age group 10-mile state championship with a time of 67 minutes. That's not a fast time for a college runner, but for a 50-year-old guy, that's pretty good."

Since his amputation, White has run several marathons, trail runs, and road races. "The thing that's hilarious is that when I go out to run, I get so much attention, and I feel goofy about it because I really don't deserve this much attention just because of my leg," he said. "I have been to marathons and there will be these big Marine guys and they're like, 'Dude!' I'm like, 'Well, OK man,' but I don't feel like I deserve that.

"Honestly, I don't do it because I'm trying to prove something. I do it just because I want to be out there running too, and that is the only way for me to do it. I think that's what Coach Vigil gave me at Adams State. Because, you know, as much as the competitions were cool, I just really missed running with the guys in Carroll's Woods, or the times that we ran across the river and got all wet and our tights froze as we were running back to Plachy Hall…"

Does anyone think Joe Vigil cares much about a win-loss record as a coach? It's unmistakably clear that he doesn't. Joe Newton. Ryan Shay. Kim McConnell. Tom White. His students from the 1950s. Their stories and their friendships—and those of many others like them—are the victories that Vigil most treasures.

"You have to love and respect the way Tom White was thinking," Vigil said, "because he was living right…and he had a plan."

15

STILL
GOING...

*I*t's early December 2018 in Green Valley, Arizona, and Vigil
has spent most of an unusually chilly Saturday running
errands, swimming laps, and barbecuing hamburgers before
settling in to his recliner to watch college football. The South-
eastern Conference championship is the day's marquee game,
featuring No. 1–ranked Alabama and legendary coach Nick
Saban against No. 4 Georgia in a much-hyped rematch of the
2017 national championship game, which Alabama won 26-23.

Late in the third quarter, Georgia has the upper hand. They
are ahead 28-14 and the Bulldog defense has just knocked Alabama starting quarterback Jalen Hurts out of the game. It looks
bleak for the defending national champs. Then, backup quarterback Tua Tagovailoa comes in and, on his second pass of the
game, throws a 51-yard laser for a touchdown. Alabama closes
the gap to 28-21.

"Oh, boy," Vigil says. "If Nick Saban can pull this off, he'll be
the king of Alabama."

Surely Vigil is joking, because if anybody would know about
beating the odds, it would be him. If anybody would know about

great comebacks and winning with depleted resources, it would be Joe Vigil.

So, it's safe to wonder: could it be that he meant to say *when* Saban pulls off the win…? Because, of course, that's what happened. Tagovailoa—whose uncle, coincidentally, is an assistant football coach at Adams State—rallied his team for three unanswered touchdowns and Alabama won 35-28.

"Well, that game sure lived up to all the hype," a satisfied Vigil says as he turns off the TV and heads to bed. It's just after 9 p.m. and Vigil is not normally awake this late; his internal alarm will get him up at 4 a.m.

These days, Vigil's life is a bit more relaxed than in the years when he coached at Adams State, though it's plenty busy. He's still up studying before the sun rises. His phone still rings constantly throughout the day. He still has workouts to plan and athletes to coach. He travels regularly, so there are arrangements to make, clothes to pack, schedules to juggle.

"I decided a long time ago that our lives are not going to completely slow down if he has his way," said his wife, Caroline. "He has things planned every day for us to do. He's on the phone a lot with people who have questions. He also makes the workouts for his athletes. He works in his office. I try to support him every way I can in keeping things up because I've decided he is so happy doing what he does that it would really be a shame for him to quit coaching."

The Vigils' Arizona home is a comfortable one-story stucco located in a gated retirement community. Most of the yard is in a classic xeriscape desert landscape, except for a small patch of grass and a row of vigilantly pruned, colorful flowers that line the backyard patio. Five Olympic rings adorn the top of a two-car garage, which contains a few dozen neatly stacked boxes, many of those containing volumes of pictures and souvenirs from a lifetime of precious memories. In a far corner is a bench press rack, with 90 pounds loaded onto the bar. "It's not much weight," Vigil says, "but I'll do three sets of ten repetitions, two or three times a week."

Inside the house, Vigil's office sits just to the left of the front-door entrance, with separate work areas and desktop computers for him and Caroline. Dozens of books fill the large bookcase, and Vigil has hung certificates signifying his academic degrees and several coaching honors, all neatly framed. His desk is tidy, but stacks of papers and a half-dozen books dotting the desk's perimeter reveal a truth that this area is likely one of the busiest in the house.

A relaxing living room with a chair and two inviting sofas looks out through large picture windows to the backyard. The modern kitchen is bright and cheery. An adjacent room with additional cozy seating fills the rest of the open-concept living space. The house represents Joe and Caroline: humble, yet stylish.

"They're certainly a power couple and they are so good at supporting each other," said Deena Kastor, who developed a special bond with Caroline while training with Vigil for nearly 15 years. "Caroline held down their house for so many years as Coach traveled and invested so many hours with his college and professional teams. Caroline has always been that rock and foundation of keeping up the household.

"I've got many great memories of sitting at their kitchen counter while Coach is chopping vegetables and Caroline and I are sipping glasses of wine, and listening to them reminiscing about trips in the past, or athletes in the past that have touched them, and their plans for the future. It's just so beautiful to see

Joe and Caroline Vigil in 2010.

how Caroline has supported Coach's travels and their lives together. They don't have children together, but I feel like they've had hundreds of children pass through their doors that she really has had to take under her wing and care for like a mother. And I was one of them."

Tom White, Vigil's former runner at Adams State, said the two have shared common ideals as well as lifestyles.

"With his integrity and his honesty, Coach Vigil is a very rich man," White said. "He has a comfortable house. He travels around the world. He has a beautiful wife that takes care of him. I don't mean to say that a wife is something you earn, but rather that by his integrity, he attracted another person of integrity, who enjoys the same kind of life and lifestyle. I think that is the best method in life. You can cheat. You can be greedy. You can try to play for the crowd and it may get you some places, but I don't think it gets you the qualities that really give you happiness."

On this particular weekend in December, Joe and Caroline are scrambling to complete their plans for a trip to Monaco, where Prince Albert and former Olympic gold medalist Sebastian Coe have summoned them to attend the annual awards banquet hosted by the International Association of Athletics Federations (IAAF, now known as World Athletics). Just over two weeks earlier, Vigil learned he would be receiving the IAAF Coaching Achievement Award, so the couple's plans for a cross-continent plane ride are coming together hurriedly.

Vigil has a handful of errands to run. The first stop is Chase Bank to get money for the upcoming trip. He is greeted by the receptionist, a loan officer, and another employee who call him 'Coach.' He reaches the teller, a young lady, who also knows him simply as 'Coach.' He takes care of his business, and as she counts out his money, she tells him her 21st birthday is coming up. "Well, what are you going to do?" Vigil asks.

"Just going out with friends," she responds.

"Well, have fun and be careful."

Vigil's next stop is Bon Voyage Travel to pick up his tickets. Three women are sitting at their desks and, almost in unison, they call out, "Hi Coach!" as Vigil comes through the door. He stops to greet each one and introduces his visitor that day. Then he sits with his agent and before the business begins, he asks how she and her family are doing.

"We're doing good," the travel agent says. "But I've got to tell you, my husband took that Vigilante shirt you gave me."

"Why did he do that?" Vigil asks.

"Well, he gets up early in the morning and takes our dog for a walk, and he likes to wear that shirt," she answers.

"What time does he get up?" Vigil asks.

"Five o'clock in the morning...every day," she says.

"Well, I think I like your husband. I've got to meet him some time. And I'll get you another shirt."

Tickets in hand, Vigil's next stop is the Safeway store across the parking lot. He grabs a few goods for dinner and heads to the checkout stand.

"Hi, Leti," he says as he puts his food on the conveyor belt.

"Hi, Coach," she says. Vigil introduces his visitor, and then cracks a joke aimed at the friendly cashier: "I don't even like her."

Leti laughs, too, and then proclaims: "That's why he's in here every day!"

Vigil goes about his day's errands in a manner reminiscent of how he used to meander through Alamosa for 70 years. He talks to most everybody, takes an interest in what they're doing, shares a little humor, and is always friendly. It's as if he simply uprooted his small hometown and moved it to southern Arizona. He interacts with people as though he has known them all his life.

Green Valley is located 35 miles north of the United States border with Mexico, about halfway between Nogales, Mexico, and Tucson, Arizona. That 63 miles of Interstate 19 is considered one of the most dangerous stretches of asphalt in the country. In a recent four-year period, there were 0.90 deaths per mile of roadway, according to the National Transportation Safety Board. It's also thought to be a major thoroughfare for drugs into the United States. In fiscal year 2016, the Tucson sector, which covers most of Arizona, accounted for nearly 60 percent of the drugs seized along the border outside of the ports of entry, according to the U.S. Customs and Border Protection agency; in other words, more than all other U.S. ports of entry combined.

The danger that lies on the adjacent highway, however, is far removed from the friendly Green Valley community, a highly desired location for retirees. In fact, an estimated 77 percent of Green Valley's 23,000 residents are living in retirement. Among the local attractions is the Titan Missile Museum, American's largest nuclear weapons museum.

After lunch and a nap, Vigil is ready for his afternoon workout. He heads to the outdoor swimming pool, about a five-minute drive from his home. He pulls up to the pool and points out that one of his good friends from Alamosa, Federal Appeals Court Judge Carlos Lucero, lives across the street. Like Vigil, Lucero was born in Antonito, graduated from Adams State College, and has never forgotten his humble background. In addition to his service as a federal judge, he and his wife, Dorothy, established the Lucero Project at Adams State, a foundation that provides funds to help college students get an education while working with underprivileged youth.

It is about 3 p.m., and normally Vigil has several workout partners, mostly women, who meet to swim laps together. But it's a cool day for Green Valley—about 50 degrees and overcast— and no one has come out to swim...except Vigil.

"A bunch of creampuffs," Vigil mutters. "They need to get tough!" He laughs and gets dressed.

In the pool, Vigil is a bit more serious. First a warmup of treading water for about 10 minutes. Then swimming 10 laps, up and back across the 25-meter pool, with scant rest in between. He powers through the first one, taking the time to strike up a conversation during the short break. Then a second one. And a third, and a fourth...

By the time Vigil reaches the eighth lap, there is very little talking going on. He's breathing much more heavily, and his eyes have become laser focused on the wall at the end of the pool. Big deep breath...eight laps down. Just like his athletes dig deep to finish repeat miles or repeat quarters, Vigil is keeping himself locked in. Nine laps down. His eyes are open wide as he takes a big deep breath. And another. Then, after a quick glance at the wall on the other end, he plunges headlong through the water. Ten laps...done.

After a cool-down and a shower, Vigil heads home to grill hamburgers, topped with a little bit of *chile verde* (green chile). Vigil makes guacamole, "with a squirt of fresh lemon," to go with tortilla chips. For dessert, there is leftover chocolate cake from the 89th birthday party that Caroline and his daughter Peggy held for him five days earlier.

Vigil's life in Arizona, though, has never pulled him too

far from his beloved Alamosa and the San Luis Valley. By the mid-2000s, a change in leadership in the Adams State athletic department helped to bridge the rift that had formed years earlier, heralding a concerted effort by the university to recognize Vigil for his contributions.

In 2010, Adams State announced it was honoring Vigil by placing a bronze statue at the entrance to Rex Field, the stadium that is home to the track and field and football teams. The weekend included an alumni reunion attended by many of Vigil's former athletes from Alamosa High School and Adams State.

Before the statue was unveiled, Vigil, then 80 years old, told the gathering, "They usually dedicate bronze statues to dead people, but I'm not done yet. I have more to learn and a lot to do. If you make one person's life better in your lifetime, then you've had a great life."

Joe Vigil standing next to the bronze statue put up in his honor at Adams State University in 2010. The statue was initially placed in front of Rex Field but currently sits at the site of the finish line for the 1968 U.S. Olympic Marathon Trials.

Then, as the crowd cheered, Vigil asked his longtime friend Boogie Romero to do the honors of unveiling the six-foot bronze statue.

The night before, Vigil was feted in front of a crowded ballroom of more than 1,000 friends, family, athletes, adorers...and even by one of his adversaries.

"As I walked into this room today, I got a lot of bad memories," said Duane Vandenbusche, Vigil's good friend and the former coach of rival Western State College. "I see all these great athletes out in the audience, and up and down the line, I remember how I got my ass kicked for 20–25 years. And I'll tell you this: I'm probably the only guy from Western State College to ever appear at a distinguished gathering like this at Adams State College."

Vandenbusche continued: "These are the things I will always remember about Joe Vigil. Number one, he always got the best out of his athletes. Mediocrity was not an option. Number two, he has this continual pursuit of excellence. Sir Isaac Newton once said, 'I only see myself as a little child walking the beach, and every once in a while picking up a pretty shell while the vast ocean of unexplored knowledge lay in front of me.' That's Joe Vigil. There's always more knowledge to be learned.

"Number three, I'll remember his great belief in the saying of Willa Cather, the great western writer, that the end is nothing, but the road is all. The journey is what has been important to Joe Vigil. And number four, he told me 40 years ago when we met in my kitchen that in cross country, [the Rudyard Kipling quote that] the strength of the pack is the wolf, and the strength of the wolf is the pack. Every team in the country is one runner short of being a national champion. You have got to have the depth."

That same evening, Randy Wilbur, a senior physiologist with the U.S. Olympic Training Center's athlete performance laboratory in Colorado Springs, lauded Vigil for 30 years as a "goodwill ambassador of the United States," having lectured in 29 countries and territories on all six of the world's habitable continents.

Let Me Tell You a Story

Duane Vandenbusche, who won two NAIA and 10 NCAA Division II national titles as head coach of the Western State men's and women's cross country teams, called Joe Vigil a great friend.

"Whenever we were at national meets, we'd always go out to get a bite to eat and we'd talk about things," Vandenbusche said. "I'd spend an hour at a time with Joe; a lot of times we wouldn't talk about track or cross country. We would talk about how we grew up and the ethics that everybody ought to have in their lives.

"We have a tremendous friendship. Joe calls me and I call him. We talk about how things are going, now that we're both semi-retired. I'm still teaching and giving a lot of talks, and Joe's still doing his thing at age 90. We have never slowed; I would not be good in retirement and neither would Joe. That's just the way we grew up. I never wanted to sit on my ass and play golf and that kind of stuff. I want to be productive and Joe wants to be productive also. I think both of us still are."

Wilbur rattled off the countries: Australia, Belgium, Brazil, Canada, China, Cuba, England, Ethiopia, Finland, Germany, Ireland, Italy, Jamaica, Japan, Kenya, Korea, Mexico, Morocco, New Zealand, Poland, Portugal, Puerto Rico, Russia, Spain, Sweden, Switzerland, Tanzania, the United States, and Venezuela. Including his travels to coach athletes, Vigil says he has been to 47 countries in his lifetime.

"In each of those countries, Coach has brought his beautiful smile, his genuine love of people, and his unselfish willingness to teach and share knowledge for the purpose of helping others, especially those less fortunate, to become better athletes and ultimately respected leaders within their nations," Wilbur said. "Many of you in this room might agree with me when I say I believe Coach's overall influence as an ambassador of the United States has been more significant than many presidents and secretaries of state.

"In 1896, Baron Pierre de Coubertin, the founder of the modern Olympic Games, said these words that remind me of Coach Vigil: 'There is no higher ideal for the human race than promoting international peace and understanding through sport.'"

Vigil has regularly returned to Alamosa since 2010, often to help with summer cross country camps at Adams State or reunions with his former runners. The trip from Green Valley is 600 miles; Joe and Caroline share the driving duties.

When Vigil is in Alamosa, the most likely time and place to find him is any morning at the Campus Cafe, his favorite restaurant ever since he was a teacher and coach across the street at the former high school building. The place hasn't changed much since the 1960s, with steel chairs and wood tabletops, and wood paneling covering the walls. The current owners, Terry and Fidella Gibbs, have adorned the walls with more than 60 plaques and trophies that Adams State's men's and women's teams have won in the past 25 years. There are pictures of Vigil, Pat Porter, Deena Kastor, Adams State's 1992 team that posted a perfect score at nationals, and others. The Gibbs have hung jerseys worn by great runners who trained in Alamosa, and even scholar-athlete awards won by Adams State teams of yesteryear.

Vigil is never alone when he's at the Campus Cafe. In fact, he is often holding court at the biggest table in the place, surrounded by several of his former athletes. As the locals walk in, they often greet him, and he in turn offers a friendly smile or story. On one day, Lisa Wilson, an Adams State employee and cheerleader at Alamosa High School in the 1980s, comes by to say hi, and Vigil is reminded that he promised to drop a picture by her office on campus. "I'll get that to you later today," he tells her.

"His loyalty to the San Luis Valley does run deep," Kastor said. "I think of the communal tables in the middle of the Campus Cafe where it didn't matter if it was a professor sitting down or a rancher or one of his athletes or a shop owner in town. He would sit down and listen and give advice if needed. And I think people trusted and respected him because of that."

The gulf between Alamosa's Haves and Have-Nots is still evident, and in fact may have grown wider in the years since Vigil played football and basketball on Ninth Street's gravel roads. The south side of town bears the scars of poverty. Just three doors down from where Vigil's daughters once staged track and field meets in the backyard is the town's homeless shelter, a haven for those down on their luck. Two blocks away and one block south of the railroad tracks, the Green Spot—a local nursery—has not changed the marquee outside the business for at least a year: "Stop the Meth and Heroine," it reads. There are many hardworking, honest people on Alamosa's south side, but the town's recent growth to the west and north has left a seismic gap in opportunity on the south end of town.

Vigil said that one of his greatest memories was returning to Alamosa in 2018 to celebrate the 50th anniversary of the U.S. Olympic Marathon Trials, the first time ever that the United States selected Olympic marathoners based on a single, head-to-head race.

"The running culture in Alamosa was just about nonexistent in 1968," Vigil said in a story written for the Road Runners Club of America by American journalist Amby Burfoot. "It was an agricultural and ranch community 50 years ago, and it still is today. It's unbelievable what the Trials did for the town, the college, the state, and also for me. I knew little at the time, but I loved running and physiology. The Trials pointed me in my life's direction."

In 2018, the folks in Alamosa who didn't get a chance to experience the 1968 Trials got a sense of what it was like. They turned out in the hundreds to watch about 300 runners—including several of the former elites who competed for an Olympic spot in 1968—line up for a five-mile race around "The Loop," the same course that was used 50 years earlier. The event ended near Plachy Hall, adjacent to a stone commemorating the 1968 race. The bronze statue of Vigil marked the finish line—a year earlier it had been moved 70 yards from its previous location near Rex Field.

In fall 2019, Vigil was invited to speak to a gathering of U.S. federal judges in Santa Fe, New Mexico. "At first, I didn't know what the hell I was going to talk to them about," Vigil said. "But my message was that it's everybody's responsibility to make this a better world in which to live.

"I spun off of that and made some comparisons to what a lawyer and a judge go through to get their education, and I told them about what I've done to get my education."

Vigil told the story of Javier Sotomayor, the Cuban high jumper who cleared 8 feet, 1/2 inch to set the world record in Salamanca, Spain, in 1993. Vigil and Sotomayor were friends, and the Cuban told Vigil how as a 10-year-old he watched countryman Alberto Juantorena win Olympic gold in 1976.

"Sotomayor had a passion and dedicated his life to 17 years of training so he also could bring glory to his country," Vigil said. "Then, I asked those judges: 'How many years have you been in school?' I told them Sotomayor's story and others like that are what motivate me to get up every day and study a little bit to learn something new. It's a lifelong pursuit of learning, or committing yourself to a passion."

Caroline Vigil (left) and U.S. Supreme Court Justice Sonia Sotomayor (center) with Joe Vigil following his talk to a group of federal judges in Santa Fe in September 2019.

Among the judges in the audience that day was U.S. Supreme Court Justice Sonia Sotomayor, the first Hispanic ever appointed to the nation's highest court. Sotomayor was enthralled by Vigil's story because of her common last name.

"So she asks me if she could use that story when she speaks," Vigil said. "I told her, 'Sure...and you can even tell people he is your nephew!'"

Earlier that year, Vigil spoke to Adams State's spring graduates. In her introduction, Adams State president Cheryl Lovell pointed to Vigil's recent recognition by the IAAF for a Coaching Achievement Award, presented by Prince Albert of Monaco.

"When I shared with Coach Vigil that we wanted to award him an honorary doctorate in human performance and physical education, I said I felt a little bit embarrassed because we don't have a prince to make that presentation," Lovell said to a handful of laughs.

Vigil responded: "The award in Monaco was nice, but a recognition from Adams State is more important to me. If it weren't for Adams State, nothing would have been possible for me. Adams State has allowed me to do everything I have done in my life."

Vigil was asked to speak for 15 minutes; he spoke for 32 minutes, yet no one seemed to mind. He received a standing ovation for nearly a minute afterward. What he said that day was a lively reflection of his life, one that has been spent in service of others:

> *I can't remember what was said at my commencement address (65 years earlier), but I can tell you that what starts here can change the world. It happened here. We established a coaching education program right here in Plachy Hall, room 101, that has been declared by the International Olympic Committee and the IAAF as the number one coaching education program in the world. You already have a head start in what you want to do because you are an American. You're the luckiest people in the world. You constitute 5 percent of the population. Ninety-five percent of the population does not have the privilege you have. There are two axioms: You have the freedom to choose what you want to do, and what you want to be, and what you want to become. That's a birthright in America. People in other countries don't have this privilege. The second axiom is that people in the United*

States have the freedom to choose how good you want to be. Do you want to be average, poor, or do you want to be excellent? What is your goal?

You have these freedoms, but you have to develop a passion. I don't know what your passions are; maybe you have one or two or maybe you have a half dozen. But have a purpose in your life; pursue something.

This is the challenge you are going to be faced with—good, bad, and indifferent. You've got to have courage, people. You have to keep going under the most difficult situations that you are confronted with. You have to learn to overcome anything that is thrown up against you. You can accomplish whatever you set out to do if you follow the right plan and you live right.

When I taught at the high school, I used to go into the coffee room, and I would hear people say, 'I don't know what I'm going to do.' They had no goal. They were mad. They didn't like their jobs. They complained about being in a rut. They didn't have a plan. They thought it was too hard to start all over again. And they lacked the confidence to try something else.

The main reason that people don't accomplish things is because of their indecision. Decide what it is you want to do and go after it. Think about this: the average American will encounter 10,000 people in their lives. As you go out and start meeting people, you will encounter 10,000 people. If every one of you changes the life of 10 people, and those 10 will change the lives of 10 others, well in five generations—125 years—you will have influenced the lives of 800 million people, which is more than twice the population that we have in the United States today.

And it can start right here. It's our responsibility to

make this world a better place, as you well know. We have so much chaos out there today, that we don't know if we're coming or going. But you have a responsibility; make it a better place to live in. We need that more than ever, people.

I have a little cliché everybody should follow: eat as though you were a poor man, do endurance training daily, and don't let your mind go to seed. Remember this saying from George Washington Carver: How far you go in life depends on your being tender with the young, compassionate with the aged, sympathetic with the striving, and tolerant of the weak and strong. Because some day in your life, you will have been all of these.

Epilogue

STORIES FOR
THE AGES

*I*n 2019, Joe Vigil was asked to list his top five memories from a life and coaching career that has taken him to all corners of the world.

No. 5

Number five on the list was the three-day celebration in Alamosa to honor the 50th anniversary of the 1968 U.S. Olympic Trials marathon.

"The Olympic Trials were a start to running in Alamosa at the championship level," Vigil said. "The people who came in influenced me a lot; I learned a lot from them. That growth pattern just continued for 50 years."

Many of the country's greatest male runners from the 1960s and 1970s attended the 2018 reunion, including George Young (who won the race in 1968) and Kenny Moore (the runner-up in 1968). Olympic gold medalists Frank Shorter (1972 marathon) and Billy Mills (1964 10,000 meters) were there. Nearly two-dozen athletes who ran the 1968 race came back to celebrate.

"To have these guys come back and talk fondly of the experience they had 50 years ago, and the way the community responded to that, was just so beautiful," Vigil said. "As Amby Burfoot (one of the participants, who later became an editor for *Runner's World* magazine) stated, Alamosa became the center of the running universe."

Among all the running royalty, Vigil made a special mention to his good friend Boogie Romero, noting how his loyalty and hard work contributed greatly to the success of Adams State and the growth of running in Alamosa.

"That reunion," Vigil said, "was all the successes we had over 50 years wrapped into one bundle."

No. 4

The fourth-greatest memory Vigil listed was the 2004 Olympic marathon in Athens, Greece, when athletes he had helped to train won gold, silver, and bronze.

Stefano Baldini of Italy, who trained in Alamosa as a teen-ager in the 1990s, won the Olympic gold in the men's marathon, while Meb Keflezighi (one of the runners training with Vigil at Mammoth Lakes, California) won silver.

Deena Kastor, who Vigil had trained for the previous nine years, won bronze in the women's marathon.

"I had a great relationship with all three of them," Vigil said. "Stefano came to Alamosa to train and run with Deena. When we moved to Mammoth, Stefano came there with the entire Italian team. I had a great relationship with their coach."

Vigil called Keflezighi's finish "a little bit of a surprise. From the get-go, he was up there and never faltered. He just kept plugging away and catching people."

For Kastor, the Olympic medal was the symbolic moment of a great athlete-coach relationship. "There's the cliché of the loneliness of the long-distance runner," Kastor said. "Luckily, I have never felt that way. I've felt nothing but being part of a team…My job on race day really was just to give back to Coach and my team for being there and encouraging me and giving good advice and taking advice. Because when I'm passing on that advice Coach gave to me, it's like paying it forward, but more importantly it's reinforcing the values that Coach taught me."

No. 3

Vigil said the third-best memory of his life was having coached 26 individual national cross country champions over a 27-year period.

He coached 10 collegiate champions: Sam Montoya (1979), Pat Porter (1980, 1981), Robbie Hipwood (1985), Rick Robirds (1986, 1987, and 1989), Craig Dickson (1988), Phil Castillo (1992), and Shane Healy (1993).

In addition, Porter won eight U.S. senior national titles (1982–1989), and Kastor won eight senior women's championships (1997–2002 and 2006 at 8000 meters, and 1999 at 4000 meters).

"All of those runners trained in Alamosa, Colorado…Can you imagine that?" Vigil said. "We had 26 national champions in cross country from one town. That's got to be some kind of record, right?

"They were all tough competitors and they all paid the price needed to succeed."

No. 2

The second-greatest memory for Vigil is the 1992 Adams State men's cross country team that posted a perfect score at the NCAA Division II national championships—the only perfect score ever at a collegiate national meet.

"I was the coach of that team, and I was there," Vigil said, "but I still can't believe what I saw that day."

Adams State's five scoring runners crossed the finish line just four seconds apart over the rain-soaked, 10,000-meter course. The perfect race capped an imperfect season in which Adams State overcame adversity and heartbreak.

"During the race, they sensed what their duty was: to be able to touch each other," Vigil said. "They kept catching each other until they were all together at the end."

No. 1

And Vigil's No. 1 memory? For anyone who has met the man, or heard about the man, or read this book, it's certainly no surprise.

"My greatest memory is the camaraderie we developed among our people," Vigil said. "No matter if they ran in the 1970s or in the 1990s, our people all had a love and respect for each other. They all came to a program that had a little culture, and they all wanted to contribute to that culture. No matter how bad they felt during a practice or a race, they would go and try to do their best, to make the team better. It was never about themselves; it was about the team and trying to keep the championship record alive.

"When I recruited kids, they were part of the program. I wanted them to be successful. Many Division I teams are allowed to carry only so many runners, so they have to cut some others. But there are kids who develop late and they can also contribute to your team. I remember one of my runners, Andrew Medina, who tried to make the team for three years. Finally, in his fourth year, he made it—and he earned All-American in cross country."

The Vigilantes, as his athletes are called, routinely get together for reunions in Alamosa. Many of Vigil's athletes from Alamosa High School also attend those get-togethers.

They bring their kids and grandkids or the athletes they are now coaching or their parents and friends to meet a man who connects them all with his positive spirit and incomparable compassion.

Maybe then it's fitting that a book about a master storyteller should end with a voice that is not his, since the tens of thousands of people he has influenced are now integrating those tales into their own lives, infusing them in others, and reminding all of us about the true value of stories.

"If you talk to Coach and listen to his stories, they are always about other people," said Larry Jeffryes, the high school and college star for Vigil's track and field teams in the 1960s. "He's always talking about this person or that person he met, or he's talking about someone over in Finland…people he's met or trained. Very few of his stories are 'I did this' or 'I did that.' He'll talk about that high school team or that relay, or those first runners. I am not sure if that's humility, but it comes from a deep interest, respect, and care for the people he's worked with and the people he's met. I think that is where it comes from more than anything else. I guess that's humility. He's other-person focused.

"We know he had a huge role in what we—his athletes and students—were able to do and become. We know that, and maybe he knows that at a certain level, too. But he doesn't take credit for it."

Appendix A

THE VIGIL FILE

A summary of Joe I. Vigil's accomplishments and awards (1954–2020)

Alamosa High School (12 years)

1 state championship team (1963) and three-time state runner-up

Adams State College (29 years)

NAIA (1965–1991) and NCAA Division II (1992–1993)

19 national collegiate team championships (cross country and track and field)
425 All-Americans
87 individual national champions
14-time national Coach of the Year
95-percent graduation rate for student-athletes during his collegiate coaching career
Professor emeritus, Adams State College (1986)

Elite Athletes (20 years)

Team USA California (2001–present)

47 individual senior champions
17 national records

20 podium medals at the Olympic Games (track and field) and
World Championships (cross country and track and field)
Only active coach with medalists at the World Championships
in both cross country and track and field (as of 2020)
Three athletes ranked No. 1 in the world
Trained and coached 22 Olympians

Patriarch of American Cross Country Running

20 World Cross Country team and individual medals*
19 NAIA and NCAA Division II cross country team
championships*
14-time national Coach of the Year*
10 individual national collegiate cross country champions*
8 senior men's USA Track & Field (USATF) cross country individual champions*
8 senior women's USATF cross country individual champions*
7-time USA World cross country coach*
2 women's individual cross country silver medals (World
Championships)
2 women's team cross country silver medals (World
Championships)
1 men's individual cross country bronze medal (World
Championships)

• *U.S. national record*

International Head Coaching Experience

2 Olympic Games (1988 and 2008)
4 Pan American Games
1 World University Games
1 World Cup
7 World Cross Country Championships

Coaching Education

One of four "founding fathers" of USATF Coaching Education
(1981)
Founding national director, USATF Coaching Education
(1981–1989)
The Athletics Congress (TAC) and USATF American Coaching
Education programs (1981–present)
Presented clinics in 43 states, 29 countries, and six continents
High-altitude consultant for nine national federations
High-altitude consultant for more than 300 individual athletes

Hall of Fame Inductions

NAIA Track and Field Coaches Association (1978)
Colorado High School Coaches Association (1989)
Colorado Sports Hall of Fame (1991)
Lasse Virén Foundation Hall of Fame (1992). The Lasse Virén
Foundation honors the former Finnish distance runner, who
swept gold medals in the 5000 and 10,000-meter runs at the
1972 and 1976 Olympics.
U.S. Track & Field and Cross Country Coaches Association (1999)
Adams State University Hall of Fame (2000)
Rocky Mountain Athletic Conference Coaches Hall of Fame (2005)
Road Runners Club of America Hall of Fame (2005)
NCAA Cross Country Coaches Hall of Fame (2007)
Adams State University Educators Hall of Fame (2015)
Latino Leadership Institute Hall of Fame (2016)

Awards

The Athletics Congress USA President's Award (1989)
U.S. Olympic & Paralympic Committee Doc Counsilman
Science Award (2005, 2012). Recognizes individuals who

apply science to sport; Vigil is the only person to have won this award twice.

USATF Master Coach Award (1993)

USATF H. Browning Ross Service and Leadership Award (2001). Recognizes individuals for service to the sport of long-distance running.

USATF Fred Wilt Award (2001). Recognizes a coach who has a distinguished record marked by sustained, exceptional performance.

USATF Coaching Education Lifetime Achievement Award (2005)

Tributes

Outstanding Leadership, State College System of Colorado (1973)

Colorado General Assembly Award of Leadership (1987)

U.S. House of Representatives, Washington, DC (2000)

U.S. Olympic Committee (2010)

USATF Legend Coach (2015)

International Association of Athletics Federations (IAAF) Continental Area Legend Coach (2015)

U.S. Track & Field and Cross Country Coaches Association George Dales Award (2018). Recognizes coaches who have enhanced the profession of coaching cross country and track and field.

IAAF Coaching Achievement Award, Monaco (2018)

Namesake Honor Awards (given annually)

Colorado High School Activities Association: Joe I. Vigil State High School Cross Country Award recognizing the state's Coach of the Year.

USATF: Joe Vigil Sport Science Coaching Education Award, for academic excellence and coaching

Peak to Peak Charter School (Lafayette, Colorado): Joe I. Vigil Award for Distance Running and Academic Excellence

U.S. Track & Field and Cross Country Coaches Association: Joe I. Vigil Award. Honors the NCAA Division II men's cross country national Coach of the Year.

Academic Degrees

Bachelor of arts, biology, Adams State College (1954)

Master of arts, education, Adams State College (1959)

Master of science, chemistry, Colorado College (1964)

Doctorate, University of New Mexico (1972)

Honorary doctoral degree, Universidad Autónoma de Zacatecas, Mexico (1976)*

Postdoctoral study, Toledo University (1979) and Louisiana Polytechnic Institute (1979)

Honorary doctoral degree, human performance and physical education, Adams State University (2019)

* In 1975, Vigil became friends with several Mexican coaches during the Pan American Games. The following year, he was invited to give a summer lecture series on coaching in Zacatecas, Mexico. The university there subsequently granted him an honorary doctorate for his service to Mexico's coaches.

Appendix B

OLYMPIC ATHLETES WHO WERE COACHED OR ADVISED BY JOE I. VIGIL (1968-2016)

Athletes listed between 1968 and 2000 trained in Alamosa, Colorado. Athletes listed between 2004 and 2012 trained at Mammoth Lakes, California. Athletes listed in 2016 trained at Big Bear Lake, California.

Olympic Year	Site	Athlete	Country	Event
1968	Mexico City	Martin Ande	Nigeria	Marathon
1980	Moscow	Antoni Niemczak	Poland	10,000m
1984	Los Angeles	Pat Porter	United States	10,000m
1984	Los Angeles	Martti Vainio	Finland	10,000m
1984	Los Angeles	Juma Ikangaa	Tanzania	Marathon
1988	Seoul	Pat Porter	United States	10,000m
1992	Barcelona	Julie Jenkins	United States	800m
1996	Atlanta	Shane Healy	Ireland	1500m

Olympic Year	Site	Athlete	Country	Event
1996	Atlanta	Martin Johns	New Zealand	1500m
2000	Sydney	Deena Kastor	United States	10,000m
2004	Athens	Deena Kastor	United States	Marathon
2004	Athens	Meb Keflezighi	United States	Marathon
2004	Athens	Jen Rhines	United States	10,000m
2008	Beijing	Deena Kastor	United States	Marathon
2008	Beijing	Jen Rhines	United States	5000m
2008	Beijing	Meb Keflezighi	United States	Marathon
2008	Beijing	Abdi Abdirahman	United States	Marathon
2008	Beijing	Ryan Hall	United States	Marathon
2008	Beijing	Ian Dobson	United States	5000m
2012	London	Diego Estrada	United States	Marathon
2016	Rio de Janeiro	Brenda Martinez	United States	1500m
2016	Rio de Janeiro	Boris Berian	United States	800m

Appendix C

In 1993, Adams State College graduate assistant coach Jay Birmingham documented a full year's worth of notes, anecdotes, and philosophical stories that he picked up while working under Joe I. Vigil. The following outlines select portions of that 21-page document, titled "Vigilante: The Legacy of Joe Vigil," exactly as they were compiled by Birmingham, including direct quotes from Coach organized by category. They are shared here with Birmingham's permission.

VIGILANTE: The Legacy of Joe Vigil

Compiled by Jay Birmingham (Autumn 1993)

Vigilante, (vee-hill-ahn-teh), Spanish noun; (a) guard, watchman; (b) keeper of the faith; (c) a follower of the teachings of Joe I. Vigil, a coach of runners at Adams State College, Alamosa, Colorado.

INTRODUCTION

I had heard of Joe Vigil, but had never met him until a blizzardy Saturday in mid-October 1991. My wife and I drove into

Alamosa after cancellation of a triathlon just 26 miles away. Adams State College was hosting a cross country meet against a half-dozen teams on its Carroll's Woods course, an undulating path along the Rio Grande river. The Adams State team stripped to their green-and-gold shorts and green singlets and proceeded to demolish the field, except for a dozen athletes also dressed in green whose shirts read, 'Vigilante.' These runners were ASC alumni, still competing, still running very fast and very tough.

One year later, I began an association with Joe Vigil—teacher, exercise physiologist, coach and inspirational leader of Adams State's world-famous distance running program. This association, as Dr. Vigil's assistant, has led to the collection of the notes, anecdotes and philosophy that follow. No booklet could do justice in capturing the essence and aura of the man; the task is too immense and each of us has had just a small amount of his time.

My intent is to refresh the memory of each of you who has known Joe Vigil, to be reminded of his ravenous appetite for life, to be re-inspired to strive for more than the commonplace, to live the best life possible. In a word, to remain forever a Vigilante, a keeper of the faith.

> "Adams State cross country—the Long Green Line—is a family made from the blood, sweat and tears of every person who has run for Coach Vigil. Every time we toe the starting line, our family is with us."
> —James Seefeldt, All American

> "Whatever problems might exist, I have to help my team win a national championship."
> —Phillip Castillo, 1992 national champion, cross country; 1993 national runner-up, cross country

TEAM

"Don't ever think of yourself over the team. Do the best job you can today for your team."

"You have something to get up for every morning. You're loved. You have a team."

"Be always compassionate of your teammates."

"Run for the good of the team. You must be with the team. You have a responsibility as a team member."

"You have a synergistic effect when you work together. You are better as a team than you can possibly be as an individual."

"Western State had their chance and they muffed it (ASC won the conference meet 25-30). I knew we were vulnerable from our competition at Arkansas and our exhausting training. It was the synergistic effect of seven guys working together to achieve a common goal."

"The bond that develops between people is based upon the joy of shared effort."

"There are no guarantees. Those of you not in the top seven, be ready to move up. If you're not dreaming about what's possible, you're in the wrong place."

"Run for something. Do the best you can possibly do—for the team. Run for something other than yourself. Your pride is on the line."

"A flashlight, unused in a drawer, can't always respond when called upon. It's meant to be used. You must always be ready to 'turn on' when you are called upon."

"Don't relegate yourself to a pecking order from which you cannot move."

LIFESTYLE

"Get up in the morning and live right."

"Take care of the process."

"This is not a program for a non-committed person. You can't afford not to be at your best all the time."

"If you're up one day, down the next, something's wrong with your lifestyle. You're not paying the price to be the best you can be!"

"You've got to pay the price now. Twenty years ago, thirty years, even a hundred years ago, the guys who won were willing to pay the price."

"Believe in yourself. Be upbeat. Positive. Live the athlete's lifestyle 24 hours a day."

"Plan your day—live your life—like a winner."

"Where do you find the time to criticize, to judge others, to complain? You don't have the time."

"Lay it on the line every day of your life. If you don't, the day will come when you'll wish you had."

"Excellence becomes a style of life and not the exception."

"Avoid a roller coaster existence; inconsistency. Your lifestyle is the key."

"You can't separate excellence from right living."

"The biggest stressor is emotional stress. The biggest emotional stress is other people's weakness. If you are married, have a roommate or partner, plan to do 90% of the work; then if the other person does more than 10%, it's easier."

"Sometimes you work awfully hard at not being winners."

"The more dedicated you become, the more self-sufficient you get. You must believe. There is no excuse for not succeeding in what I have chosen to do."

"He who would ignite a fire in others must himself glow."

"Constantly remind yourself what you're supposed to do. Develop a sense of responsibility."

"Associate yourself with things positive. You don't have the strength and energy to associate with negative people."

"Great deeds are performed by individual people who have determined to accomplish something."

"If you apply all these ethical values to your abilities, you'll become a fountainhead of strength."

MISCELLANEOUS

"How did such a handsome coach get stuck with such an ugly bunch of runners?"

"*Repetitio est mater studiorum* (Latin)—Repetition is the Mother of Learning"

"What a beautiful day!"

"Let's go have a cup of coffee."

"When excellence is in sight, good is not enough!"

"In athletics, 1 + 1 = 2; not 1 + 1 = 5. You get exactly what you put into it."

COMPETING

"Never, never be afraid of competition. It will bring out the best in you, if you have it in you."

"He wanted to beat them; he wasn't thinking about himself or how he felt." (Referring to Shane Healy, who beat every member of the Arkansas cross country team at their own invitational, October 1993)

"Run with a vengeance."

"You guys have more than you're laying on the line."

"Don't ever run a race just to run it; give it your best shot."

"You're never going to find out what you can do if you don't stick your neck out."

"At the start, become mesmerized. The race is the only thing in your life that matters at that time."

"Nobody likes a noisy athlete. Prove yourself on the day of the race."

"If somebody passes you, don't pat them on the butt…let them know they've been in a race."

"Nobody should be able to break you in a race. Most races are won in the last mile. If you are up there with a mile to go, it is mental courage that prevails. If we lack courage, it will come out in the results."

"When the moment of truth comes, do the best you can, under whatever conditions you are faced with. Don't be reaching into Bag 13 for an excuse."

"Just race. The more you think, the more inhibitory the stimuli."

"You can't ever worry about how you feel. Become one with the race. Feel the desire to do something better than ever before."

"Everyone's going to be after our ass. We've been Number One all year! The only thing that counts is what we finish at the championship."

"During competition, think of nothing else. Be relentless. Have an unshatterable belief in what you're doing."

ADVERSITY

Regarding injuries: "Listen to your body, but don't wimp out! You can run with your injuries. Some of you have no pain tolerance."

"If something is bugging you—a sore head, a sore throat, a sore leg—you've got to work a little harder, that's all."

"Tom White has never had an excuse—for anything."

"There is no equality. You're going to lose sometimes. It's the person who learns to deal with his failures who becomes a success."

"When something is wrong with you, you can use it for an excuse, or you can try a little harder."

"When you sit back and develop a game plan of excuses, you're a loser."

"Mobilize your energies to overcome adverse environmental conditions. You have to be the master. You control your body."

"Don't let little things get to you."

AMERICA AND THE WORLD

"Ours is a narcissistic culture; Americans are egocentric."

"Americans have lost their courage—the courage to challenge to be the world's best."

"American culture as a whole stinks. There is apathy. No one is accountable. People have an excuse for everything."

"75% of the people wallow in mediocrity and self-pity. Only about 25% see life's difficulties as a challenge; they have direction, they have goals. Crowd into that upper 25%. Do the best job you know how."

"Compared to athletes in third world countries, Americans are lazy. They lack self discipline."

"Miminski (a Polish Olympian and 8:09 steeplechaser) is here in Alamosa to train. I want you to see it (being an Olympian) everyday in your mind. Do a little dreaming."

ATTITUDE

"Attitude is our magic."

"We are going to coach for excellence. We can get you ready physically. You have to get yourself together mentally."

"What does it take to place in the Olympics? Dedication. Commitment."

"Your success depends on your mental level of aspiration. If your standards are not high, you'll wallow in mediocrity."

"The committed will survive. The rest will be blown away like dust."

"Don't have 'druthers.' A true athlete will run in all conditions and think nothing of it."

"Be grateful for what you have."

"I'm concerned that some of you are not able to get to a higher level of thinking. Be introspective. Get into the run. Don't be worried about the pain, the fatigue, the pace. Get into your workout and give yourself to it. If you're scared about something, you're not going to do it."

"Be mesmerized. Get immersed in the process of the workout."

"You set your own limits by the way you think."

"It's cold and wet today for our miles. I hope we have bad weather every Thursday to make you tough."

"Don't let anybody drag you down. Some people out there are vampires; they'll drain you. Seek people who are positive."

"You have to let go. You can't hold onto the past and reach for the future at the same time. Look ahead. Don't lament your decisions."

"You have great capacities but weak minds. Train without placing limitations on yourself."

"Continue to strive. You can't accomplish it with a weak mind."

"Work harder at the workout you don't like. Work harder in a class that you don't like."

"You have endurance. You have muscular strength. Enjoy the joy of effort!"

"The spirit that moves you can be developed."

"The one thing that we cannot control is a passive mind. Be stronger mentally when dealing with adverse weather and fatigue. You've got backbones. You're tough. We're proud of you."

"People who have hardships—illnesses, toil, loneliness, problems—are constantly whittled away by death of the spirit.

We need to be rock-like; to be strong. The only way is to avoid being whittled away by negative people and negative lifestyles."

"Don't be satisfied. You are one in 4 billion!"

"Poor attitudes bring on diseases. Few people die of old age. They die from diseases of the spirit."

"Spirit—Vision—Personal challenge."

"Surround yourself with constructive positivity all the time."

"What is possible is all in your mind."

"Roger Bannister was asked, 'How did you become the first four-minute miler instead of someone else?' Bannister said, 'Others work as hard; others are more talented. I believe it rests in the quality of the mind. I believed I could be the one to do it.'"

"You make impossible happen by virtue of your drive."

"Some of you have not yet appreciated the strength you can derive from your mental capacity. Desire! You are the limiting factor. Be a potential realizer."

"Setbacks: It's your ability to come back which makes the difference."

"We all have a lot to learn about increasing our ambitions."

"Don't think (that) Castillo and Healy are lucky... They work, they listen to their bodies, they perform. You'll not reach your goals if you work hard just part of the time. You have to work hard all the time."

"This is not a scolding; just an analysis of the workout you did yesterday."

"You have all the power you need in that 1455 c.c.'s (your brain). It is an awesome force. You can't have any doubts about yourself."

"Dennis Conner, winner of America's Cup in sailing, put it this way: First, you have to make a commitment. Then, you have to commit yourself to the commitment."

PHYSIOLOGY AND TRAINING

"Other coaches ask me how we succeed year after year. They want to know about our training so I give them the workouts. They can't believe we do what we do."

"Running VO_2 max pace—repeat miles and repeat 1000s—is the way your highest endurance value is built."

"Most literature focuses on lactate threshold and ventilator threshold training. I disagree. I believe that 6 X 1 mile is the best indicator of 10K pace (VO_2 max)."

"When we follow the two-mile time trial with repeat miles, you elicit the Hering-Breuer reflex. You exceed your ventilator threshold and improve it. You have to run your miles faster than your VO_2 max."

"Focus. Prepare yourself for the workout. Execute it."

"To want to do something, mentally, and to have your body ready to do it, is a different thing."

"Performance is a vindication of your training."

"Get excited about your workouts. Don't cheat on yourself."

"We have to challenge ourselves with a difficult workout sometimes to challenge the energy systems."

"Get your body ready for that golden moment when opportunity arrives."

"In the physical context, maintaining is most important for distance runners. Build/improve when you get the opportunity. In the mental context, have positive thoughts about everything. You don't have the energy to waste on negativity."

"'I'm tired!' You have no patent on that word."

"Hurt, hurt, hurt—adapt!"

"You must say to yourself, 'I want to do that workout. I want to go out there and do my best on that workout.'"

"Results are a direct result of the level of enthusiasm you bring to a task."

"The higher the intensity, the longer the period of adaptation."

"One day a runner does not make."

"Eat to run. Eat only to run."

"Tell yourself, 'I'VE GOT TO GET THE JOB DONE, NO MATTER WHAT IT TAKES.' Be relentless. Do the job."

"Worry mitigates against muscular relaxation. Lower frequency brain waves lead to parasympathetic dominance and relaxation."

"One of the big observations of human nature is that when people get close to the end, they tend to relax. Get away from that disease of relaxing. Run through the finish line, as in a track race. When there is a goal in sight, work hard toward it. You should work harder the last several weeks." [Vigil said this three weeks before the national meet in 1993].

TRADITION

"We run up front. That's the way we do things."

"Adams State is the only team in cross country history to have seven All Americans in a race— and we've done it three times." [As of 2019, Adams State has accomplished this feat seven times.]

"When you're wearing the green and gold, you're running for all the guys back home and all the men who have gone before you."

REFLECTION

"Things didn't go as planned this season (injuries, upsets, etc...) but we didn't change horses in the middle of the stream. We executed our plan. There is no reason to be devastated by anything in life."

SUCCESS

More than 30 years ago, Vigil coached the Alamosa High school track team. All the best runners on the team were from the south side of the (railroad) tracks, the poorer part of town. They had t-shirts made up which read 'U.C.L.A.' which stood for 'Upper Crust, Lower Alamosa.'

At the beginning of the season, Vigil charged two of the boys with the challenge of becoming state champions at 440 yards and 880 yards. At the district meet, both placed a disappointing third. One week later, both won at the state championships and ran on two champion relays to take the team title.

When Vigil asked them how they accomplished such a reversal of form in one week, they answered: "You told us we would win at state!"

Appendix D

INTERNATIONAL CLINICS WHERE JOE I. VIGIL HAS PRESENTED

Dr. Joe I. Vigil has lectured and/or coached in 29 countries and territories on all six habitable continents. In addition, he has given hundreds of clinics to American coaches at state association meetings or clinics sponsored by various groups. Below is a sampling of the clinics he has given around the world, and the coaches who brought Vigil to speak.

Brazil	Luis Noriega
Brazil	Carlos Cavachertto
Brazil	Pedro Toledo
England	Sebastian Coe
England	Peter Coe
Ethiopia	Yilma Berta
Finland	Kari Sinkkonen
Finland	Lasse Mikkelsen
Germany	Günter Lange
Ireland	Jim Kilty
Italy	Renato Canova
Japan	Yoo Honda

Japan	Yasunori Hamada
Mexico	Rafael Quesada
Morocco	Habeeb Alm
New Zealand	Arthur Lydiard
Poland/Mexico	Thaddeus Kempka
Poland/Mexico	Houseliber
Portugal	Carlos Perea
Portugal	Arthur Ramos
Spain	Manuel Ballesteros
Sweden	James Sven-Ake
United States	Randy Wilbur
United States	Jack Daniels
United States	Jim Ryun
United States	Joe Newton

In addition to the countries listed, Vigil has presented clinics or coached in the following countries and territories: Australia, Belgium, Canada, China, Cuba, Jamaica, Kenya, Korea, Puerto Rico, Russia, Switzerland, Tanzania, and Venezuela.

INDEX

ABOUT THE AUTHOR

*P*at Melgares was born in Alamosa, Colorado, in 1967 and was raised on the south side of town just four blocks from where Joe I. Vigil grew up. Like Vigil, Pat graduated from Alamosa High School and Adams State College, and was a four-time All-American in cross country and track and field while running for Vigil from 1985 to 1989. Pat was also a member of four NAIA cross country championship teams and two The Athletics Congress (TAC) junior cross country championship teams.

At Adams State, Pat studied journalism and began his career as sports editor of the hometown *Valley Courier*. He advanced to editor of that newspaper before landing the job as public information officer at Adams State in 1994. Since 1998, he has been a communications specialist and public information officer at Kansas State University in Manhattan, Kansas.

Pat had the unique experience of watching Vigil's Adams State teams as a small child, and many of the athletes who competed for Vigil in the 1970s and early 1980s became his running idols. None of them loomed larger than

Pat Melgares wearing a Vigilante T-shirt atop Mount Blanca, the majestic fourteener that marks the eastern end of the San Luis Valley.

Joe I. Vigil, who he first admired as a coach but came to know and love as an even greater human being and friend.

Want to read more stories about
Adams State and Joe I. Vigil's life?

Go to: **melgares.wixsite.com/ChasingExcellence**

THE JOE I. VIGIL SCHOLARSHIP
AT ADAMS STATE UNIVERSITY

A portion of net proceeds from the sale of this book will go to establish the Joe I. Vigil Scholarship at Adams State University. This initiative to benefit student-athletes in the ASU cross country and track and field programs grew out of this book project. The scholarship is administered by the Adams State Foundation. The publisher and author are grateful for this partnership.

ABOUT THE PUBLISHER

SOULSTICE PUBLISHING brings to life "books with soul" that inspire readers with stories of human potential realized and celebrate our unique position in the Southwest.

Soulstice took root in our mountain town of Flagstaff, Arizona, which sits at the base of the San Francisco Peaks, on homelands sacred to Native Americans throughout the region. We honor their past, present, and future generations, as well as their original and ongoing care for the lands we also hold dear.

Surrounded by ponderosa pines, enriched by diverse cultures, and inspired by the optimistic Western spirit, Flagstaff abounds with scientists, artists, athletes, and many other people who love the outdoors. It is quite an inspiring place to live. Considering the dearth of oxygen at our 7,000-foot elevation, you might even say it leaves us breathless.

Learn more at **soulsticepublishing.com**.

Soulstice Publishing, LLC
PO Box 791
Flagstaff, AZ 86002
(928) 814-8943
connect@soulsticepublishing.com